Outlook® 2003

FOR

DUMMIES®

Outlook® 2003 For Dummies®

Outlook Toolbars

Clicking a button in a toolbar is a super-speedy way to do many jobs in Outlook. Many toolbar buttons disappear when they're not needed, so don't be surprised if your toolbars look different. If you want more tools to choose from, choose View⇨Toolbars⇨Advanced.

Message tools — Standard toolbar buttons

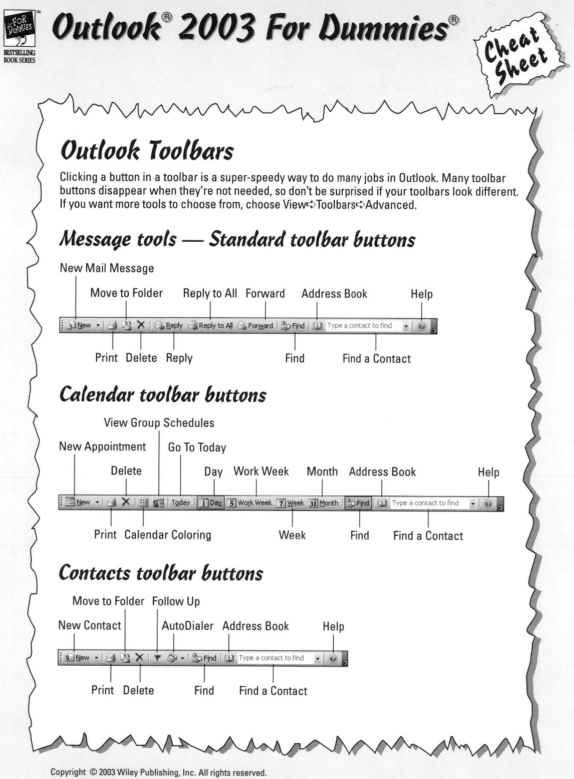

New Mail Message
Move to Folder   Reply to All   Forward   Address Book   Help

Print   Delete   Reply   Find   Find a Contact

Calendar toolbar buttons

View Group Schedules
New Appointment   Go To Today
Delete   Day   Work Week   Month   Address Book   Help

Print   Calendar Coloring   Week   Find   Find a Contact

Contacts toolbar buttons

Move to Folder   Follow Up
New Contact   AutoDialer   Address Book   Help

Print   Delete   Find   Find a Contact

For Dummies: Bestselling Book Series for Beginners

Outlook® 2003 For Dummies®

Tasks toolbar buttons

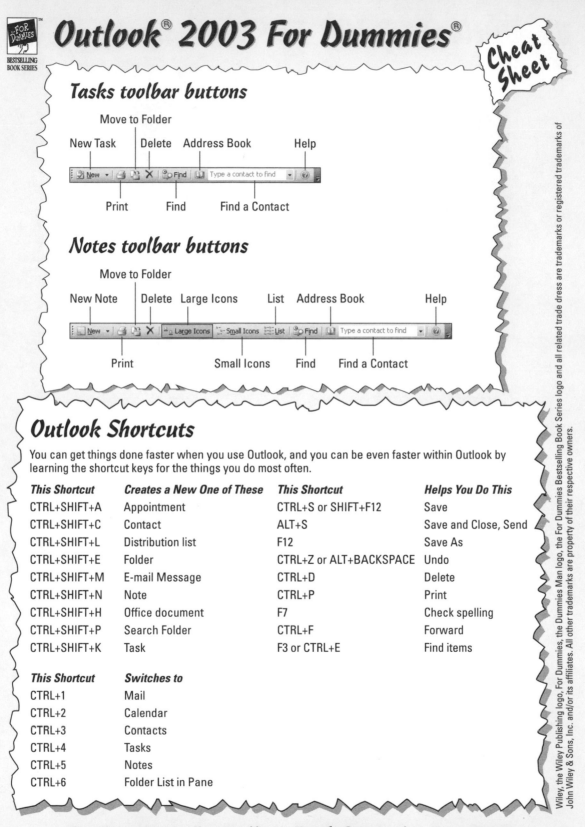

Move to Folder

New Task — Delete — Address Book — Help

Print — Find — Find a Contact

Notes toolbar buttons

Move to Folder

New Note — Delete — Large Icons — List — Address Book — Help

Print — Small Icons — Find — Find a Contact

Outlook Shortcuts

You can get things done faster when you use Outlook, and you can be even faster within Outlook by learning the shortcut keys for the things you do most often.

This Shortcut	Creates a New One of These	This Shortcut	Helps You Do This
CTRL+SHIFT+A	Appointment	CTRL+S or SHIFT+F12	Save
CTRL+SHIFT+C	Contact	ALT+S	Save and Close, Send
CTRL+SHIFT+L	Distribution list	F12	Save As
CTRL+SHIFT+E	Folder	CTRL+Z or ALT+BACKSPACE	Undo
CTRL+SHIFT+M	E-mail Message	CTRL+D	Delete
CTRL+SHIFT+N	Note	CTRL+P	Print
CTRL+SHIFT+H	Office document	F7	Check spelling
CTRL+SHIFT+P	Search Folder	CTRL+F	Forward
CTRL+SHIFT+K	Task	F3 or CTRL+E	Find items

This Shortcut	Switches to
CTRL+1	Mail
CTRL+2	Calendar
CTRL+3	Contacts
CTRL+4	Tasks
CTRL+5	Notes
CTRL+6	Folder List in Pane

Wiley, the Wiley Publishing logo, For Dummies, the Dummies Man logo, the For Dummies Bestselling Book Series logo and all related trade dress are trademarks or registered trademarks of John Wiley & Sons, Inc. and/or its affiliates. All other trademarks are property of their respective owners.

For Dummies: Bestselling Book Series for Beginners

Outlook® 2003 FOR DUMMIES®

by Bill Dyszel

WILEY

Wiley Publishing, Inc.

Outlook® 2003 For Dummies®

Published by
Wiley Publishing, Inc.
111 River Street
Hoboken, NJ 07030-5774
www.wiley.com

Copyright © 2003 by Wiley Publishing, Inc., Indianapolis, Indiana

Published by Wiley Publishing, Inc., Indianapolis, Indiana

Published simultaneously in Canada

For general information on our other products and services or to obtain technical support, please contact our Customer Care Department within the U.S. at 800-762-2974, outside the U.S. at 317-572-3993, or fax 317-572-4002.

Wiley also publishes its books in a variety of electronic formats. Some content that appears in print may not be available in electronic books.

Library of Congress Control Number: 2003101889

ISBN: 0-7645-3759-8

Manufactured in the United States of America

10 9 8 7 6 5 4 3 2 1

1B/RY/QZ/QT/IN

About the Author

Bill Dyszel writes frequently for leading magazines, including *PC Magazine* and *Computer Shopper,* while also working as a consultant and trainer to many of New York's leading firms in the securities, advertising, and publishing industries. He appears regularly as a guest on national television programs on the CNNfn and the TechTV networks. An award-winning public speaker, he enjoys entertaining audiences with talks about the pleasures and pitfalls of using modern technology. He is also the author of *Palm For Dummies* and *Handspring Visor For Dummies.*

The world of high technology has led Mr. Dyszel to grapple with such subjects as Multimedia (or how to make your $2,000 computer do the work of a $20 radio), Personal Information Managers (how to make your $3,000 laptop computer do the work of a $3.00 date book), and graphics programs (how to make your $5,000 package of computers and peripheral devices do the work of a 50-cent box of crayons). All joking aside, he has found that after you figure out the process, most of this stuff can be useful, helpful, and yes, even cool.

Before entering the computer industry, Mr. Dyszel sang with the New York City Opera and still works regularly on the New York stage as a singer, actor, and writer in numerous plays, musicals, and operas. His opera spoof — *99% ARTFREE!* — won critical praise from *The New York Times,* New York *Daily News,* and the Associated Press when he performed the show Off-Broadway.

Author's Acknowledgments

I'd like to thank all the wonderful people who helped me make this book entertaining and useful to the reader, especially Tiffany Franklin, Barry Childs-Helton, Andy Cummings, Geoff Mukhtar, Carmela DellaRipa, and the whole staff of Wiley Publishing, Inc. that makes this series possible. Thanks also to my agent, Laura Lewin of Studio B Productions.

Publisher's Acknowledgments

We're proud of this book; please send us your comments through our online registration form located at www.dummies.com/register/.

Some of the people who helped bring this book to market include the following:

Acquisitions, Editorial, and Media Development

Senior Copy Editor: Barry Childs-Helton

(Previous Edition Project Editor: Linda Morris)

Acquisitions Editor: Tiffany Franklin

Technical Editor: Michael J. Zulich

Editorial Manager: Leah Cameron

Media Development Manager: Laura VanWinkle

Media Development Supervisor: Richard Graves

Editorial Assistant: Amanda Foxworth

Production

Project Coordinator: Ryan Steffen

Layout and Graphics: Seth Conley, Carrie Foster, Joyce Haughey, Stephanie D. Jumper, Lynsey Osborn, Heather Ryan, Jacque Schneider

Proofreaders: Andy Hollandbeck, Carl William Pierce, TECHBOOKS Production Services

Indexer: Lynnzee Elze

Publishing and Editorial for Technology Dummies

    Richard Swadley, Vice President and Executive Group Publisher

    Mary C. Corder, Editorial Director

    Andy Cummings, Vice President and Publisher

Publishing for Consumer Dummies

    Diane Graves Steele, Vice President and Publisher

    Joyce Pepple, Acquisitions Director

Composition Services

    Gerry Fahey, Vice President of Production Services

    Debbie Stailey, Director of Composition Services

Contents at a Glance

Table of Contents

Introduction

●●●

Deep space adventurers have control panels on their spaceships, explorers in the Wild West had their faithful guides, and detectives have their little black books. Why? Because every adventurer knows how important it is to have good information. Knowing about the people with whom you're dealing, the things you need to do, and when you have to do those things can make the difference between triumph and failure.

Okay, maybe your daily adventures aren't exactly life-and-death struggles, but having a tool to help you keep a handle on whom and what you need to take care of from day to day is really nice. Even if your daily challenges are limited to dealing with a phone and a personal computer, having one place to look for all your daily details is convenient and timesaving.

Microsoft Outlook was designed to make organizing your daily information easy — almost automatic. You already have sophisticated programs for word processing and number crunching, but Outlook pulls together everything you need to know about your daily tasks, appointments, e-mail messages, and other details. More important, Outlook enables you to use the same methods to deal with many different kinds of information — so you have to learn only one program to deal with the many kinds of details that fill your life, such as

- ✔ Finding a customer's phone number
- ✔ Remembering that important meeting
- ✔ Planning your tasks for the day and checking them off after you're done
- ✔ Recording all the work you do so you can find what you did and when you did it

Outlook is a Personal Information Manager (Microsoft calls it a Desktop Information Manager) that can act as your assistant in dealing with the flurry of small-but-important details that stand between you and the work you do. You can just as easily keep track of personal information that isn't business-related and keep both business and personal information in the same convenient location.

About This Book

As you read this book and work with Outlook, you discover how useful Outlook is, as well as new ways to make it more useful for the things you do most. If you fit any of the following categories, this book is for you:

- ✔ Your company just adopted Outlook as its e-mail program and you need to learn how to use it in a hurry.

- ✔ You're planning to purchase (or have just purchased) Outlook and want to know what you can do with Outlook — as well as how to do it.

- ✔ You want an easier, more efficient tool for managing tasks, schedules, e-mail, and other details in your working life.

Even if you don't fall into one of these groups, this book gives you simple, clear explanations of how Outlook can work for you. It's hard to imagine any computer user who wouldn't benefit from the features that Outlook offers.

If all you want is a quick, guided tour of Outlook, you can skim this book; it covers everything you need to get you started. Getting a handle on most major Outlook features is fairly easy — that's how the program is designed. (You can also keep the book handy as a reference for the tricks that you may not need every day.)

The first part of this book gives you enough information to make sense of the whole program. Because Outlook is intended to be simple and consistent throughout, when you've got the big picture, the details are fairly simple (usually).

Don't be fooled by Outlook's friendliness, though — you can find a great deal of power in it if you want to dig deeply enough. Outlook links up with your Microsoft Office applications, and it's fully programmable by anyone who wants to tackle a little Visual Basic script writing (I don't get into that in this book). You may not want to do the programming yourself, but finding people who can do that for you isn't hard; just ask around.

Foolish Assumptions

I assume that you know how to turn on your computer and how to use a mouse and keyboard. In case you need a brush up on Windows, I throw in reminders as I go along. If Windows and Microsoft Office are strange to you, I recommend picking up (respectively) Andy Rathbone's *Windows For Dummies,* or Wally Wang's *Microsoft Office For Dummies,* both published by Wiley Publishing, Inc.

If all you have is a copy of this book and a computer running Outlook, you can certainly do basic, useful things right away, as well as a few fun ones. And after some time, you'll be able to do *many* fun and useful things.

How This Book Is Organized

To make it easier to find out how to do what you want to do, this book is divided into parts. Each part covers a different aspect of using Outlook. Because you can use similar methods to do many different jobs with Outlook, the first parts of the book focus on *how* to use Outlook. The later parts concentrate on *what* you can use Outlook to do.

Part 1: Getting the Competitive Edge with Outlook

I learn best by doing, so the first chapter is a quick guide to the things that most people do with Outlook on a typical day. You find out how easy it is to use Outlook for routine tasks such as handling messages, notes, and appointments. You can get quite a lot of mileage out of Outlook even if you do only the things our fictional detective does in the first chapter.

Because Outlook allows you to use similar methods to do many things, I go on to show you the things that stay pretty much the same throughout the program: how to create new items from old ones by using drag-and-drop; ways to view items that make your information easy to understand at a glance; and the features Outlook offers to make it easier to move, copy, and organize your files.

Part II: Taming the E-Mail Beast

E-mail is now the most popular function of computers. Tens of millions of people are hooked up to the Internet, an office network, or one of the popular online services, such as MSN or AOL.

The problem is that e-mail can still be a little too complicated. As I show you in Part II, however, Outlook makes e-mail easier. Computers are notoriously finicky about the exact spelling of addresses, correctly hooking up to the actual mail service, and making sure that the text and formatting of the message fit the software you're using. Outlook keeps track of the details involved in getting your message to its destination.

Outlook also allows you to receive e-mail from a variety of sources and manage the messages in one place. You can slice and dice your list of incoming and out-going e-mail messages to help you keep track of what you send, to whom you send it, and the day and time you send it.

Part III: Managing Contacts, Dates, Tasks, and More

Outlook takes advantage of its special relationship with your computer and your office applications (Microsoft Outlook with Microsoft Office, Microsoft Internet Explorer, and Microsoft Windows — notice a pattern emerging here?) to tie your office tasks together more cleanly than other such programs — and make it easier for you to deal with all the stuff you have to do. The chap-ters in Part III show you how to get the job done with Outlook.

If you've got yellow sticky notes covering your monitor, refrigerator, desktop, or bathroom door, you'll get a great deal of mileage out of Outlook's Notes feature. Notes are little yellow (or blue, or green) squares that look just like those handy paper sticky notes that you stick everywhere as reminders and then lose. About the only thing that you can't do is set your coffee cup on one and mess up what you wrote.

Part IV: Beyond the Basics: Tips and Tricks You Won't Want to Miss

Some parts of Outlook are less famous than others, but no less useful. Part IV guides you through the sections of Outlook that the real power users take advantage of to stay ahead of the pack.

There are parts of Outlook that many people never discover. Some of those parts are obscure but powerful — others aren't part of Outlook at all (techni-cally speaking) — but you'll get a lot of mileage from knowing how to do things like create custom forms and set up Outlook to get e-mail from the Internet. If you use Outlook at home, in your own business, or just want to soup up your copy of Outlook for high-performance work, you'll find useful tips in Part IV.

Part V: Outlook at the Office

Beyond planning and scheduling, you probably spend a great deal of your working time with other people, and you need to coordinate your schedule with theirs (unless you make your living doing something strange and anti-social, like digging graves or writing computer books). Outlook allows you to share schedule and task information with other people and synchronize information with them. You can also assign tasks to other people if you don't want to do them yourself (now *there's* a timesaver). Be careful, though; other people can assign those tasks right back to you.

Part VI: The Part of Tens

Why ten? Why not! If you must have a reason, ten is the highest number you can count to without taking off your shoes. A program as broad as Outlook leaves a great deal of flotsam and jetsam that doesn't quite fit into any category, so I sum up the best of that material in groups of ten.

Conventions Used in This Book

Outlook has many unique features, but it also has lots in common with other Windows programs — dialog boxes, pull-down menus, toolbars, and so on. To be productive with Outlook, you need to understand how these features work — and recognize the conventions I use for describing these features throughout this book.

Dialog boxes

Even if you're not new to Windows, you deal with dialog boxes more in Outlook than you do in many other Microsoft Office programs because so many items in Outlook are created with dialog boxes, which may also be called *forms*. E-mail message forms, appointments, name and address forms, and plenty of other common functions in Outlook use dialog boxes to ask you what you want to do. The following list summarizes the essential parts of a dialog box:

- ✔ **Title bar:** The title bar tells you the name of the dialog box.

- ✔ **Text boxes:** Text boxes are blank spaces into which you type information. When you click a text box, you see a blinking I-beam pointer, which means that you can type text there.

- ✔ **Control buttons:** In the upper-right corner of a dialog box, you find three control buttons:

    • The *Close button* looks like an X and makes the dialog box disappear.

    • The *Size button* toggles between maximizing the dialog box (making it take up the entire screen) and resizing it (making it take up less than the entire screen).

    • The *Minimize button* makes the dialog box seem to go away but really just hides it in the taskbar at the bottom of your screen until you click the taskbar to make the dialog box come back.

- ✔ **Tabs:** Tabs look like little file-folder tabs. If you click one, you see a new page of the dialog box. Tabs are just like the divider tabs in a ring binder; click one to change sections.

The easiest way to move around a dialog box is to click the part that you want to use. If you're a real whiz on the keyboard, you may prefer to press the Tab key to move around the dialog box; this method is much faster if you're a touch typist. Otherwise, you're fine just mousing around.

Links

Links are special pictures or pieces of text that you can click to change what you see on-screen. If you're used to surfing the Internet, you're used to clicking blue, underlined text to switch from one Web page to another. Outlook has some links that work just like links on the Internet. When you see underlined text, the text is most likely a link — click that text if you want to see where it leads.

Keyboard shortcuts

Normally, you can choose any Windows command in at least these three ways (and sometimes more):

- ✔ Choose a menu command or click a toolbar button.

- ✔ Press a keyboard combination, such as Ctrl+B, which means holding down the Ctrl key and pressing the letter B (you use this command to make text bold).

✔ Press the F10 key or the spacebar to pull down a menu, press an arrow key to choose a command, and press Enter (way too much trouble, but possible for those who love a challenge).

You often tell Outlook what to do by choosing from menus at the top of the screen. I normally simplify menu commands by saying something like "Choose Yeah⇨Sure," which means "Choose the Yeah menu; then, choose the Sure command."

One rather confusing feature of Outlook is the way each menu appears in two different views. When you first click the name of a menu in the menu bar, a short menu appears to show the most popular choices from that menu. If you leave the menu open for about two seconds, the menu suddenly doubles in length, showing you every command available on that menu. Don't worry, your eyes aren't going bad — that's how the product was designed. Microsoft programmers believe that some people are more comfortable with shorter menus, whereas others prefer longer menus, so this "Jack-in-the-box" scheme will either make everyone equally happy or equally confused.

Icons Used in This Book

Sometimes the fastest way to go through a book is to look at the pictures — in this case, icons that draw your attention to specific types of information that's useful to know. Here are the icons I use in this book:

The Remember icon points out helpful information. (Everything in this book is helpful, but this stuff is even *more* helpful.)

A hint or trick for saving time and effort, or something that makes Outlook easier to understand.

The Warning icon points to something that you may want to be careful about in order to prevent problems.

The Technical Stuff icon marks background information that you can skip, although it may make good conversation at a really dull party.

The Timesaver icon points out a trick that can save you time.

The Network icon points out information that applies primarily to people using Outlook on a computer network at the office.

The Internet icon points out a feature of Outlook that helps you connect to the Internet or use the Internet more effectively.

Where to Go from Here

A wise person once said, "The best way to start is by starting." Okay, that's not all that wise, but why quibble? Plunge in!

Part I

Getting the Competitive Edge with Outlook

In this part . . .

*O*utlook is an all-in-one information management system that lets you organize and manage your appointments, activities, e-mail, and office life with a few clicks of the mouse. In this part, I give you a basic vision of how Outlook works to improve the way you manage your days.

Chapter 1

Fundamental Features: How Did You Ever Do without Outlook?

*O*utlook is easier to use than you might think; it also does a lot more than you might realize. Even if you use only about 10 percent of Outlook's features, you'll be amazed at how this little program can streamline your life and spiff up your communications. People get pretty excited about Outlook — even if they take advantage of only a tiny fraction of what the package can do. I'm kicking off this book with "Outlook's Greatest Hits," the things you'll want to do with Outlook every single day. The list sounds simple enough: sending e-mail, making appointments, and so on. But there's more here than meets the eye; Outlook does ordinary things extraordinarily well. I know you want to do the same, so read on.

Easy Ways to Do Anything in Outlook

Well, okay, maybe you can't use Outlook to decipher hieroglyphics — but if you learn a little about some basic techniques, you can do a lot in Outlook — click an icon to do something, view something, or complete something. Using Outlook is so simple, I can sum it up in just a few how-to sentences to cover the most common tasks:

- ✔ **Open an item and read it:** Double-click the item.

- ✔ **Create a new item:** Click an icon in the Navigation Pane, click the New button in the Toolbar at the top of the screen, and fill out the form that appears. When you're done, click the button labeled Send — or, alternatively, Save and Close.

- ✔ **Delete an item:** Click the item once to select it, and then click the Delete icon in the Toolbar at the top of the screen. The Delete icon contains a black X.

- ✔ **Move an item:** Use your mouse to drag the item to where you want it.

Does that seem too simple? No problem. If you have an itch to complicate things, you *could* try to use Outlook while hopping on a pogo stick or flying the space shuttle. But why? These four tricks can take you a long way.

Outlook can also do some sophisticated tricks, such as automatically sorting your e-mail or creating automated form letters, but you'll need to learn a few details to take advantage of those tricks. The other 300 pages of this book cover the finer points of Outlook. If you only wanted the basics, I could've sent you a postcard.

The pictures I show you in this book and the instructions I give you assume you're using Outlook the way it comes out of the box from Microsoft — with all the standard options installed. If you don't like the way the program looks (or what things are named) when you install Outlook, you can change nearly everything. If you change too much, however, some instructions and examples I give you won't make sense, because then the parts of the program that I talk about may have names you gave them, rather than the ones Microsoft originally assigned. The Microsoft people generally did a good job of making Outlook easy to use. I suggest leaving the general arrangement alone until you're comfortable using Outlook.

Reading E-Mail

E-mail is Outlook's most popular feature. I've run across people who didn't know Outlook could do anything but exchange e-mail messages. It's a good thing Outlook makes it so easy to read your e-mail.

When you start Outlook, normally you see a screen with three columns. The center column is your list of messages; the right-hand column (called the Reading Pane) contains the text of one of those messages. If the message is short enough, you may see its entire text in the right-hand column, as shown in Figure 1-1. If the message is longer, you'll have to open it to see the whole thing.

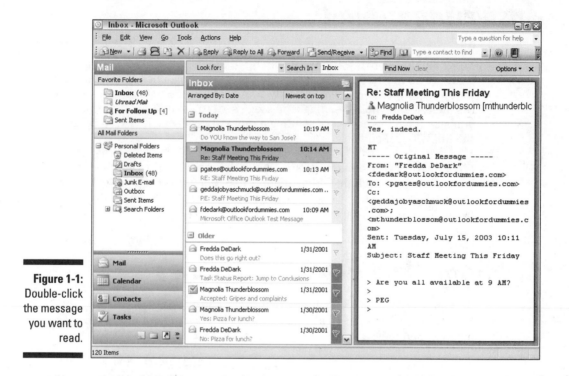

Figure 1-1: Double-click the message you want to read.

Here's how to see the entire message:

1. **Click the Mail button in the Navigation Pane.**

   You don't need this step if you can already see the messages, but it doesn't hurt.

2. **Double-click the title of the message.**

   Now you can see the entire message.

3. **Press Esc.**

A quick way to skim the messages in your Inbox is to press the up-arrow or down-arrow key on your keyboard. You can move through your message list as you read the text of your messages in the Reading Pane.

If you feel overwhelmed by the number of e-mail messages you get each day, you're not alone. Billions and billions of e-mail messages fly around the Internet each day, and lots of people are feeling buried in messages. You discover the secrets of sorting and managing your messages in Chapter 6.

Answering E-Mail

When you open an e-mail message in Outlook to read it, buttons labeled Reply and Reply to All appear at the top of the message screen. That's a hint. When you want to reply to a message you're reading, click the Reply button. A new message form opens, already addressed to the person who sent you the message. If you're reading a message sent to several people besides you, you also have the option of sending a reply to everyone involved by clicking the Reply to All button.

When you reply to a message, the text of the message that was sent to you is automatically included. Some people like to include original text in their replies, some don't. In Chapter 5, I show you how to change what Outlook automatically includes in replies.

Creating New E-Mail Messages

At its easiest, the process of creating a new e-mail message in Outlook is ridiculously simple. Even a child can do it. If you can't get a child to create a new e-mail message for you, you can even do it yourself.

To create a new e-mail message, follow these steps:

1. **Click the Mail button in the Navigation Pane.**

   Your message list appears.

2. **Click the New button in the Toolbar.**

   The New Message form appears.

3. **Fill out the New Message form.**

   Put the address of your recipient in the To box, a subject in the Subject box, and type a message in the main message box.

4. **Click Send.**

   Your message is on its way.

If you want to send a plain e-mail message, that's all you have do. If you prefer to send fancy e-mail, Outlook provides the bells and whistles — some of which are actually useful. You might (for example) send a High Priority message to impress some big shots or send a Confidential message about a hush-hush topic. (Discover the mysteries of confidential e-mail in Chapter 4.)

Sending a File

Call me crazy, but I suspect you have more to do than exchange e-mail all day. You probably do lots of daily work in programs other than Outlook. You might create documents in Microsoft Word or build elaborate spreadsheets with Excel. When you want to send a file by e-mail, Outlook gets involved, although sometimes it works in the background.

To e-mail a document you created in Microsoft Word, for example, follow these steps:

1. **Open the document in Microsoft Word.**

   The document appears on-screen.

2. **Choose File⇨Send To⇨Mail Recipient (as attachment).**

   The New Message form appears with your document listed on the Attachment line (as pictured in Figure 1-2).

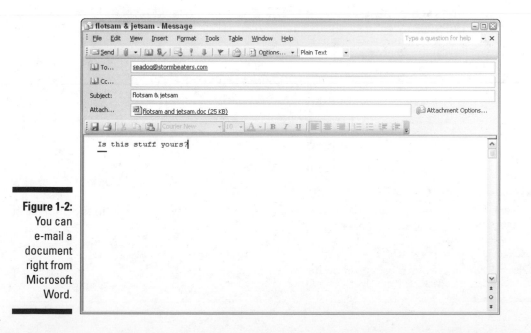

Figure 1-2:
You can e-mail a document right from Microsoft Word.

3. **Type the e-mail address of your recipient on the To line.**

   The address you enter appears on the To line.

4. **Click Send.**

   Your file is now en route.

When you're just sending one Word file, these steps are the easiest way to go. If you're sending more than one file, I describe a more powerful way to attach files in Chapter 5.

Entering an Appointment

If you've ever used an old-fashioned paper planner, the Outlook Calendar will look familiar to you. When you click the Calendar icon, you see a grid in the middle of the screen with lines representing each half-hour of the day (as in Figure 1-3). To enter an appointment at a certain time, just click the line next to the time you want your appointment to begin, type a name for your appointment, and press Enter.

If you want to enter more detailed information about your appointment — such as ending time, location, category, and so on — see Chapter 8 for the nitty-gritty about keeping your Calendar.

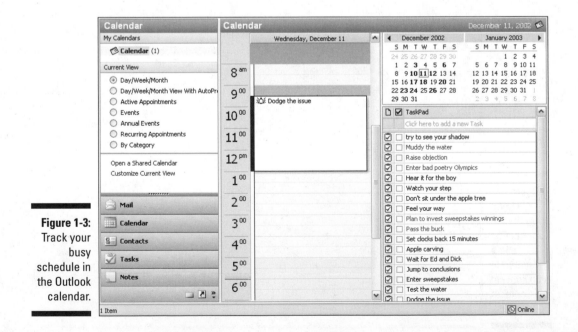

Figure 1-3:
Track your busy schedule in the Outlook calendar.

Checking Your Calendar

Time management involves more than just entering appointments. If you're really busy, you want to manage your time by slicing and dicing your list of appointments to see when you're free enough to add even more appointments. You can choose from several different views of your calendar by clicking the Day, Week, and Month buttons at the top of the Calendar screen. If you need a more elaborate collection of calendar views, choose one of the views listed in the Current View section of the Navigation Pane. To really master time management, see Chapter 8 to see the different ways you can view your Outlook Calendar.

Adding a Contact

When it's not *what* you know but *who* you know, you need a good tool for keeping track of who's who. Outlook is a great tool for managing your list of names and addresses, and it's just as easy to use as your Little Black Book. To enter a new contact, click the Contacts button in the Navigation Pane; then click the New button on the toolbar to open the New Contact entry form. Fill in the blanks on the form (an example appears in Figure 1-4), and then click Save and Close. Presto — you have a Contacts list.

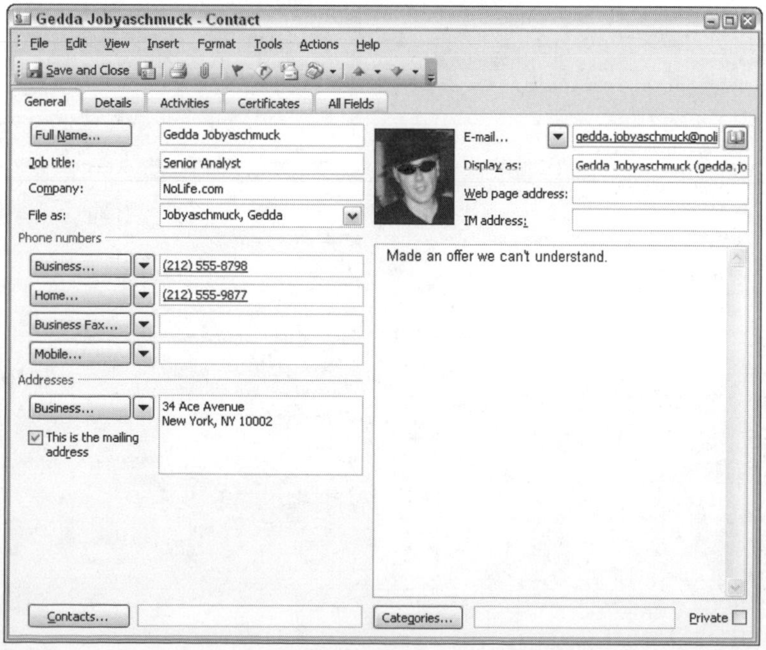

Figure 1-4:
Keep detailed information about everyone you know in the Contacts list.

Outlook does a lot more than your little black book — if you know the ropes. Chapter 7 reveals the secrets of searching, sorting, and grouping the names on your list — and of using e-mail to keep in touch with all the important people in your life.

Entering a Task

Entering a Task in Outlook isn't much of a task itself. You can click either the Task button or the Calendar button to see a list of your tasks. If you see the words `Click here to add a new Task,` you've got a clue.

To enter a new task, follow these steps:

1. **Click the text that says** `Click here to add a new Task.`

   The words disappear, and you see the Insertion Point (a blinking line).

2. **Type the name of your task.**

   Your task appears in the block under the Subject line on the Tasks list (which in turn appears in Figure 1-5).

3. **Press the Enter key.**

   Your new task moves down to the Tasks list with your other tasks.

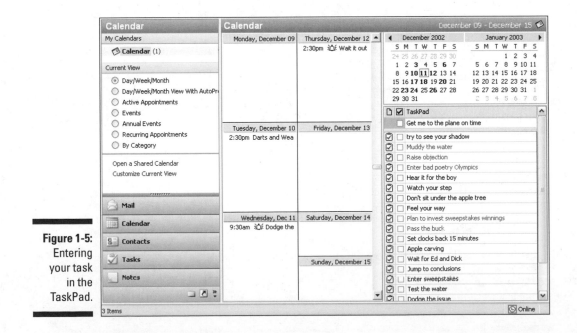

Figure 1-5:
Entering your task in the TaskPad.

Outlook can help you manage anything from a simple shopping list to a complex business project. In Chapter 9, I show you how to deal with recurring tasks, regenerate tasks, and also how to mark tasks complete (and earn the right to brag about how much you've accomplished).

Taking Notes

I have hundreds of little scraps of information that I need to keep somewhere, but until Outlook came along, I didn't have a place to put them. Now all the written flotsam and jetsam I've decided I need goes into my Outlook Notes collection — where I can find it all again when I need it.

To create a new Note, follow these steps:

1. **Click the Notes button in the Navigation Pane (or press Ctrl+5).**

   Your list of Notes appears.

2. **Click the New button in the toolbar.**

   A blank note appears.

3. **Type the text you want to save.**

   The text you type appears in the note (see Figure 1-6).

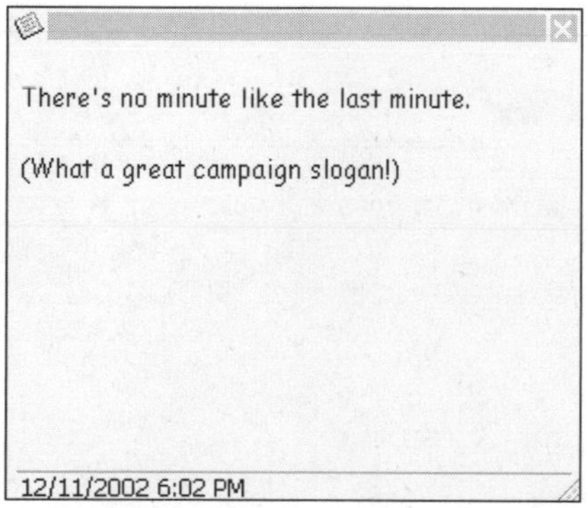

Figure 1-6: Preserve your prose for posterity in an Outlook Note.

There's no minute like the last minute.

(What a great campaign slogan!)

12/11/2002 6:02 PM

4. **Press Esc.**

   The note you created appears in your list of Notes.

An even quicker way to enter a note is to press Ctrl+Shift+N and type your note text. You can see how easy it is to amass a large collection of small notes. Chapter 10 tells you everything you need to know about Notes, including how to find the notes you've saved, as well as how to sort, categorize, and organize your collection of notes and even how to delete the ones you don't need anymore.

After you're in the habit of using Outlook to organize your life, I'm sure you'll want to move beyond the basics. That's what the rest of this book shows you. When you're ready to share your work with other people, send e-mail like a pro, or just finish your workday by 5:00 p.m. and get home, you'll find ways to use Outlook to make your job — and your life — easier to manage.

Chapter 2

Inside Outlook: Mixing, Matching, and Managing Information

- -

In This Chapter

▶ Examining the many faces of Outlook

▶ Choosing menus: One from column A and one from column B

▶ Using the tools of the trade

▶ Taking the shortcut: Speedier keystrokes

▶ Getting the big picture from the Information Viewer

▶ Fine-tuning with the Folder List

- -

Computer companies love new stuff. Every so often, they beef up their products with new names and new features and release them just before I've figured out how to use the old products. It's kind of confusing, but I can't deny that many of these newfangled features make my life easier after I get a handle on them.

In the old days B.C. (Before Computers), every task in an office required a different machine. You typed letters on a typewriter, calculated on an adding machine, filed names and addresses in a card file, and kept your appointments in a datebook. It would be very difficult to add up your monthly sales on the typewriter and even harder to type a letter on the calculator.

When computers started creeping in, they took over each of these functions, one by one. A different program replaced each machine. First, the word-processing program eliminated the typewriter; next, the spreadsheet replaced the calculator. After a brief flirtation with the giant record-keeping database, the frequent job of keeping track of names, addresses, and dates slowly (but not completely) gave way to a program called the Personal Information Manager (PIM). Microsoft claims to take the information manager concept one step further with Outlook.

Outlook and Other Programs

Outlook is a part of Microsoft Office. It's called an Office *suite,* which means it's a collection of programs that includes everything you need to complete most office tasks. Ideally, the programs in a suite work together, enabling you to create documents that you couldn't create as easily with any of the individual programs. For example, you can copy a chart from a spreadsheet and paste it into a sales letter that you're creating in your word processor. You can also keep a list of mailing addresses in Outlook and use the list as a mailing list to address form letters (see Chapter 20).

Microsoft Office includes six programs that cost less to buy together than you would pay to buy them separately. The concept is a little like buying an encyclopedia; it's cheaper to buy the entire set than it is to buy one book at a time. Besides, who wants just one volume of an encyclopedia (unless you're interested only in aardvarks)?

Outlook turns up in connection with several other Microsoft products, as well. Microsoft Exchange Server is the backbone of the e-mail system in many corporations, and Outlook is often the program that employees of those corporations use to read their company e-mail. Outlook's first cousin, Outlook Express, is included free when you install Internet Explorer and as a part of Windows XP, as well as all future versions of Windows. Outlook is also linked strongly to Internet Explorer, although technically they're separate programs. You don't need to worry about all this, though. You can start up Outlook and use it the same way no matter which other programs it's bundled with.

Enter the PIM

When it comes to the basic work of managing names, addresses, appointments, and e-mail, the word processing and spreadsheet programs just don't get it. If you're planning a meeting, you need to know with whom you're meeting, what the other person's phone number is, and when you can find time to meet.

Several small software companies recognized the problem of managing addresses and appointments long ago and offered Personal Information Managers (PIMs) to fill in the gap. PIMs, such as Lotus Organizer, SideKick, and Act!, specialized in names, addresses, dates, and tasks, leaving the word processing and number crunching to brawnier business applications, such as Microsoft Word and Excel.

In designing Outlook, Microsoft took advantage of the fact that many people use Microsoft products for most of the work they do. The company created a

PIM that speaks a common language with Microsoft Word, Excel, and the rest of the Microsoft Office suite. Microsoft also studied what kind of information people use most often, and tried to make sure that Outlook could handle most of it. The program also has scads of *customizability* (a tongue-twister of a buzz-word that just means you can set it up however you need, after you know what you're doing). Outlook is so ambitious that Microsoft doesn't even call it a PIM — instead, it's a *Desktop Information Manager*. (Yeah, that's right — it's a DIM. Microsoft doesn't always come up with the brightest names for things.)

Whatever the terminology, Outlook is — above all — easy to understand and hard to mess up. If you've used any version of Windows, you can just look at the screen and click a few icons to see what Outlook does. You won't break anything. If you get lost, going back to where you came from is easy. Even if you have no experience with Windows, Outlook is fairly straightforward to use.

There's No Place Like Home: Outlook's Main Screen

Outlook's appearance is very different from the other Microsoft Office applications. Instead of confronting you with a blank screen and a few menus and toolbars, Outlook begins by offering you large icons with simple names and a screen with information that's easy to use and understand. If you've spent much time surfing the Web, you'll find the Outlook layout pretty similar to many pages on the Web. Just select what you want to see by clicking an icon on the left side of the screen, and the information you selected appears on the right side of the screen.

Feeling at home when you work is nice. (Sometimes, when I'm at work, I'd rather *be* at home, but that's something else entirely.) Outlook makes a home for all your different types of information: names, addresses, schedules, to-do lists, and even a list to remind you of all the stuff you have to do today (or didn't get done yesterday). You can customize the main screen as easily as you rearrange your home furnishings. Even so, to make it easier to find your way around at first, I recommend waiting until you feel entirely at home with Outlook before you start rearranging the screen.

The Outlook main screen — which looks remarkably like Figure 2-1 — has all the usual parts of a Windows screen (see the Introduction if you're not used to the Windows screen), with a few important additions. At the left side of the screen, you see the Navigation Pane. Next to the Navigation Pane is the Information Viewer, the part of the screen that takes up most of the space.

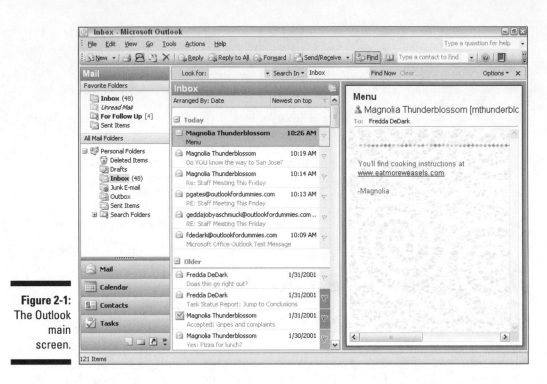

Figure 2-1:
The Outlook
main
screen.

Outlook modules

All the work you do in Outlook is organized into *modules,* or sections. Each
module performs a specific job for you: The Calendar stores and manages
your schedule, the Tasks module stores and manages your to-do list, and so
on. Outlook is always showing you one of its modules in the main screen (also
known as the Information Viewer). Whenever you're running Outlook, you're
always using a module, even if the module contains no information — the
same way your television can be tuned to a channel even if nothing is showing
on that channel. The name of the module you're currently using is displayed
in large type at the top of the Information Viewer part of the screen, so you
can easily tell which module is showing.

Each module is represented by a button in the Navigation Pane on the left side
of the screen. Clicking any button takes you to a different module of Outlook:

- **The Mail button** takes you to the Inbox, which collects your incoming
  e-mail.

- **The Calendar button** shows you your schedule and all your appointments.

- **The Contacts button** calls up a module that stores names and addresses
  for you.

- ✔ **The Tasks button** displays your To Do list.

- ✔ **The Notes button** takes you to a module you can use to keep track of random tidbits of information that don't quite fit anywhere else.

To change Outlook modules, do either of the following things:

- ✔ Click Go in the menu bar, and then choose the module you want from the menu that appears (as in Figure 2-2).

- ✔ For faster action, simply click the module's button in the Navigation Pane.

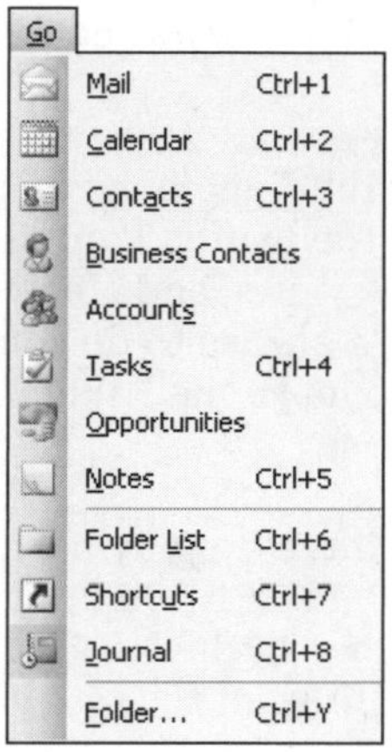

Figure 2-2:
Click Go and
choose from
the menu if
you want to
see a new
module.

Go		
Mail	Ctrl+1
Calendar	Ctrl+2
Contacts	Ctrl+3
Business Contacts	
Accounts	
Tasks	Ctrl+4
Opportunities	
Notes	Ctrl+5
Folder List	Ctrl+6
Shortcuts	Ctrl+7
Journal	Ctrl+8
Folder...	Ctrl+Y

If you're using Outlook on your company network, your network's system administrator may have created a different set of buttons for you to work with. You may have a few more (or a few less) than you see in this book, but the buttons should work the same way.

Finding your way with the Navigation Pane

Navigating your way through some computer programs can be a pain, but Outlook can ease your discomfort somewhat with the help of the Navigation Pane. This part of the Outlook screen was formerly called the Outlook Bar, but to prevent anybody from committing EWI (E-mailing While Intoxicated), Microsoft changed the name of this critter to the Navigation Pane. Now you'll have to do your tippling in some other program.

The column on the left side of the Outlook screen is the one called the Navigation Pane. It contains several buttons with names such as Mail, Calendar, Contacts, Tasks, and Notes — the basic Outlook modules. I explain these modules later, but the names alone already tell you the story.

The Navigation Pane is made up of two sections: an upper window section and a bottom section made up of buttons. Each button in the bottom section is connected to one of Outlook's main modules — mail, calendar, contacts, tasks, and so on. Just click a button, any button, and you'll see what it sets in motion. Clicking the button changes the stuff on the main screen to fit what that button describes. Click the Calendar button, for example, and a Calendar screen shows up. Click Contacts, and you get a screen for names and addresses. The process is like changing the channels on the TV set. If you switch to a channel you don't want, switch to another — no problem.

The top section of the Navigation Pane displays different kinds of information at different times. Sometimes the top half of the Navigation Pane shows the Folder List, sometimes it shows a list of available views, and sometimes it contains phrases in blue lettering. You can click a phrase to do something such as "Open a Shared Calendar." If you want to make the Folder List appear in this top window section, choose Go⇨Folder List.

Just above the Mail icon in the Navigation Pane there's a gray border separating buttons on the bottom from the top part of the bar. If you drag that gray borderline downward with your mouse, the buttons in the Navigation Pane disappear one by one. That's something you might want to do to get a better view of your Folder List. You can make those buttons reappear by simply dragging the gray border upward again.

The Information Viewer: Outlook's hotspot

The Information Viewer is where most of the action happens in Outlook. If the Navigation Pane is like the channel selector on your TV set, the Information Viewer is like the TV screen. When you're reading e-mail, you look in the Information Viewer to read your messages; if you're adding or searching for contacts, you see contact names here. The Information Viewer is also where you can do all sorts of fancy sorting tricks that each module in Outlook lets you perform. (I talk about sorting Contacts, Tasks, and so forth in the chapters that apply to those modules.)

Because you can store more information in Outlook than you want to see at any one time, the Information Viewer shows you only a slice of the information available. The Calendar, for example, can store dates as far back as the year 1601 and as far ahead as 4500. (Got any plans on Saturday night 2,500 years from now?) That's a lot of time, but Outlook breaks it down and shows it to you in manageable slices in the Information Viewer. The smallest Calendar slice you can look at is one day; the largest slice is a month.

The Information Viewer organizes the items it shows you into units called *views.* You can use the views that are included with Outlook when you install it, or you can create your own views and save them. (I go into more details about views in Chapter 16.)

You can navigate among the slices of information that Outlook shows you by clicking different parts of the Information Viewer. Some people use the word *browsing* for the process of moving around the Information Viewer — it's a little like thumbing through the pages of your pocket datebook (that is, if you have a million-page datebook).

To see an example of how to use the Information Viewer, look at the Calendar module in Figure 2-3.

To browse the Calendar data in the Information Viewer, follow these steps:

1. **Click the Calendar button in the Navigation Pane (or press Ctrl + 2).**

   The Calendar appears.

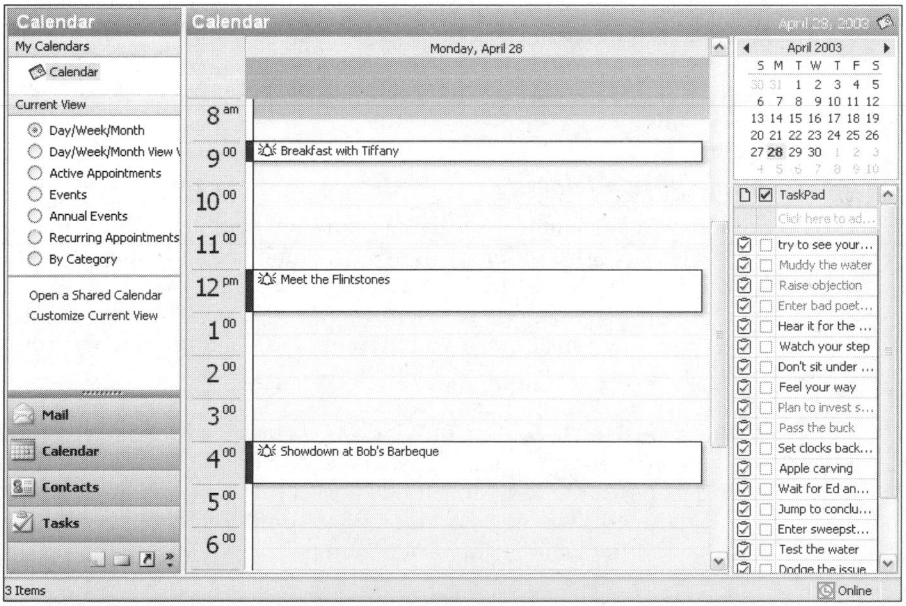

Figure 2-3:
A calendar
in the
Information
Viewer.

   2. Choose View⇨Week.

    The weekly view of the Calendar appears.

Try these tricks to see how the Information Viewer behaves:

  ✔ Click a date in the small calendar in the upper-right corner.

    The large calendar changes to a one-day view.

  ✔ Click the *W* for *Wednesday* at the top of one of the small calendars.

    The large calendar changes to a monthly view.

You can change the appearance of the Information Viewer an infinite number of ways to make the work you do in Outlook make sense to you. For example, you may need to see the appointments for a single day, or only the items you've assigned to a certain category. Views can help you get a quick look at exactly the slice of information you need.

Navigating the Folder List

If you want to navigate Outlook in a more detailed way than you can with the Navigation Pane, you can use the Folder List. If you think of the Navigation Pane buttons as being like a car's radio buttons for picking favorite stations, then the Folder List is like the fine-tuning button that tunes in the stations between your favorite ones. The Folder List simply shows you the folders — your Windows folders or your Outlook folders — where your files and Outlook items are stored.

A tale of two folders

Folders can seem more confusing than they need to be because, once again, Microsoft gave two different things the same name. Just as two kinds of Explorer (Windows and Internet) exist, more than two kinds of Outlook exist, and more than two kinds of Windows (3.1, 95, 98, 2000, CE, NT, Me, and XP) exist. You may run across two different kinds of folders when you use Outlook — and each behaves differently.

You may be used to folders in Windows 95 or 98, which are the things you look in to organize files. You can copy, move, and delete files to and from folders on your disk drive. Outlook doesn't deal with that kind of folder. If you need to manage the files you've created on your computer, click the Windows XP Start Button, and then choose My Documents.

Outlook has its own special folders for storing items (calendar items, contact names, tasks, and so on) that you create in the various Outlook modules. Each module has its own folder, and the Folder List gives you immediate access to any of them.

If you're looking at an Outlook module, such as the Inbox, for example, and you turn on the Folder List by choosing Go➪Folder List, you see a list of folders that represent the other standard Outlook modules, such as the Tasks List, Contacts, Calendar, and so on.

Using the Folder List

The only time you absolutely must use the Folder List is when you want to create a new folder for a separate type of item (such as a special contact list or a folder for filing e-mail) or find that folder again to use the items you've stored there.

You may quite possibly never use the Folder List at all. The Navigation Pane includes the folder choices that most people use most of the time. You may never need to get a different one. Fortunately, the Folder List appears all by itself when you're likely to need it. If you don't see the Folder List but want to, choose Go➪Folder List (or press Ctrl + 6). It's a matter of taste, so take your pick.

Clicking Once: Outlook Toolbars

Tools are those little boxes with pictures in them all lined up in a row just below the menu bar. Together, they're called a *toolbar,* and they're even more popular than menus when it comes to running Windows programs. Outlook has three toolbars to choose from: the Standard toolbar, the Advanced toolbar, and the Web toolbar. If you don't do anything special, the Standard toolbar is the one you see, and it will probably do everything you need. If you want to get fancy and open another toolbar (or customize any toolbar), see Chapter 20. Toolbars are great timesavers; one little click on a little picture, and voilà — your wish is granted and you're off to lunch.

Viewing ToolTips

Like menus, tools in Microsoft Office programs get a little drop shadow when you hover the mouse pointer over them. The shadow tells you that if you click there, the tool will do what it's there to do: paste, save, launch missiles (just kidding) — whatever.

Another slick thing about tools is that when you rest the mouse pointer on any of them for a second or so, a little tag pops up to tell you the tool's name (see Figure 2-4). Tags of this sort, called *ToolTips,* are very handy for deciphering the hieroglyphics on those tool buttons.

Figure 2-4:
A ToolTip
tells you the
name of the
tool you're
using.

To view a ToolTip, follow these steps:

1. **Place the mouse pointer on the word File in the menu bar.**

2. **Slide the mouse pointer straight down until it rests on the icon just below the word File.**

    After about half a second, you see a little tab that says "New Office Document" or "New *Something-or-Other.*" (The text changes, depending on what section of Outlook you're in.)

Some tools have a little down-pointing triangle to their right. This triangle means the tool has a pull-down menu. The first tool at the left end of any Outlook toolbar is the New tool. Click the triangle to pull down its menu and see all the glorious new stuff you can create — a new appointment, a new e-mail message, or even a new Office document.

Using the New tool

You can use the New tool, which is available in any module of Outlook, to create an item in any other module. Perhaps you're entering the name and address of a new customer who is also mentioned in an interesting article in today's paper. You want to remember the article, but it doesn't belong in the customer's address record. Although you're still in the Contacts module (see Figure 2-5), you can pull down the New button's menu and create a quick note, which gets filed in the Notes section. Using the New tool to create a new note when you're looking at the Contacts screen can get confusing. At first, you may think the note isn't entered, but it is. Outlook just files it in the Notes module, where it belongs.

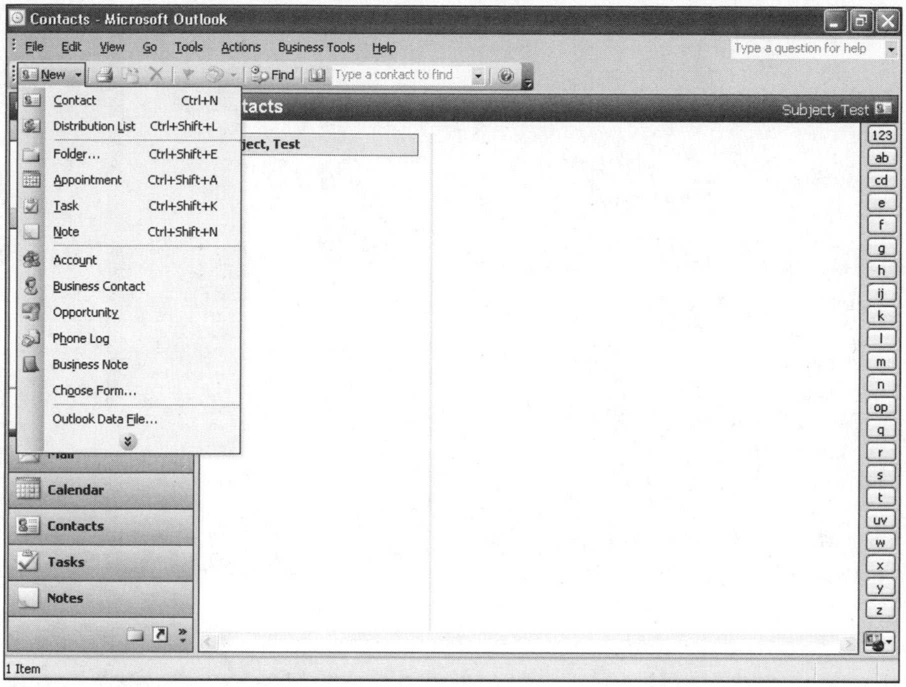

Figure 2-5:
Use the
New tool to
create a
note,
request a
meeting, or
perform a
variety of
new tasks
without
switching to
another
Outlook
module.

Getting Help in Outlook

Even though Outlook is as user-friendly a program as you could hope to find,
at times you may want to take advantage of the efficient Windows online help
system when you're temporarily stumped (of course, you can turn to this
book for help, but sometimes online help is faster).

The Windows Help system appears on the right side of the Outlook screen
(as shown in Figure 2-6) whenever you press F1. The Windows Help system
finds answers to any question you type in the text box at the top of the
screen. When you type a question in the text box and press Enter, a list of
possible answers appears in the box following the text box. Click the answer
that seems best related to your question, and a full explanation appears in a
new window. The Help system includes lots of blue underlined text, just like
you see in your Web browser, which you can click to make the Help system
show you more information about the underlined topic.

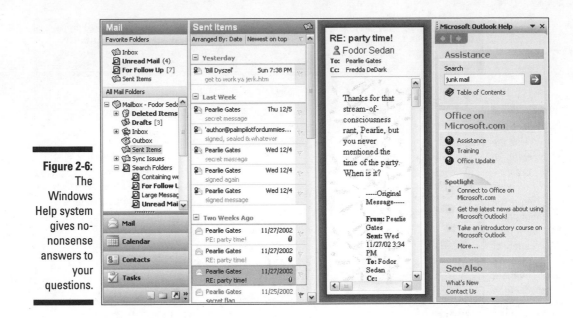

Figure 2-6:
The
Windows
Help system
gives no-
nonsense
answers to
your
questions.

Using the Office Assistant

The Windows Help system is always helpful, but maybe you long for something a little more sociable. If so, your prayers have been answered (if not, skip ahead to the next section). A little animated character called the *Office Assistant* is available to pop up and cavort around when you ask for help; it even does little tricks when you do things, such as save a file or search for text. Try it!

To bring the Office Assistant into your life, choose Help⇨Show the Office Assistant. When the Office Assistant appears, you can change the type of character you use as your Office Assistant: You can use the Clippit character that Office begins with, The Genius character, Links the Cat, or others. All you have to do is right-click the Office Assistant character, choose a new character, and click OK.

The Office Assistant character is included because research shows that people treat their computers pretty much like people. No kidding. Most people, for example, would rather gripe about a computer to a *second* computer than enter those complaints into the computer they're slamming; it's as though they're trying not to hurt the computer's feelings.

You don't have to worry about hurting the Office Assistant's feelings. Just press the F1 key anytime; your Office Assistant pops up and invites you to ask a question. Just type your question in plain English, and the Assistant scratches its head and returns with a list of help topics that are likely to answer your question. If you want to forward a message, for example, just press F1 and type **forward a message**. The list of choices includes everything that has to do with forwarding messages.

If you keep the Office Assistant open, some questions that you usually answer through dialog boxes are asked by the Assistant. Click the response you want, just as you would in a regular dialog box.

The Office Assistant will get smarter with time; it's supposed to notice what you do wrong repeatedly and chime in with suggestions about how to do them better. Microsoft calls this system the Social Interface; some people call it nagging. **Remember:** The Office Assistant only means to be helpful (just like your mother-in-law).

Getting rid of the Office Assistant

Believe it or not, some hard-nosed, no-nonsense people out there actually find the Office Assistant annoying. Some of them don't even believe in Santa. If you're an Office Assistant hater, you can make the Office Assistant stay away (but please don't make Santa stay away; I'm still waiting for my two front teeth). Just choose Help⇨Hide Office Assistant and the little critter will disappear. If you get mushy and sentimental later on and want to bring the Office Assistant back, just choose Help⇨Show the Office Assistant.

Chapter 3

On the Fast Track: Drag 'til You Drop

*T*yping — ugh! Who needs it? It's amazing to think that we still use a nineteenth-century device — the typewriter keyboard — to control our computers in the twenty-first century. We appear to be stuck with the QWERTY keyboard (the standard keyboard we all know and, uh, *love*) for a while longer, but we can give our carpal tunnels a rest now and then — by using the mouse, trackball, or touchpad, we can drag and drop rather than hunt and peck.

How to Drag

When I say *drag,* I'm not referring to Monty Python's men in women's clothing. I mean the process of zipping items from one place to another with quick, easy mouse moves rather than slow, laborious menu choices. Throughout the rest of this book, I tell you how to do nearly everything in Outlook by the menu method only because it's the clearest way to explain how to do most things reliably. But if you want to work quickly in Outlook, drag-and-drop is the ticket to the simple and speedy completion of your tasks.

Before you can drag an item, you have to *select* it — which simply means to click the item once. Then the rest of the process is straightforward:

✔ *Dragging* means clicking your mouse on something and moving the mouse to another location while holding the mouse button down at the same time. The item you're dragging moves with the mouse pointer.

✔ *Dropping* means letting go of the mouse button. The mouse pointer detaches from the object you dragged and leaves it in its new location.

When you drag an item, you see an icon hanging from the tail of the mouse pointer as you move the pointer across the screen. The icon makes the pointer look like it's carrying baggage, and to some degree, that's true; dragging your mouse between Outlook modules "carries" information from one type of item to another.

When you drag and drop items between different Outlook modules, you can keep creating new types of items from the old information, depending on what you drag and where you drop it.

Everything you can do by using the drag-and-drop method can also be done through menu choices or keystroke shortcuts, but you lose the advantage of having the information from one item flow into the new item, so you have to retype information. I'm too lazy for that, so I just drag and drop.

Because I'm using this chapter to extol the benefits of drag-and-drop, I describe every action in terms of a drag-and-drop movement rather than through menu choices or keyboard shortcuts. Throughout the rest of the book, however, I describe how to do things in terms of menu choices. That's because the menus never change, whereas you *can* change the names of the buttons in the Navigation Pane if you customize them. So when you read other parts of the book, don't think I'm discouraging you from trying drag-and-drop; I'm just trying to offer you the clearest explanation I can. (Whew! I'm glad that's off my chest.)

Creating E-Mail Messages

Anything you drag to the Inbox becomes an outgoing e-mail message. If the item you drag to the Inbox contains an e-mail address (for example, a contact), Outlook automatically creates the message with that person's e-mail address filled in.

If the item you drag to the Inbox contains a subject (for example, a task), Outlook automatically creates the message with that subject filled in.

From a name in your Address Book

Addressing messages is one of the most useful drag-and-drop techniques in Outlook. E-mail addresses can be cumbersome and difficult to remember, and if your spelling of an e-mail address is off by even one letter, your message won't go through. It's best to just keep the e-mail addresses of the people to whom you sent messages in your Contacts list and use those addresses to create new messages.

To create an e-mail message from your Contacts list:

1. **Click the Contacts button in the Navigation Pane (or press Ctrl + 3).**

   The Contacts list appears, as shown in Figure 3-1. You can use any view, but Address Cards view is easiest; you can click the first letter of the person's name to see that person's card. (For more about viewing your Contacts list, see Chapter 7.)

2. **Drag a name from your Contacts list to the Mail button in the Navigation Pane.**

   The Message form appears, with the address of the contact filled in.

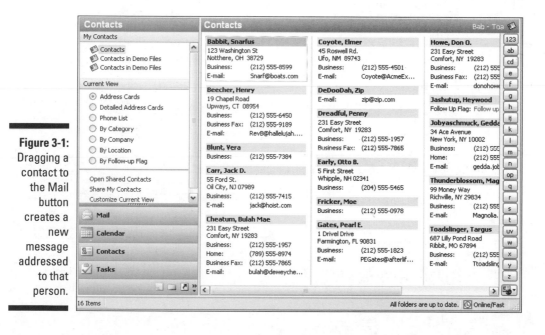

Figure 3-1: Dragging a contact to the Mail button creates a new message addressed to that person.

   3. **Type a subject for your message.**

      Keep it simple; a few words will do.

   4. **Click in the text box and type your message.**

      You can also format text with bold type, italics, and other effects by clicking the appropriate buttons on the toolbar.

   5. **Click Send.**

      The display returns to the Contacts list and your message is sent.

From an appointment

After you enter the particulars about an appointment, you may want to send that information to someone to tell that person what the appointment is about, where it occurs, and when it occurs.

To send an e-mail message with information about an appointment:

   1. **Click the Calendar button in the Navigation Pane (or press Ctrl +2).**

      The Calendar appears, as shown in Figure 3-2.

   2. **Drag the appointment you're interested in from the Calendar to the Mail button.**

      The Message form appears. The subject of the message is already filled in.

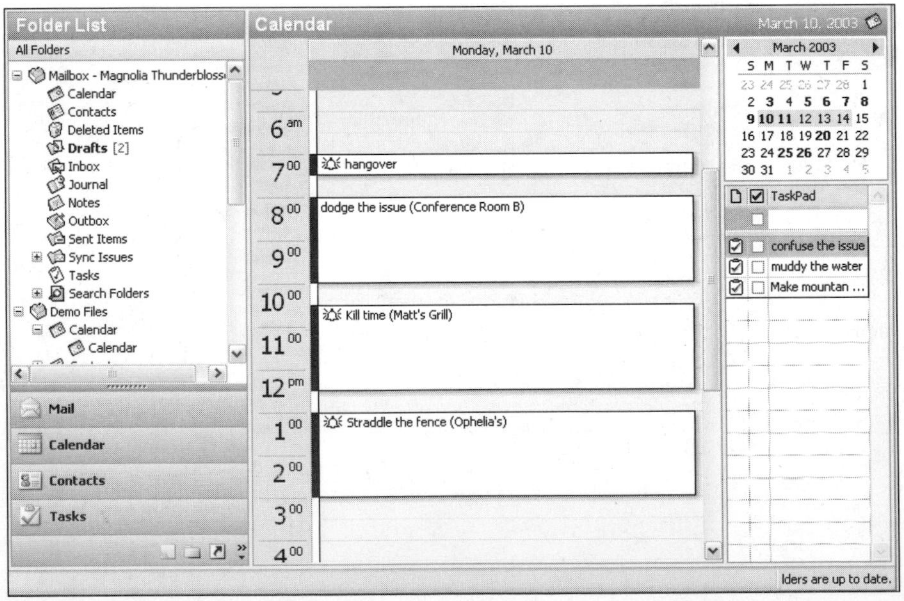

Figure 3-2:
Dragging an appointment to the Mail button creates a new message.

3. **In the To text box, type the name of the person to whom you want to send a copy of the appointment.**

    Alternatively, you can click the To button and choose the person's name from the Address Book. If you use the Address Book, you have to click To again and then click OK.

4. **Click the Send button.**

    Your recipient gets an e-mail message with details about the meeting. You can add additional comments in the text box.

If you plan to invite other people in your organization to a meeting, and you want to check their schedules to plan the meeting, you can also use the Attendee Availability tab of the Appointment form. For this method to work, the people whom you plan to invite to the meeting must be sharing their schedules through Microsoft Exchange Server.

Creating Appointments from E-Mail

The most popular way to announce an event is by e-mail; it's cheap, fast, and complete. Whether you are inviting people to a meeting, a party, a show, or a conference, you probably already know how convenient e-mail can be for organizing events where people get together.

When you receive an announcement about an event and you want to plug its details into your calendar, you can do that in Outlook by following these steps:

1. **Click the Mail button in the Navigation Pane (or press Ctrl+1).**

    A list of your current incoming e-mail messages appears.

2. **Select the message from which you want to make an appointment.**

3. **Drag the selected message to the Calendar button.**

    The New Appointment form opens with the text from the message you dragged in the note section of the New Appointment form. Figure 3-3 shows an appointment created in this way.

4. **If you want to include more information about the event, type that information in the appropriate box on the New Appointment form.**

    You probably want to fill in the Start Time and End Time boxes to reflect the actual time of your appointment.

5. **Click the Save and Close button.**

    You now have all the event information stored right in your calendar for future reference.

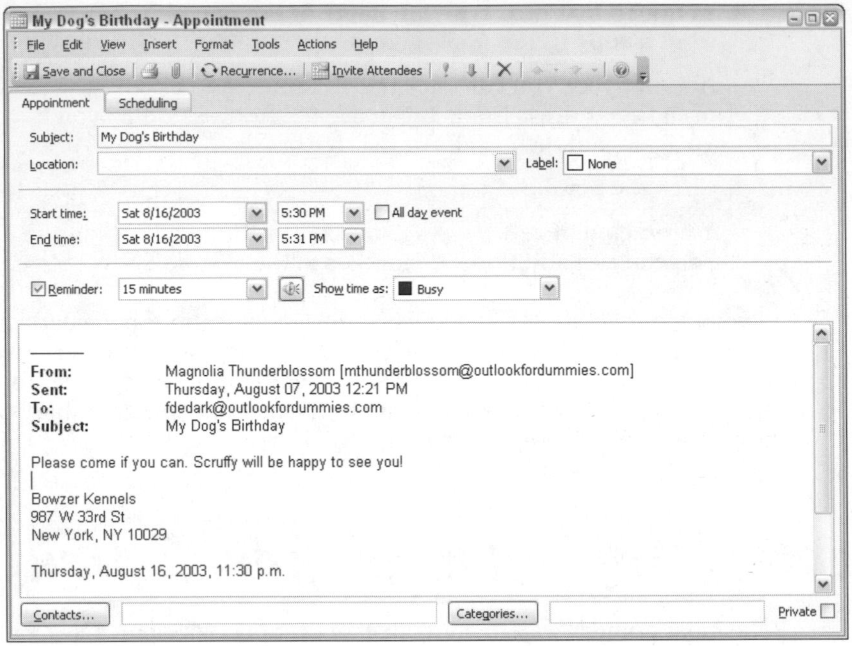

Figure 3-3:
When you drag an e-mail message to your calendar, the message text is stored with your new appointment.

The great thing about creating an appointment from an e-mail message is that all the details included in your message end up right in your calendar. If you need driving directions, agenda details, or whatever information was included in the message, just double-click the appointment in your calendar to get the lowdown. And if you synchronize a Palm or other handheld computer to Outlook, all the information from your Outlook calendar ends up on your handheld. As a result, you'll have your appointment details handy wherever you go. For more tips on dealing with your Palm device, I humbly suggest you read *Palm For Dummies,* 2E (Wiley Publishing, Inc.) written by (yes) yours truly.

Creating Contact Records from E-Mail

You can drag an item from any other Outlook module to the Contacts button, but the only item that makes sense to drag there is an e-mail message. That is, you can drag an e-mail message to the Contacts button in order to create a Contact record that includes the e-mail address. You not only save work by dragging a message to the Contacts button, but also eliminate the risk of misspelling the e-mail address.

To create a new Contact record, follow these steps:

1. **Click the Mail button in the Navigation Pane (or press Ctrl +1).**

   A list of your current incoming e-mail messages appears.

2. **Select the message for which you want to make a Contact record.**

3. **Drag the selected message to the Contacts button in the Navigation Pane.**

   The New Contact form opens, with the name and e-mail address of the person who sent the message filled in. Figure 3-4 shows a New Contact form created this way.

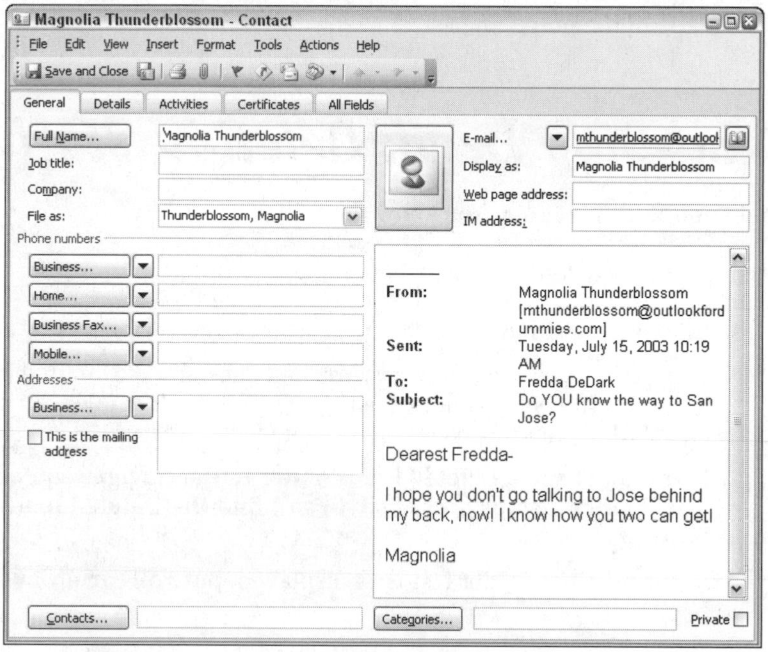

Figure 3-4: Somebody is about to receive a Contact record.

4. **If you want to include more information than the e-mail address of the contact, type that information in the appropriate box on the New Contact form.**

   You can change existing information or add information — the company for whom the person works, the postal mail address, other phone numbers, personal details (say, whether to send a complimentary gift of freeze-dried ants for the person's pet aardvark), and so on.

If the body of the e-mail message contains information you want to use as contact information, select that information and drag it to the appropriate box of the New Contact form.

5. **Click the Save and Close button.**

   You now have the e-mail address and any other information for the new contact stored for future reference.

Another quick way to capture an e-mail address from an incoming message is to right-click the name of the sender in the From line of the incoming message block. The From line is not a normal text box, so you may not think that right-clicking it would do anything, but it does: A shortcut menu appears. Click Add to Contacts to open the New Contact form and then follow the last two steps of the preceding list.

Drag and Drop Dead: Deleting Stuff

If in doubt, throw it out. You know the drill.

Here's how to delete an item using drag-and-drop:

1. **Click the Mail button in the Navigation Pane (or press Ctrl+1).**

   Your list of messages appears. You can click any button that has items you want to delete. (I'm just using e-mail as an example; you can delete any Outlook item by using the Drag and Drop feature.)

2. **If you don't see a Deleted Items folder in the Navigation Pane, Choose Go➪ Folder List (or press Ctrl+6) and find the Deleted Items folder there.**

   Sometimes the Folder List isn't displayed, but you can always bring it back.

3. **Drag an e-mail message to the Deleted Items folder in the Folder List.**

   Kiss it goodbye — it's gone.

If you change your mind after deleting something, just click the Deleted Items folder. The folder opens and a list of everything you've deleted is there. It's like being a hit man in the afterlife — you get another chance to see everyone you've disposed of. Except in this case, you can bring items back to life. Just drag them back to where they came from. (Even Don Corleone couldn't do that.)

Right Button Magic

So far I've talked about holding down your mouse button as if your mouse has only one button. But most up-to-date PC mice have two buttons; some have even more. Many people use only the left button and they get along just fine.

Just to confuse matters, you can change your mouse into a left-handed mouse by adjusting some settings in Windows. When you do that, the left and right buttons exchange functions. Shazam!

When you right-drag an item, or drag it by holding down the right button instead of the left button, something different happens when you drop the item off: A menu appears asking you exactly what result you want. For example, if you right-drag a contact to the Mail button, a menu with a half-dozen choices appears. The choices include

- Copy here as message with text
- Copy here as message with shortcut
- Copy here as message with attachment
- Move here as message with attachment

I don't always remember what's going to happen when I drag an item and drop it off, so I like to use the right-drag feature just to be sure.

Part II
Taming the E-Mail Beast

The 5th Wave   By Rich Tennant

"TELL THE BOSS HE'S GOT MORE FLAME MAIL FROM YOU-KNOW-WHO."

In this part . . .

E-mail . . . everybody's doing it, but not everybody's doing it well. In this part, you'll learn to harness the power of Outlook to dress up your e-mail, stay in touch with your contacts, and span the globe through the Internet without leaving your desk.

Chapter 4

The Essential Secrets of E-Mail

*I*f you're as lazy as I am, electronic mail — e-mail — is a dream. I love getting mail — fan mail, junk mail, official mail, anything except bills. But regular paper mail stacks up in ugly piles, and I always lose the important stuff. E-mail is quick to read, easy to find, and simple to answer. Outlook makes e-mail even easier to read, create, and answer. You don't even have to organize your e-mail in Outlook; it organizes itself!

Front Ends and Back Ends

You need two things to send and receive e-mail:

- ✔ A program that helps you create, save, and manage your messages
- ✔ A program that actually transports the messages to or from the other people with whom you exchange messages

Some technical people call these two parts the front end and the back end, respectively. Outlook is a front end for e-mail; it helps you create, format, store, and manage your messages, but it has little to do with actually getting your messages to your destination. That work is done by a back-end service (such as Microsoft Exchange Server in your office), by your Internet Service Provider (ISP), or by an online service such as CompuServe or The Microsoft Network (MSN).

If you feel that you're the last person on earth without Internet e-mail capability, you've got that capability now with Outlook. Microsoft has made it fiendishly simple to sign up for several online services through the Windows desktop. Remember, though, that your easiest choice isn't always your best choice. Literally hundreds of companies are out there ready to give you Internet access, so it pays to shop around. (I tell you more about online services in Chapter 12.)

You may already be set up on an office e-mail system, such as Microsoft Exchange. If so, I assume that you have a computer guru around to set you up — because that stuff can get kind of messy. You can definitely use Outlook to exchange e-mail via nearly any regular Internet Service Provider. Usually the ISP's technical support people can help you set up Outlook.

Creating Messages

In many ways, electronic mail is better than regular paper mail (also known to e-mail aficionados as *snail mail*). E-mail is delivered much faster than paper mail — almost instantaneously. I find that speedy delivery is really handy for last-minute birthday greetings. E-mail is also incredibly cheap; in fact, it's free most of the time.

The quick and dirty way to create a message

Creating a new message is insanely easy. You can probably figure it out without my help, but here's a hint: Start Outlook, click the New button, enter an address in the To box, a subject in the Subject box, a message in the message box, and click Send. (Nailed that one, didn't you? Was that easy or what?)

The slow, complete way to create a message

You may prefer a more detailed approach to creating an e-mail message. If you have a yen for fancy e-mail — especially if you want to take advantage of every bell and whistle Outlook can add to your message — follow these steps:

1. **Click the Mail button in the Navigation Pane (or press Ctrl+1).**

   The e-mail Inbox appears.

2. **Choose File⇨New⇨Mail Message (or press Ctrl+N).**

   The New Message form appears (as shown in Figure 4-1).

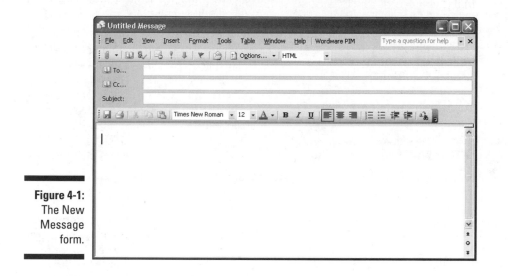

Figure 4-1:
The New
Message
form.

3. **Click the To text box and type the e-mail address of the person to whom you're sending your message.**

   You can also click the To button itself, find the name of the person to whom you're sending the message in the Address Book, and then click OK. (Or you can use the AutoName feature, which I describe in the "What's in a name? AutoName!" sidebar in this chapter.)

4. **Click the Cc text box and type the e-mail addresses of the people to whom you want to send a copy of your message.**

   If you're sending messages to multiple people, separate their addresses; you can use either commas or semicolons.

5. **Type the subject of the message in the Subject box.**

   Your subject can be quite long, but keep it brief. A snappy, relevant subject line makes someone want to read your message; a long or weird subject line doesn't. (Well, you never know with a weird subject line — but don't send weird e-mail at the office unless everybody does.)

6. **Type the text of your message in the text box.**

   If you use Microsoft Word as your word processor, you can also set up Outlook to use Word as your e-mail editor. You can include formatting, graphics, tables, and all the tricks available in Word to make your e-mail more attractive.

What's my e-mail address?

When you have an e-mail account, you want to tell other people your e-mail address so they can send stuff to you. E-mail addresses are a little like long-distance telephone numbers. If you live in Chicago, and you're calling someone in New York, you tell that person your number is (312) 555-9780; if the other person lives in Chicago, you leave off the (312) and just tell him or her to call you at 555-9780. If you work in the same office, you say you're at extension 9780; the other person knows the rest.

Likewise, your e-mail address comes in short, medium, and long versions for different people,

depending on how much of the address they share with you. If you use The Microsoft Network and your account name is Jane_Doe, your e-mail address to the world at large is Jane_Doe@msn.com.

The same is true if you're on an office e-mail system. If you work for International Widgets Corporation, you may be Jdoe@widgets.com. (Check with your company's computer guru about your corporate e-mail address.) Your coworkers can send you messages at Jdoe.

When you use Word as an e-mail editor, you don't do anything different — you just see the Word toolbars in the Outlook e-mail form when you're creating e-mail. You can use all the tools you see to add formatting to your e-mail. I've listed a few formatting tricks you can use in Chapter 20. You can also read Dan Gookin's *Word 2003 For Dummies* (Wiley Publishing, Inc.) for more complete information about using Microsoft Word. If you're completely at home with Microsoft Word, you can just create messages in Word and send them right out without even opening Outlook. Simply type a message in Word by choosing File⇨Send To⇨Mail Recipient, type an address and subject, and then click Send.

Be careful how you format e-mail to send to people on the Internet. Not all e-mail systems can handle graphics or formatted text, such as bold-face or italics, so the masterpiece of correspondence art that you send to your client on the Internet may arrive as gibberish. If you don't know what the other person has on his or her computer, go light on the graphics. When you're sending e-mail to your colleagues in the same office, or if you're sure the person you're sending to also has Outlook, the formatting and graphics should look fine.

7. Click the Send button.

Your mail is sent to the Outbox. If you're on an office network, your mail automatically goes from your Outbox to the Inbox of the person to whom you're sending the message. If you're using an online service such as MSN or CompuServe, press F5 to send the e-mail message along.

Setting the priority of a message

Some messages are more important than others. The momentous report you're sending to your boss demands the kind of attention that wouldn't be appropriate for the wisecrack you send to your friend in the sales department. Setting the importance level to High tells the recipient that your message requires some serious attention.

Here's how you set the priority of a message:

1. **While composing your message, click the Options button in the toolbar (refer to Figure 4-1).**

   The Message Options dialog box appears (as in Figure 4-2).

   You can also open the Message Options dialog box by choosing View⇨ Options if you're not using Microsoft Word as your e-mail editor. The Message Options dialog box enables you to define qualities about your message as, well, *optional* (clever name, eh?).

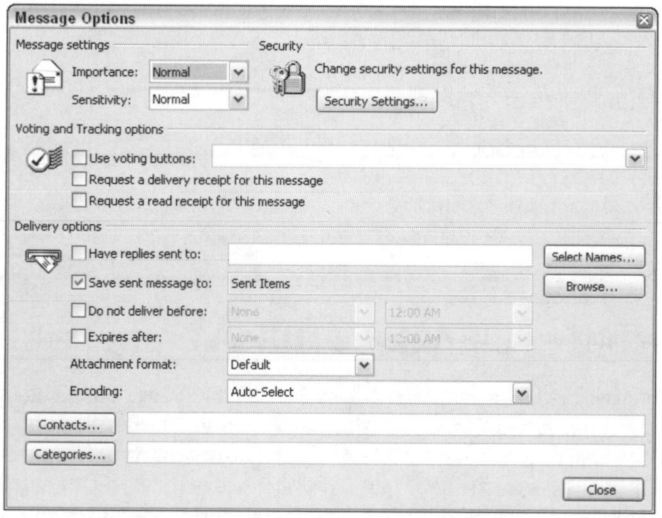

Figure 4-2:
Use the
Message
Options
dialog box
to set the
priority of
your
message.

2. **Click the triangle at the right end of the Importance box.**

   A menu of choices drops down.

3. **Choose High, Normal, or Low.**

   Usually Importance is set to Normal, so you don't have to do anything. Putting a Low importance on your own messages seems silly, but you can also assign importance to messages received in your Inbox, to tell yourself which messages can be dealt with later, if at all.

4. **To close the Message Options dialog box, click Close (or press Esc).**

An even quicker way to set the priority of a message is to use the buttons in the message toolbar. The button with the red exclamation point marks your message as a High importance message. The button with the arrow pointing downward marks your message as a Low importance message. You might wonder why anyone would mark a message as a Low importance message. After all, if it's so unimportant, why send the message in the first place? Apparently, some bosses like their employees to send in routine reports with a Low importance marking so the bosses know to read that stuff *after* all those exciting new e-mail messages they get to read every day.

Setting the sensitivity of a message

You may want your message to be seen by only one person, or you may want to prevent your message from being changed by anyone after you send it. Sensitivity settings enable you to restrict what someone else can do to your message after you send it and who that someone else can be.

To set the sensitivity of a message:

1. **While composing your message, click the Options button in the toolbar.**

The Message Options dialog box appears.

What's in a name? AutoName!

One neat feature of Outlook is that you can avoid memorizing long, confusing e-mail addresses of people to whom you send mail frequently. If the person to whom you're sending a message is entered in your Contact list (see Chapter 7 for more information about contacts) and you've included an e-mail address in the Contact record, all you have to type in the To box of your e-mail form is the person's name or even just a part of the person's name. Outlook helps you fill in the rest of the person's name and figures out the e-mail address. You know you got it right when Outlook underlines the name with a solid black line after you press the Tab key or click outside the To box. If Outlook underlines the name with a wavy red line, that means Outlook thinks it knows the name you're entering but the name isn't spelled quite right — so you have to correct the spelling. If Outlook doesn't put any underline below the name, it's telling you it has no idea to whom you're sending the message — but it will still use the name you typed as the literal e-mail address. Making doubly sure that the name is correct is a good habit to cultivate.

2. Click the scroll-down button (the triangle) at the right end of the Sensitivity box.

A menu scrolls down, showing the words *Normal*, *Personal*, *Private*, and *Confidential* (as in Figure 4-3). Most messages you send will have Normal sensitivity, so that's what Outlook uses if you don't say otherwise. The Personal and Confidential settings only notify the people getting the message that they may want to handle the message differently from a Normal message. (Some organizations even have special rules for dealing with Confidential messages.) Marking a message Private means no one can modify your message when forwarding or replying to it.

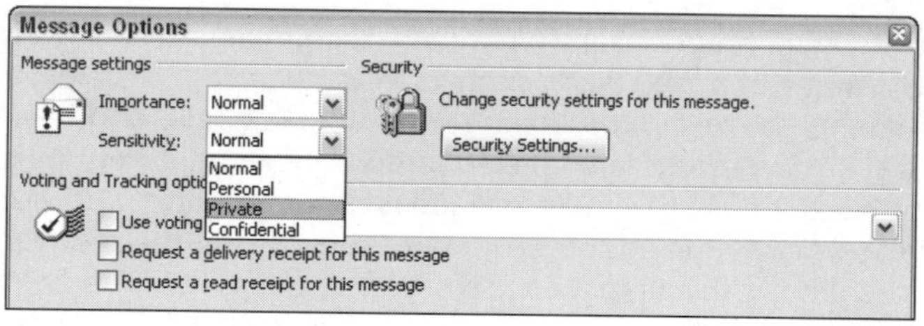

Figure 4-3:
Set the
sensitivity
of your
message
from the
Message
Options
dialog box.

3. Choose Normal, Personal, Private, or Confidential.

4. To close the Message Options dialog box, click Close.

5. When you finish composing your message, click Send (or press Alt+S).

Outlook sends your message off.

Setting the sensitivity of a message to Private or Confidential doesn't make the message any more private or confidential than any other message; it just notifies the recipient that the message contains particularly sensitive information. Many corporations are very careful about what kind of information can be sent by e-mail outside the company. If you use Outlook at work, check with your system administrators before presuming that the information you send by e-mail is secure.

Setting other message options

When you click the Options button and open the Options page the way I describe in the previous section, you may notice a number of strange-sounding options. The other options include Request Read Receipt (which notifies you when your recipient reads your message) and Expires After (which makes a message disappear if your recipient doesn't open it before a time you designate). Those are handy options, but if you want to use them, there's a catch: Both your e-mail system and your recipient's mail system must support those features, or they won't work at all. If you and your recipient are both on the same network using Microsoft Exchange Server, then everything should work just fine. If you're not using Outlook on an Exchange Network, then (frankly) it's a gamble. (See Chapter 14 for more about how to use the features of Outlook that work only on Exchange Server.)

Adding an Internet link to an e-mail message

All Microsoft Office programs automatically recognize Internet addresses. If you type the name of a Web page, such as www.outlookfordummies.com, Outlook changes the text color to blue and underlines the address, making it look just like the hypertext you click to jump between different pages on the Web. That makes it easy to send someone information about an exciting Web site; just type or copy the address into your message. If the recipient is also an Outlook user, he or she can just click the text to make the Web browser pop up and open the page you mentioned in your message.

Reading and Replying to E-Mail Messages

Outlook has a couple of ways to tell you when you receive an e-mail message. The Status Bar in the bottom left corner of the Outlook screen tells you how many e-mail messages you have overall and how many of those are unread (see Figure 4-4). The word *Inbox* in the Folder List changes to boldface type when you have unread e-mail, and when you look in the Inbox, you see titles of unread messages in bold as well. Also, when you log on to Windows XP, you'll see a little notice.

To open and read an e-mail message, follow these steps:

1. **Click the Mail button in the Navigation Pane (or press Ctrl+1).**

   The Inbox screen opens, showing your incoming mail.

2. **Double-click the title of the message you want to read.**

   The message opens, and you can see the text of the message (as in Figure 4-5). If the message is really long, press the down-arrow key or the PgDn key to scroll through the text.

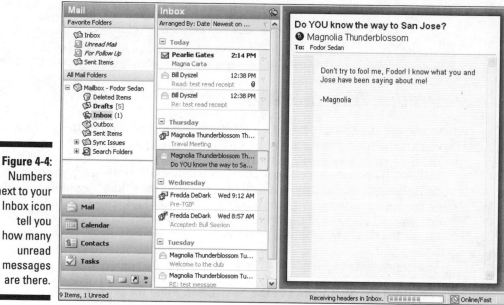

Figure 4-4:
Numbers next to your Inbox icon tell you how many unread messages are there.

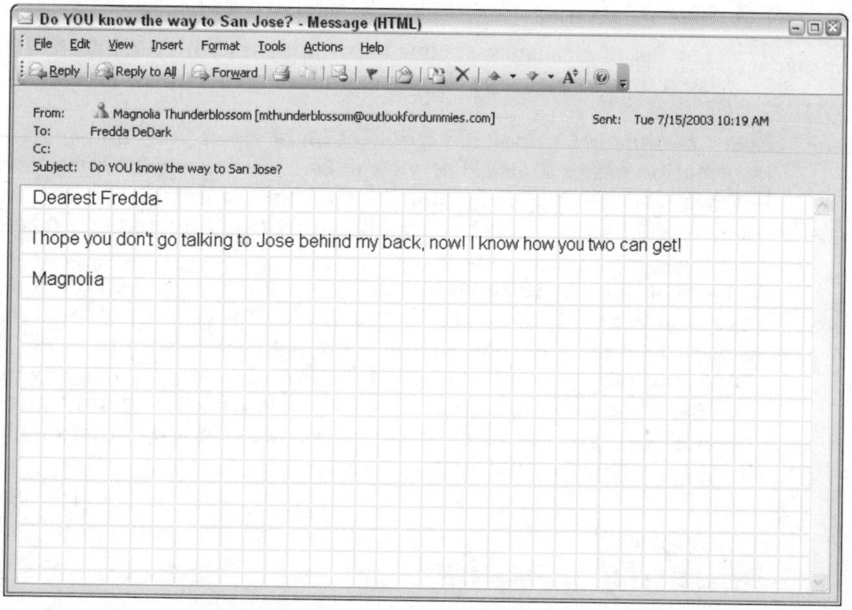

Figure 4-5:
Double-click a message to open it and read the contents.

3. **To close the Message screen, choose File⇨Close (or press Alt+F4).**

   The Message screen closes, and you see the list of messages in your Inbox.

Previewing message text

When you start getting lots of e-mail, some of it will be important, but some of it will be relatively unimportant — if not downright useless. When you first see the mail in your Inbox, it's nice to know which messages are important and which are not so you can focus on the important stuff. You can't count on the people who send you e-mail to say, "Don't read this; it's unimportant" (although a Low priority rating is a good clue). Outlook tries to help by enabling you to peek at the first few lines of a message so you know right off the bat whether it's worth reading.

To see previews of your unread messages:

1. **Click the Mail button in the Navigation Pane (or press Ctrl+1).**

   The Inbox screen opens, showing your incoming mail.

2. **Choose View⇨ AutoPreview (see Figure 4-6).**

   The list of messages in your Inbox appears with the first few lines of each unread message displayed in blue.

Every module in Outlook has a collection of views you can use to make your information easier to use. The view called Messages with AutoPreview is the best way to look at your incoming e-mail. In Chapter 16, I show you some other views that can make your collection of e-mail messages more useful.

An even better way to zoom through your Inbox is to open the Reading Pane, an area of the Outlook screen that displays the contents of any message you select. To set up your Reading Pane, choose View⇨Reading Pane, then choose either Right, Bottom, or Off. You can't go wrong with any of the three choices; if you don't like one, change to another. When you've turned on the Reading Pane, you can skim through your messages by pressing either your up-arrow or down-arrow keys.

Sending a reply

The thing I love about e-mail is that sending a reply is so easy. You don't even need to know the person's address when you're sending a reply; just click the Reply button and Outlook takes care of it for you.

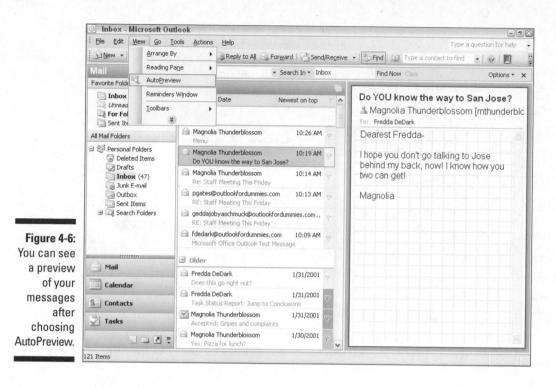

Figure 4-6:
You can see
a preview
of your
messages
after
choosing
AutoPreview.

Here's how you reply to a message:

1. **Click the Mail button in the Navigation Pane (or press Ctrl+1).**

   The Inbox screen opens, showing your incoming mail.

2. **Double-click the title of the message to which you want to reply.**

   The message you double-clicked opens, and you can see the contents of the message.

   If the message is already open, you can skip the first two steps and go directly to Step 3.

3. **To reply to the people who are named in the From line, click the Reply button.**

4. **To reply to the people who are named in the Cc line as well as the From line, click the Reply to All button.**

   The Reply screen appears (as shown in Figure 4-7).

   You may get (or send) e-mail that's addressed to a whole bunch of people all at one time. At least one person must be named in the To line; more than one person can be in the Cc line, which is for people to whom you're sending only a copy. Little difference exists between what happens to mail that's going to people in the To line and mail that's going to the people in the Cc line — all of them can reply to, forward, or ignore the message. You don't always need to reply to the people on the Cc line, or you may want to reply to only some of them. If you do that, you must click the Reply button (not Reply to All) and add them again to the Cc line.

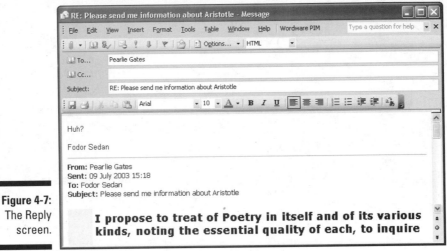

RE: Please send me information about Aristotle - Message

File   Edit   View   Insert   Format   Tools   Table   Window   Help   Wordware PIM

Type a question for help

Options...   HTML

To...   Pearlie Gates
Cc...
Subject: RE: Please send me information about Aristotle

Arial   10

Huh?

Fodor Sedan

From: Pearlie Gates
Sent: 09 July 2003 15:18
To: Fodor Sedan
Subject: Please send me information about Aristotle

I propose to treat of Poetry in itself and of its various kinds, noting the essential quality of each, to inquire

Figure 4-7:
The Reply
screen.

5. **Type your reply in the Message box.**

   Don't be alarmed when you discover some text already in the text box — it's part of the message to which you're replying. Your blinking cursor is at the top of the screen, so anything you type precedes the other person's message. (This arrangement means the person who gets your message can review the original message as a memory-jogger when your reply comes back.)

6. **Click the Send button.**

   On your office network, clicking Send speeds the message to its intended recipient.

   If you're a standalone user who's sending mail on an online service, such as The Microsoft Network or CompuServe, you must also choose Tools⇨ Send/Receive⇨Send/Receive All or press F9 to send your message out over the Internet. See Chapter 12 for more about sending e-mail from your home computer with Outlook.

7. **Choose File⇨Close (or press Esc) to close the Message screen.**

   The Message form disappears and your Inbox reappears.

Using a link to the Web from your e-mail

When you open a message, sometimes you see blue, underlined text with the name of a Web page or other Internet resource, such as `www.outlookfor dummies.com`. If you want to look at that page, all you have to do is double-click the text — if everything is installed correctly, your Web browser pops up and opens the Web page whose name you've clicked.

After you open the page, you can save the page to your Favorites folder so you can find it again easily.

That's Not My Department: Forwarding E-Mail

You may not always have the answer to every e-mail message you get. You may need to pass a message along to somebody else to answer, so pass it on.

To forward a message, follow these steps:

1. **Click the Mail button in the Navigation Pane (or press Ctrl+1).**

   The Inbox screen opens, showing your incoming mail.

2. **Double-click the title of the message you want to forward.**

   The Message screen opens (see Figure 4-8). You can forward the message as soon as you read it. If you've already opened the message, you can skip the first two steps.

3. **Click the Forward button.**

   The Forward screen appears (see Figure 4-9). The subject of the original message is now the subject of the new message, except the letters *FW:* (for Forward) are inserted at the beginning.

4. **Click the To text box and type the e-mail address of the person to whom you're forwarding the message.**

   If the person to whom you're forwarding is entered in your Contact list, just type the person's name — Outlook figures out the e-mail address for you.

5. **Click the Cc text box and type the e-mail addresses of the people to whom you want to forward a copy of your message.**

   Many people forward trivia (such as jokes of the day) to scads and scads of their friends by e-mail. Most recipients are included as Cc addresses.

Remember, business e-mail etiquette is different from home e-mail etiquette. Many employers have strict policies about appropriate use of their corporate e-mail systems. If you work for such a company, be aware of your company's policies.

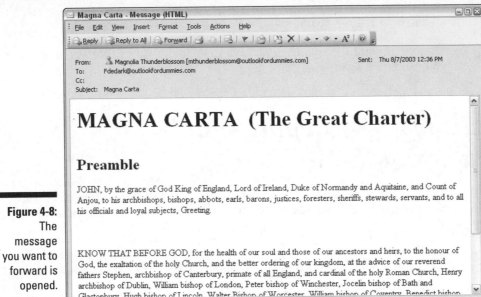

Figure 4-8:
The message you want to forward is opened.

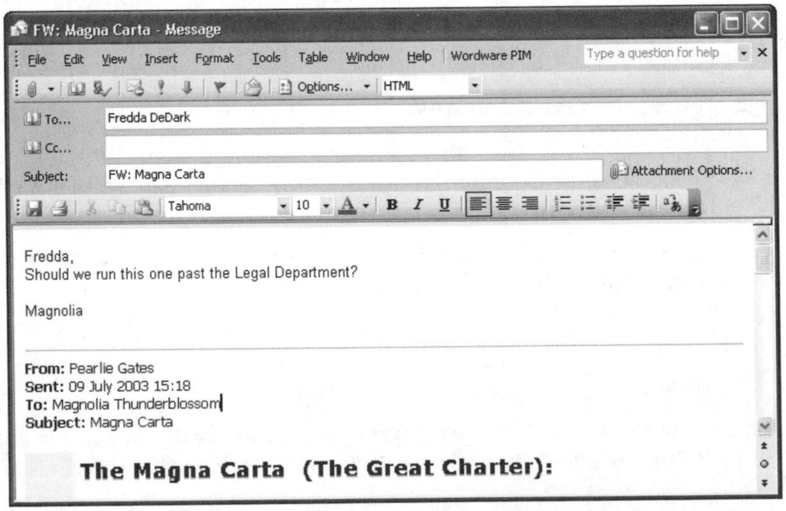

Figure 4-9:
The Forward screen.

If you want to pester your friends by sending silly trivia from your home computer to their home computers (as I do), that's your own business.

6. **In the text box, type any comments you want to add to the message.**

   The text of the original message appears in the text box, preceded by the words Original Message and a couple of blank lines. You can preface the message that you're forwarding if you want to give that person a bit of explanation — for example, **This is the 99th message I've had from this person; somebody needs to get a life.**

7. **Click the Send button.**

   Your message is on its way.

Deleting Messages

You can zap an e-mail message without a second thought; you don't even have to read the thing. As soon as you see the Inbox list, you know who's sending the message and what it's about, so you don't have to waste time reading Burt's Bad Joke of the day. Just zap it.

If you accidentally delete a message you didn't want to lose, click the Deleted Items icon; you find all the messages you've deleted in the last few months. To recover a deleted message, just drag it from the Deleted Items list to either the Inbox icon or the Outbox icon.

Here's how you delete a message:

1. **Click the Mail button in the Navigation Pane (or press Ctrl+1).**

   The Inbox screen opens, showing your incoming mail.

2. **Click the title of the message you want to delete.**

   You don't have to read the message; you can just delete it from the list.

3. **Choose Edit⇨Delete (or press Delete).**

When you delete messages, Outlook doesn't actually eliminate deleted items; it moves them to the Deleted Items folder. If you have unread items in your Deleted Items folder, Outlook annotates the Deleted Items icon with the number of unread items, the same way it annotates the Inbox with the number of unread items. You can get rid of the annotation by choosing Tools⇨Empty Deleted Items Folder. Or you can just ignore the annotation. After you empty your Deleted Items folder, the messages that were in it disappear forever.

Saving Interrupted Messages

If you get interrupted while writing an e-mail message, all is not lost. You can just save the work you've done and return to it later. Just choose File⇨Save (or press Ctrl+S), and your message is saved to the Drafts folder, as shown in Figure 4-10 (unless you had reopened the message from the Outbox, in which case Outlook saves the unfinished message to the Outbox).

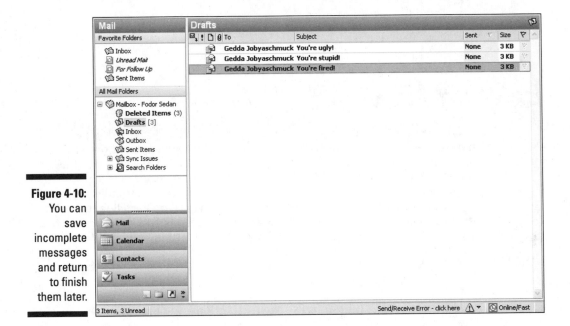

Figure 4-10:
You can save incomplete messages and return to finish them later.

When a message is ready to be sent, its name appears in the Outbox in italics. If you've saved it to work on later, its name appears in normal text, not italics. If you're not finished with the message and plan to return to it later, save it (press Ctrl+S). If the message is ready for prime time, send it (press Alt+S).

Saving a Message as a File

You may create or receive an e-mail message that's so wonderful (or terrible) that you just have to save it. You may need to print the message and show it to someone else, save it to a floppy disk, or export it to a desktop-publishing program.

To save a message as a file, follow these steps:

1. **Choose File⇨Save As (or press F12).**

   The Save As dialog box appears.

2. **Click the triangle at the end of the Save In box (called the *scroll-down* button) to choose the drive to which you want to save your file.**

   If you do all your work on drive C, Outlook chooses drive C first, so you don't have to do anything. To save to a floppy disk, choose the A drive.

3. **Click the name of the folder in which you want to save the file.**

   A list appears of all files in the folder you select.

4. **Click the File Name text box and type the name you want to give the file.**

   Type any name you want, up to 256 characters.

5. **If you want to change the type of the file, click the triangle at the end of the Save as Type box and choose a file type.**

   If you're using Word as your e-mail editor, you see the entire range of file types you can create in Word. If not, the list offers text, the Outlook message format, Outlook Template, and the Internet standard format, HTML (see Figure 4-11). Use HTML. The Outlook Template format is for a message you want to use repeatedly in Outlook.

6. **Click Save (or press Enter).**

   The message is saved to the file and folder you specified in Steps 2 through 4.

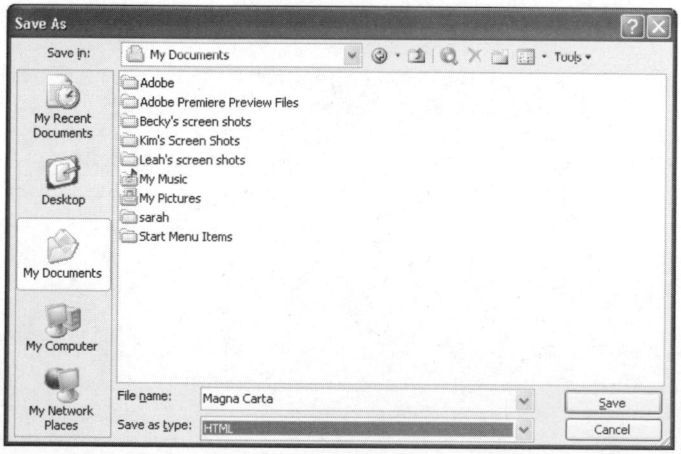

Figure 4-11: The Save As dialog box.

Postscript

Sending e-mail is simple. Keeping track of all the tens of millions of people to whom you want to send e-mail is a bigger task. Fortunately, Outlook does both things, so you can go to one program to get the names of the people you know, find what you know about them, and send them e-mail asking them to tell you more. Don't forget to stop when you know enough.

Chapter 5

E-Mail Tools You Can't Do Without

In This Chapter

▶ Using flags with messages

▶ Saving copies of messages you send

▶ Including your name with your remarks in replies

▶ Setting options for replies

▶ Attaching files to messages

▶ Setting up a signature

---

*O*utlook can do all sorts of tricks with the mail you send out, as well as with the messages you receive. You can flag messages with reminders, customize your messages with a signature, or add special formatting to the messages you send as replies.

As the automobile ads say, "Your mileage may vary." Outlook is just the pretty face on an elaborate arrangement of programs that make e-mail work. Outlook is like the dashboard of your car; you can use the dashboard to make the car do what you want it to do, but what your car *can* do depends more on what's under the hood than what's on the dashboard. In the same way, some features of Outlook work only if the system that's backing it up supports those same features. In addition, some Outlook features work only if the person to whom you're mailing uses a system that supports the same features you're using.

Microsoft Exchange Server — a program that runs on many corporate networks — adds a number of features to Outlook, such as delaying delivery of messages or diverting messages to someone else. In this chapter, I don't discuss features you may not have, but if you want to know more about the features you may have on a corporate network with Microsoft Exchange Server, see Chapter 14. If you're not among the fortunate ones who have Exchange Server, don't worry — Outlook can do plenty all by itself.

Nagging by Flagging

Over time, flags have become my favorite Outlook feature. Back when I received only a few dozen e-mail messages a week, flags didn't matter that much. Now that I get thousands of messages each week, I need help remembering to get back to important messages that otherwise might get lost in the shuffle. If I can't respond to an important message right away, I like to flag that message as soon as I read the message. Then I'm sure to get back to it. You can also plant a flag in a message you send to others to remind them of a task they have to do if both you and the other person are on an Exchange network.

Adding a flag to an e-mail message with one click

Why flag a message? To help get your work done faster! So you need to know the fastest possible way to flag a message, right? Of course.

When you look at the list of messages in your Inbox (shown in Figure 5-1), you see a little box at the right end of each subject line containing a little, gray outline of a flag, sort of a shadow flag. When you click that little shadow, it changes from gray to beautiful living color to show you've flagged it. Now whenever you look at your list of messages, you know which messages need further attention.

Once you've attended to your flagged message, click the flag again. That replaces the flag with a check mark to show you've taken care of that message.

Adding flags of different colors

If you only click once on a message to add a flag, a flag will appear in whatever lovely default color is set in Outlook, usually red. But maybe you don't want to use a red flag for some reason. Perhaps you don't want to irritate your pet bull. Maybe you're still afraid of Soviet spies hiding in the broom closet, whatever. So pick another color by right-clicking the little flag to display a list of alternate flag colors. You'll find many attractive choices (sorry, no paisley). If you want to choose different colored flags for different occasions, feel free.

Changing the default flag color

If you want to avoid red flags altogether, perhaps because they clash with your décor, you can change the default color of your flags by following these steps:

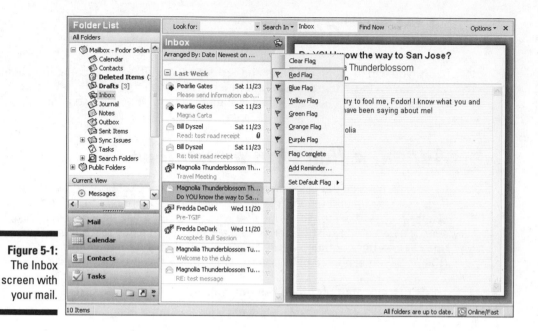

Figure 5-1:
The Inbox
screen with
your mail.

1. **Right-click any flag.**

   The flag shortcut menu appears.

2. **Choose Set Default Flag.**

   Another shortcut menu appears, offering several color choices (see Figure 5-2).

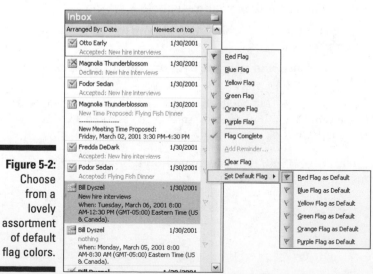

Figure 5-2:
Choose
from a
lovely
assortment
of default
flag colors.

3. **Pick the color that suits you.**

   The color you choose becomes the default flag color.

Sadly, you can't get the old Stars and Stripes as an Outlook flag color. But then you'd have a hard time seeing either the stars or the stripes, and you'd have to salute and sing "The Star-Spangled Banner" every time you used one. . . .

Adding a flag with a reminder

Of course, flags can do a lot more than stand there looking pretty. Outlook flags can pop up and remind you to do something at a preset time. They can also pop up and pester someone *else* when you put a flag on a message you send. (Who could resist that?) Adding a reminder to a flag takes more than one click — but not much more. To attach a flag to your e-mail messages (the ones you send and ones you're sent), follow these steps:

1. **Click the Mail button in the Navigation Pane (or press Ctrl+1).**

   The Inbox screen opens, showing your incoming mail.

2. **Right-click the flag on the message you want to flag.**

   The flag shortcut menu appears.

3. **Choose Add Reminder.**

   The Flag for Follow Up dialog box appears. At this point, if you click OK (or press Enter), your message is flagged. You can set more detailed options by using the next three steps.

4. **Click the triangle at the right end of the Flag To text box and choose one of the menu items (or type your own choice).**

   One handy flag is "Follow Up," which reminds you to confirm an appointment or other arrangement.

5. **Click the Reminder box and type the date on which you want the reminder flag to appear.**

   You can type the date **3/3/04**; Outlook understands. You can type **first wednesday of march**; Outlook understands. You can type **a week from Wednesday**; Outlook understands that to mean "seven days after the Wednesday that comes after today." You don't even have to worry about capitalization. (Don't type **I hate mondays,** though — Outlook doesn't understand that. But I do.)

If you'd rather just pick a date from a calendar, you can click the little down arrow next to the Reminder box to reveal a calendar, and then just click the date you want.

6. Click OK.

When the date you entered in the Flag for Follow Up dialog box arrives, a reminder dialog box pops up to help jog your memory.

Changing the date on a flag

Procrastination used to be an art; Outlook makes it a science. When someone nags you with flags, you can still put it off. Yes, dear, you *can* do it later.

To change the date on a flag, follow these steps:

1. Click the Mail button in the Navigation Pane (or press Ctrl+1).

The Inbox screen opens, showing your incoming mail (see Figure 5-3).

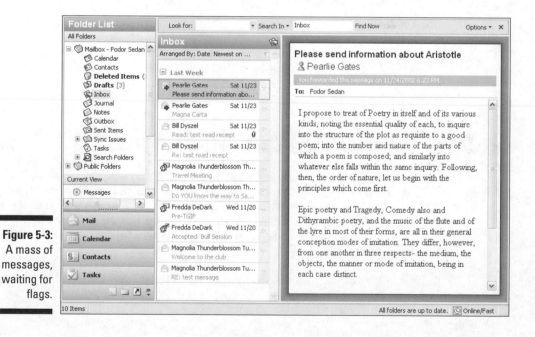

Figure 5-3:
A mass of messages, waiting for flags.

  2. **Click the message that has a flag you want to change.**

     The Message appears highlighted to show that you've selected it.

  3. **Choose Action➪Follow Up➪Add Reminder (or press Ctrl+Shift+G).**

     The Flag for Follow Up dialog box appears (see Figure 5-4).

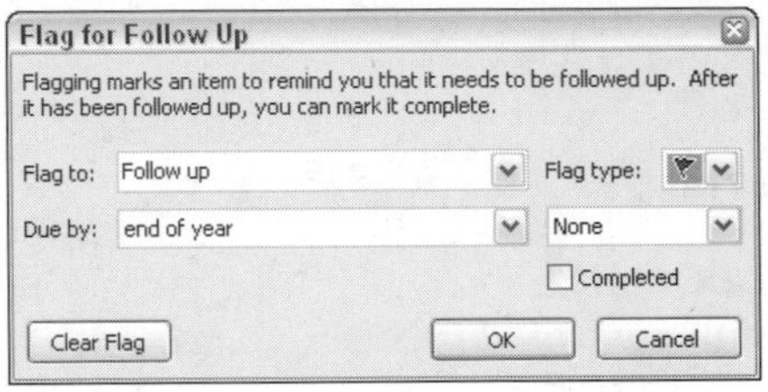

Figure 5-4:
The Flag for
Follow Up
dialog box.

  4. **Click the Due by box and type the new date when you want the reminder flag to appear.**

     Type the date when you think you'll feel ready to be flagged again. Typing **999 years from now** will work — really!

  5. **Click OK.**

Of course, you can always put something off if you really try. When a flag reminder pops up, hit the snooze button to put it off for a while, as you do with your alarm clock.

Saving Copies of Your Messages

Nothing is handier than knowing what you've sent and when you sent it. You can save all your outgoing mail in Outlook so you can go back and look up the messages you've sent. Outlook starts saving sent items when you first install the program, but you can turn this feature on and off. So before you go changing your options, look in your Sent Messages folder to see whether it contains messages.

To save copies of your messages, follow these steps:

  1. **Choose Tools➪Options.**

     The Options dialog box appears.

  2. **Click the E-mail Options button.**

     The E-mail Options dialog box appears (shown in Figure 5-5).

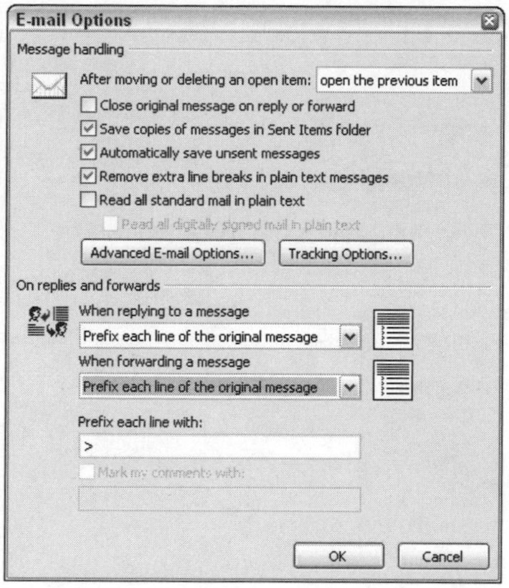

E-mail Options

Message handling

After moving or deleting an open item: open the previous item ▾

☐ Close original message on reply or forward
☑ Save copies of messages in Sent Items folder
☑ Automatically save unsent messages
☑ Remove extra line breaks in plain text messages
☐ Read all standard mail in plain text
☐ Read all digitally signed mail in plain text

[Advanced E-mail Options...] [Tracking Options...]

On replies and forwards

When replying to a message
Prefix each line of the original message ▾

When forwarding a message
Prefix each line of the original message ▾

Prefix each line with:
>

☐ Mark my comments with:

[OK] [Cancel]

Figure 5-5:
You can decide whether to save copies of the messages you send by using the E-mail Options dialog box.

3. **Click the Save Copies of Messages in Sent Items Folder check box.**

   If the box already contains a check mark, leave it alone. (That's the way Outlook is set up when you first install it.) If you click the box when it's already checked, you turn off your option for saving messages. Don't worry if you make a mistake; you can always change it back. Just make sure a check appears in the box if you want to save messages.

4. **Click OK.**

Outlook saves two months' worth of saved messages and sends older messages to an archive file to save disk space on your computer.

Automatically Adding Your Name to a Reply

When you reply to a message, it helps to include parts of the original message you're replying to so the person reading your message knows exactly what you're responding to. The trick is, how will the reader know which comments are his or hers and which are yours?

Outlook enables you to preface your comments with your name or any text you choose. If you want to be understood, it's best to use your name. (If you want to confuse the issue, you could always use a phrase such as "Simon says.")

To tag your replies with your name, follow these steps:

1. **Choose Tools⇨Options.**

   The Options dialog box appears.

2. **Click the E-mail Options button.**

   The E-mail Options dialog box appears (as in Figure 5-6).

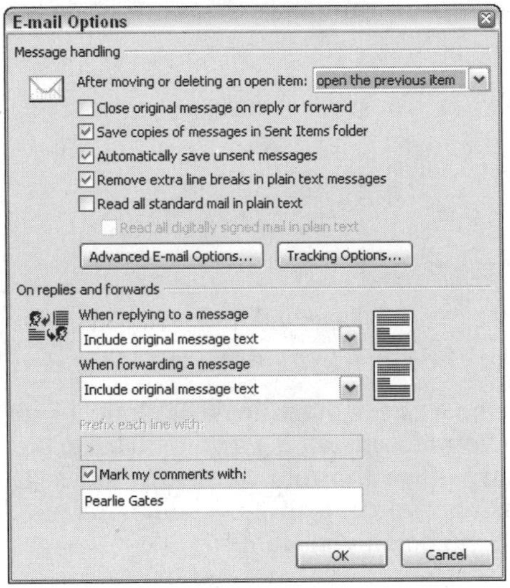

Figure 5-6:
Preface
your replies
with your
name by
checking
the box at
the bottom
of the E-mail
Options
dialog box.

E-mail Options
Message handling
After moving or deleting an open item: [open the previous item ▾]
☐ Close original message on reply or forward
☑ Save copies of messages in Sent Items folder
☑ Automatically save unsent messages
☑ Remove extra line breaks in plain text messages
☐ Read all standard mail in plain text
☐ Read all digitally signed mail in plain text
[Advanced E-mail Options...]   [Tracking Options...]
On replies and forwards
When replying to a message
[Include original message text ▾]
When forwarding a message
[Include original message text ▾]
Prefix each line with:
[>]
☑ Mark my comments with:
[Pearlie Gates]
[OK]   [Cancel]

3. **Click the Mark My Comments With check box to put a check there.**

   If the check box is already checked, don't click it; doing so would remove the check.

4. **In the Mark My Comments With text box, type the text you want to accompany your annotations.**

   Your best bet is to enter your name here. Whatever you enter will be used as the prefix to all text you type when you reply to messages.

5. **Click OK.**

You can select and delete the text of the original message when you create a reply, but including at least a part of the message you're replying to makes your response easier to understand. You also have the option of selecting and deleting the parts of the original text that aren't relevant to your reply.

Setting Your Options

You can control the appearance of the messages you forward, as well as your replies. If all your e-mail stays in your office among other Microsoft Office users, you can make your text look pretty incredible in messages you send to one another by adding graphics, wild-looking fonts, or special effects, such as blinking text. If you're sending mail to poor ol' Internet users or to people on an online service, such as CompuServe (see Chapter 12 for more about sending e-mail to online services and the Internet), pay attention to how messages look to those people.

To set your options, follow these steps:

1. **Choose Tools⇨Options.**

   The Options dialog box appears.

2. **Click the E-mail Options button.**

   The E-mail Options dialog box appears (looking a lot like Figure 5-7).

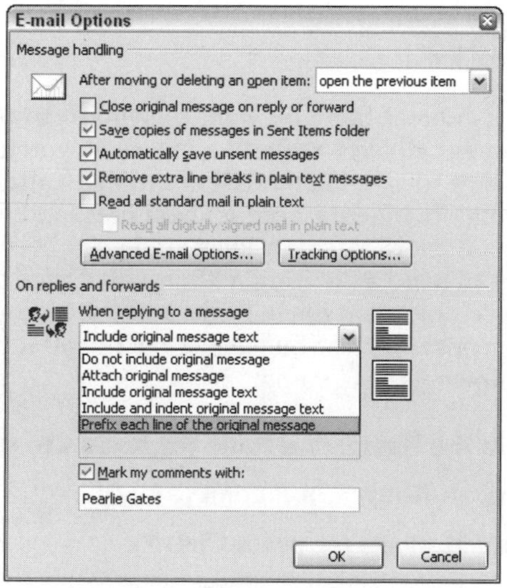

Figure 5-7:
Change the appearance of your outgoing messages by selecting what you need in the E-mail Options dialog box.

3. **Click the scroll-down button (triangle) at the right end of the When Replying to a Message box.**

   A menu of options drops down. When Outlook is first installed, Include and Indent Original Message Text is the default option. The diagram to the right of the scroll-down menu illustrates how the message will be laid out when you choose each option.

4. **Choose the style you prefer to use for replies.**

   The little diagram to the right of the menu changes when you make a choice to show you what your choice will look like. If you don't like the choice you've made, try another and see how it looks in the diagram.

5. **Click the triangle at the right end of the When Forwarding a Message box.**

   The When Forwarding a Message box has one choice fewer than the When Replying to a Message box does, but the two menus work the same way. Also, they both have that little diagram of the page layout off to the right.

6. **Choose the style you prefer to use for forwarding messages.**

   Just pick one; you can always change it.

7. **Click OK.**

You can do all sorts of fancy, exciting, and even useful tricks with e-mail by taking advantage of Outlook's options. If the advanced options seem confusing, you can easily ignore them. Just click Reply and type your answer.

Sending Attachments

If you've already created a document that you want to send to somebody, you don't have to type the document all over again in a message; you just send the document as an attachment to an e-mail message. You can attach any kind of file — word-processing documents, spreadsheet files, and presentations from programs, such as PowerPoint. Any kind of file can be sent as an attachment. The easiest way to send a file from a Microsoft Office program (such as Microsoft Word) is to open that file in Word and then choose File⇨Send To. If you'd rather not do that, you can send a file attachment straight from Outlook by following these steps:

1. **Click the Mail button in the Navigation Pane (or press Ctrl+Shift+I).**

   The Inbox screen opens, showing your incoming mail.

2. **Choose File⇨New⇨Mail Message (or press Ctrl+N).**

   The New Message form appears.

3. **Choose Insert⇨File or click the paper-clip button in the Message Form toolbar.**

   The Insert File dialog box appears (see Figure 5-8). It looks like the dialog box you use for opening files in most Windows programs, and it works like opening a file, too. Just click the name of the file you want to send and press Enter.

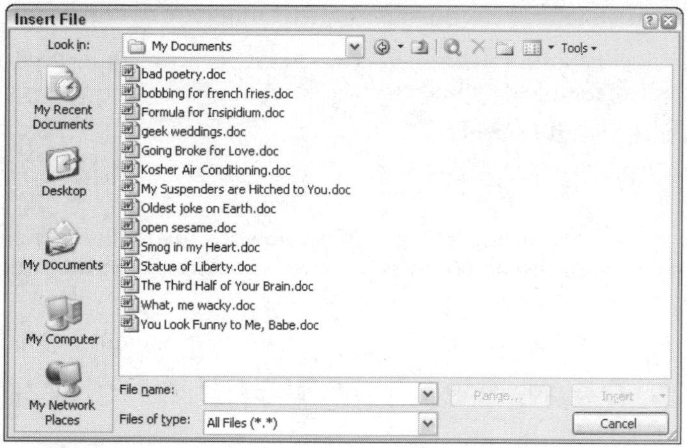

Figure 5-8:
The Insert
File dialog
box.

4. **In the list of files, click the name of the file you want to send.**

   An icon appears in your text, representing the file you attached to your message.

5. **Click OK.**

   Your Message form now contains an icon that has the same name as the file you selected — which means the file is attached. When you send this e-mail message, a copy of the file you selected goes to your recipient.

6. **Type your message (if you have a message to send).**

   You may not have a message; perhaps you want to send only the attachment. If what you want to say is in the attachment, that's fine, but remember that the contents of an attachment don't show up on the recipient's screen until he or she double-clicks to open the attachment.

7. **Click the To button in your Message form.**

   The Select Names dialog box appears.

8. **Select a name from your address book.**

   If the name of the person to whom you want to send your message isn't in the list, you can click the Cancel button and return to the Message form. Then just type the person's e-mail address in the To text box.

9. **Click the To button in the Select Names dialog box.**

   The name of the selected person appears in the Message Recipients box of the Select Names dialog box.

10. **Click OK.**

    The name of the selected person is now in the To box of the message.

11. Click the Subject text box and type a subject for your message.

A subject is optional, but if you want somebody to read what you send, including a subject helps.

12. Click the Send button.

Your message and its attachment are sent.

Those are just a few of the tricks you can do with the mail you send. You can also do tricks with the mail you get; I cover those tricks in Chapter 9.

Creating Signatures for Your Messages

Many people like to add a *signature* to the end of every message they send. A signature is usually a small piece of text that identifies you to everyone reading your message and tells something you want everyone to know. Many people include their name, the name of their business, their motto, a little sales slogan, or some squib of personal information.

You can tell Outlook to add a signature automatically to all your outgoing messages, but first you must create a signature file. Here's how to create your signature file, follow these steps:

1. Choose Tools⇨Options.

The Options dialog box appears.

2. Click the Mail Format tab.

The Mail Format dialog box appears.

3. Click the Signature button.

The Create Signature dialog box appears (as shown in Figure 5-9).

4. Click the New button.

The Create New Signature dialog box appears.

5. Type a name for your new signature.

The name you type appears in the Signature box. You can name a signature anything you want.

6. Click the Next button.

The Edit Signature dialog box appears.

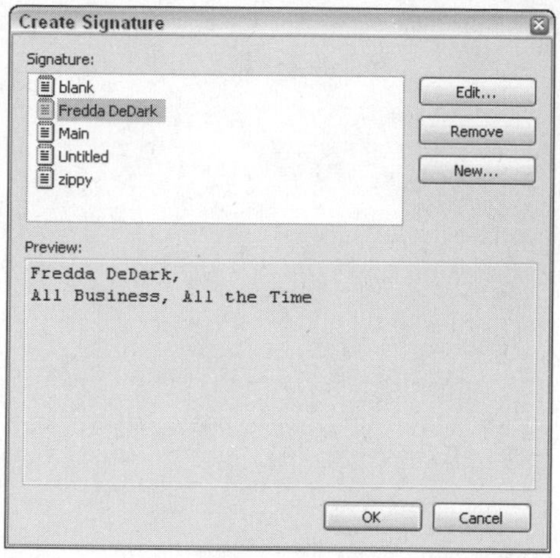

Create Signature

Signature:
- blank
- Fredda DeDark
- Main
- Untitled
- zippy

Edit...
Remove
New...

Preview:

Fredda DeDark,
All Business, All the Time

OK   Cancel

Figure 5-9:
The Create
Signature
dialog box.

7. **Type the text of the signature you want to create.**

   The text you type appears in the Signature text box. You can put anything you want in a signature, but try to be brief. You don't want your signature to be longer than the message to which it's attached.

8. **Click the Finish button.**

   The Signature Picker dialog box appears.

9. **Click OK.**

   The Mail Format dialog box appears.

10. **Click OK.**

    The Options dialog box appears.

11. **Click OK.**

    Your new signature will now appear on every message you send. If you create more than one signature, you can switch between signatures by following Steps 1 and 2 and then choosing the signature you want from the scroll-down menu next to the words *Use this signature by default.*

If you use more than one e-mail address, you can set up Outlook to use different signatures on different e-mail addresses. For example, if you have one e-mail address you use for business and a different address you use for personal messages, you can designate a businesslike signature to the messages you send from the business address and a more casual signature for your personal messages. To designate which signatures go with which address, click the scroll-down menu labeled "Select the signatures to use with the following account," and then pick the signatures you want to use.

Chapter 6

Conquering Your Mountain of Messages

I have good news and bad news about e-mail. The good news is that e-mail is free; you can send as much as you want for virtually no cost. The bad news is that e-mail is free; anybody can easily send *you* more e-mail than you can possibly read. Before long, you need help sorting it all out so you can deal with the messages that actually need immediate action.

Outlook has some handy tools for coping with the flood of electronic flotsam and jetsam that finds its way into your Inbox. You can create separate folders for filing your mail, and you can use Outlook's view feature to help you slice and dice your incoming messages into manageable groups.

Even better than the View feature is the Rules Wizard, which automatically responds to incoming messages according to your wishes. You can move all messages from certain senders to the folder of your choice — for instance, consigning everything from Spam-O-Rama.com to oblivion — send automatic replies to messages about certain subjects, or delete messages containing words that offend you.

Speaking of spam, an even more effective way to deal with offensive or aggressively useless messages is to use the new junk e-mail filters built into Outlook. You turn the filters on only once — after you do, you'll have a lot less junk mail cluttering up your Inbox.

Creating a New Mail Folder

The simplest way to manage incoming mail is just to file it. Before you file a message, you need to create at least one folder in which to file your messages. You have to create a folder only once; it's there for good after you create it. You can create as many folders as you want; you may have dozens or just one or two.

I have folders for filing mail from specific clients, for example. All the e-mail I've received in connection with this book is in a folder called *Outlook For Dummies* (clever title, eh?). Another folder called *Personal* contains messages that aren't business-related.

To create a folder for new mail, follow these steps:

1. **Click the Mail button in the Navigation Pane (or press Ctrl+1).**

   The list of messages in your Inbox appears.

2. **Choose Go⇨Folder List.**

   The Folder List appears on the left side of the screen.

3. **Right-click the word Inbox in the Folder List.**

   A shortcut menu appears.

4. **Choose New Folder from the shortcut menu.**

   The Create New Folder dialog box appears (as in Figure 6-1).

4. **In the Name text box, type a name for your new folder, such as Personal.**

   You can name the subfolder anything you like. You can also create many folders for saving and sorting your incoming e-mail. Leaving all your mail in your Inbox gets confusing. On the other hand, if you create too many folders, you may be just as confused as if you had only one.

5. **Click OK.**

   Your new folder appears in the Folder List.

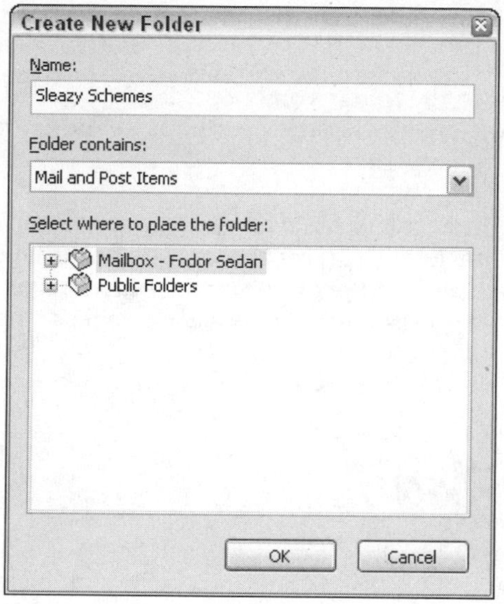

Create New Folder

Name:

Sleazy Schemes

Folder contains:

Mail and Post Items

Select where to place the folder:

⊞ 🌐 Mailbox - Fodor Sedan
⊞ 🌐 Public Folders

OK   Cancel

Figure 6-1:
The Create
New Folder
dialog box.

You now have a new folder named Personal (or whatever name you entered) for filing messages you want to save for future reference. I like to use three or four mail folders for different types of mail to make finding what I'm looking for easier.

Moving messages to another folder

Filing your messages is as easy as dragging them from the folder they're in to the folder where you want them. Just click the Inbox to look at your messages when they arrive, and then drag each message to the folder where you want your messages to stay.

To move messages to another folder, follow these steps:

1. **Click the Mail button in the Navigation Pane (or press Ctrl+Shift+I).**

   Your list of incoming mail messages appears.

2. **Click the title of the message you want to move.**

   The message is highlighted.

3. **Choose Edit⇨Move to Folder.**

   The Move Items dialog box appears.

4. **Click the name of the folder to which you want to move your message, and then click OK.**

   Your message is moved to the folder you chose. If you created a folder named *Personal* (or anything else) in the preceding section of this chapter, you can drag the message there.

The Outlook toolbar has a button called *Move to Folder* that you can click to move a selected message to the folder of your choice. The best thing about the Move to Folder button is that it remembers the last ten folders to which you moved messages. That feature makes it easy to move messages to folders that may be tricky to find in the Folder List.

Organizing Your E-Mail with Search Folders

The Search Folders feature in Outlook is designed to help you organize the messages in your inbox. Search Folders provide a single place where you can always look to find a certain kind of message.

A Search Folder doesn't actually move your messages; it's really a kind of imaginary location for your messages so you only have to look at one type of message at a time. When you first start Outlook, you'll find three Search Folders already installed.

- ✔ **For follow-up:** This folder shows only the messages you've flagged. When you remove the flag from a message, you'll no longer see it in this Search Folder, but you can still find it in your Inbox.

- ✔ **Large Messages:** This Search Folder organizes your messages in order of how much storage space they require. Normally, you're probably not too concerned with the size of the messages you receive — but don't be surprised if the system administrators where you work ask you not to store too much mail in your inbox. If you have lots of messages with attachments (or messages in which friends include their photographs), you may find your inbox filling up quickly.

  You can use the Large Messages Search Folder to figure out which messages are taking up the most space — and eliminate the largest ones. The messages you'll see in this folder are categorized by size, starting with Large and moving up to Huge and Enormous.

- ✔ **Unread mail:** This folder shows you only the messages you haven't read yet. When you read a message in this folder, it disappears from the folder, but you'll still be able to find it in your Inbox.

Using a Search Folder

You don't need to do anything special to use a Search Folder; just click the name of the search you want to look at, and those messages appear in the Reading Pane. When you're ready to go back to your inbox, just click the Mail button in the Navigation Pane to see your whole collection of messages again.

Setting up a new Search Folder

You need not limit yourself to the Search Folders that Outlook provides. You can create your own custom folders as well. For example, if you receive regular messages about sales in a certain region, you can set up a Search Folder that automatically shows you all the messages you've received containing that information.

To set up a new Search Folder, follow these steps:

1. **Choose File⇨New ⇨Search Folder.**

   The New Search Folder Dialog Box appears.

2. **Select the type of Search Folder you'd like to create from the list in the New Search Folder dialog box.**

   About a dozen different kinds of folders are available. You can either use a predefined folder or create your own type of Search Folder (by choosing Create Custom Search Folder).

3. **If a button appears at the bottom of the New Search Folder dialog box, click the button and fill in the requested information.**

   When you click one of the folder types to select it, the bottom of the New Search Folder dialog box changes, offering you a choice suitable to the type of folder you're creating.

4. **When you finish filling in all the information requested, click OK.**

   The New Search Folder dialog box closes.

Deleting a Search Folder

After your Search Folder has served its purpose, there's no reason for you to keep it. Remember, the contents of the Search Folder are really just imaginary; deleting this folder does not delete the messages it contains. Just click the Search Folder you want to delete and then click the Delete button (the button with the big black X) in the toolbar to make your Search Folder disappear.

Using (Electronic) Stationery

It has been only a few centuries now since preprinted stationery came into fashion for paper mail, so I suppose it's not too early for the same idea to catch on for electronic mail.

Stationery is designed to convey a visual impression about your message. With the right choice of stationery, you can make your message look uniquely important, businesslike, or just plain fun.

Unlike paper stationery, an unlimited selection (and supply!) of stationery is available for your e-mail messages — and you don't have to spend any money on printing and paper. Just pick the design you want from a menu, and there you are! Correspondence Art!

To use stationery, follow these steps:

1. **Choose Actions⇨New Mail Message Using⇨More Stationery.**

   The Select a Stationery dialog box appears, containing a list of stationery types you can choose (as shown in Figure 6-2). Each time you click the name of a type of stationery, you see what that stationery looks like in the Preview window.

Figure 6-2:
The Select a
Stationery
dialog box.

If the New Mail Message Using command on the Actions menu isn't black and doesn't work when you click it, turn the feature on. Choose Tools⇨ Options, click the Mail Format tab, and choose HTML from the scroll-down menu at the top of the Mail Format page.

2. Click the name of the stationery you want to use.

The name of the stationery you click is highlighted to show you've selected it.

3. Click OK.

The stationery you choose appears. For this example (see Figure 6-3), I chose the Citrus Punch Stationery.

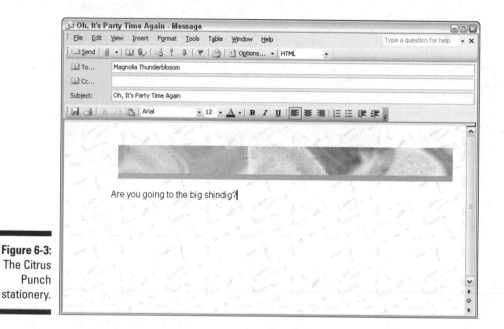

Figure 6-3:
The Citrus Punch stationery.

4. Fill in the information in the form.

You can customize stationery to fit any need. Just click any box where you can put information and type your desired text. You can replace any existing text on a piece of stationery; just select the text you want to replace by dragging the mouse pointer over the text, and then type the text you want.

5. Click the To button.

The Select Names dialog box appears (as shown in Figure 6-4).

6. Select the name of the person to whom you want to send the message.

The name you click is highlighted to show you've selected it.

7. Click the To button.

Yes, I know, you clicked the To button before. This time it's for entering the person's name into your e-mail message.

Select Names

Type Name or Select from List: Show Names from the:

Global Address List

Name	Business Phone	Office
Bill Dyszel		
BillDyszelList		
Fodor Sedan		
Fredda DeDark		
Gedda Jobyaschmuck		
Magnolia Thunderblossom		
Pearlie Gates		
TopBrass		

Message Recipients

To ->

Cc ->

Bcc ->

Advanced ▼   OK   Cancel

Figure 6-4:
The Select
Names
dialog box.

8. **Click OK.**

   The Select Names dialog box disappears and the stationery reappears.

9. **Click Send.**

   If your computer is on a network at your office, your message is on its way. If you're using Outlook at home, you have to send your message by choosing Tools➪Send/Receive. You can also press F5.

Not everyone uses Outlook to read his or her e-mail, which means the beauty of your stationery may be lost on some people to whom you send messages. Don't be offended if your stationery design is lost in shipment as long as the text of your message arrives.

Using the Reading Pane

If you want to skim through a whole bunch of messages quickly, the Reading Pane can help. When you choose View➪Reading Pane➪Right, the Inbox screen divides into two sections. The left section shows your list of messages; the right shows the contents of the message you've selected (see Figure 6-5). To move from one message to the next, just press the down-arrow key. You can also view any message in your Inbox by clicking the title of the message. If you prefer to see the text of your messages on the bottom of the screen, you can also choose View➪Reading Pane➪Bottom, but you can't see as much of your message. I recommend setting your Reading Pane to appear on the right.

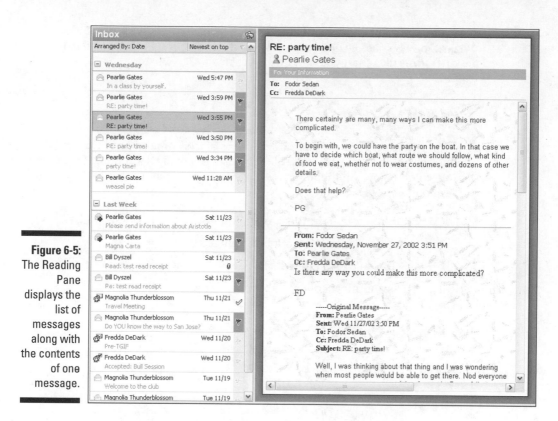

Figure 6-5:
The Reading
Pane
displays the
list of
messages
along with
the contents
of one
message.

The difference between looking at messages in the Reading Pane and looking at them in AutoPreview mode is that you can see graphics and formatting in the Reading Pane, but you can see only the text of a message in the AutoPreview mode. If your friends send you messages using Outlook stationery, for example, you can appreciate their graphic genius by viewing their messages in the Reading Pane.

Using Rules

Rules are probably my favorite feature in Outlook. The rules feature lets you make Outlook act on certain kinds of e-mail messages automatically. For example, I get tons of e-mail messages, and I can easily waste the whole day sorting through them. So, I set up rules in Outlook to automatically sort my incoming mail into different folders so I can waste a little less time wading through all the messages.

The question of how many different rules you can create with the Rules Wizard may be one of those vast cosmic mysteries, but I'm sure you can create more rules than you and I will ever need.

Creating a rule

The Rules Wizard is called a wizard because of the way the program leads you step by step to create each rule. The process is pretty simple. To create a simple rule to move an incoming message from a certain person to a certain folder, follow these steps:

1. **Click the Inbox icon in the Navigation Pane (or press Ctrl+Shift+I).**

   The list of messages in your Inbox appears.

2. **Choose Tools⇨Rules and Alerts.**

   The Rules and Alerts dialog box appears (see Figure 6-6).

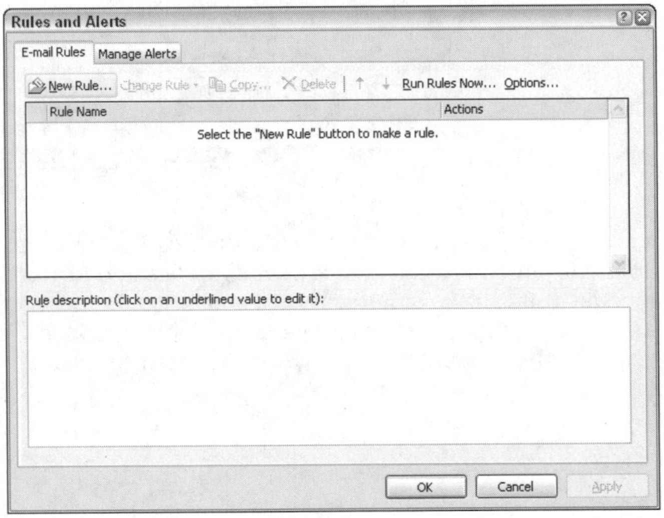

Figure 6-6:
The Rules
Wizard
dialog box
enables you
to make
the rules.

3. **Click the New Rule button.**

   A dialog box for creating new rules appears. The dialog box contains a list of the types of rules you can create.

4. **Choose the type of rule you want to create.**

   The Rules Wizard offers several common types of rules you may want to create, such as Move messages from someone to a folder, Move messages with specific words in the subject to a folder, or Move messages sent to a distribution list to a folder (as shown in Figure 6-7). For this example, I suggest choosing Move messages from someone to a folder. I look in the Rule Description box at the bottom of the dialog box, and behold there the words *Apply this rule after the message arrives from people or distribution list ... move it to the specified folder.* (That's a mouthful, but Outlook understands.)

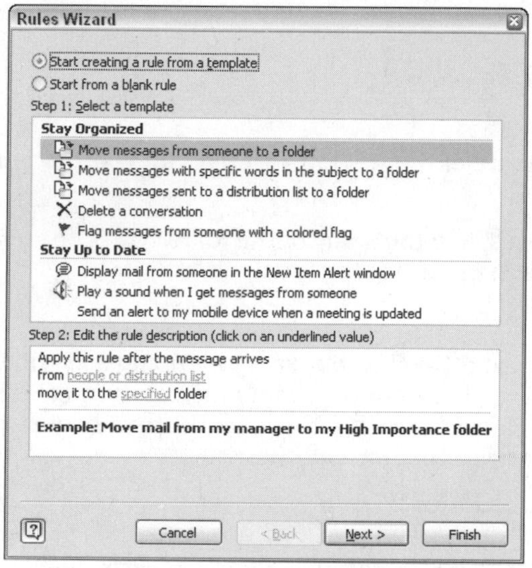

Figure 6-7:
Choose the type of rule you want to create.

```
Rules Wizard                                                    ⊠

⊙ Start creating a rule from a template
○ Start from a blank rule
Step 1: Select a template
  Stay Organized
    📩 Move messages from someone to a folder
    📩 Move messages with specific words in the subject to a folder
    📩 Move messages sent to a distribution list to a folder
    ✗  Delete a conversation
    ▼  Flag messages from someone with a colored flag
  Stay Up to Date
    📩 Display mail from someone in the New Item Alert window
    🔊 Play a sound when I get messages from someone
       Send an alert to my mobile device when a meeting is updated
Step 2: Edit the rule description (click on an underlined value)
  Apply this rule after the message arrives
  from people or distribution list
  move it to the specified folder

  Example: Move mail from my manager to my High Importance folder


  [?]         Cancel      < Back    Next >      Finish
```

5. **Click the first piece of underlined text in the Rule Description box, which says people or distribution list.**

   The Rules Address dialog box appears.

6. **Double-click the name of each person whose messages you want to move to a new folder.**

   The name of each person you chose appears in the right column of the Rules Address dialog box.

7. **Click OK when you've chosen all the people whose messages you want to move.**

   The Rules Address dialog box closes and the names you've selected replace the words people or distribution list.

8. **Click the next piece of underlined text in the Rule Description box, which is the word specified.**

   Another dialog box opens, offering you a choice of folders to which you can move the message (as shown in Figure 6-8).

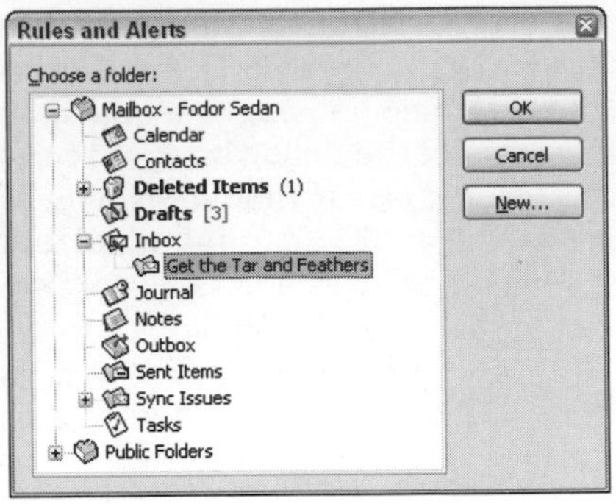

Figure 6-8:
Choose the
folder to
which your
messages
will go.

9. **Double-click the name of the folder to which you want to move messages.**

   The dialog box closes, and the name of the folder you choose appears in the sentence in the Rule Description box.

10. **Click Finish.**

    The first Rules Wizard dialog box appears, providing a list of all your rules. Each rule has a check box next to it. You can turn rules on and off by clicking the check boxes. If a check mark appears next to a rule, it's turned on; otherwise the rule is turned off.

11. **Click OK to close the Rules Wizard.**

Rules can do much more than just sort incoming messages. You can create rules that automatically reply to certain messages, flag messages with a particular word in the subject, delete messages about specific topics . . . the sky's the limit.

Running a rule

Normally, rules go into action when messages arrive in your Inbox. When you create a rule to move messages from a certain person to a certain folder, the messages that arrive after you create the rule get moved, but the messages sitting in your Inbox keep sitting there. If you want to apply a rule to the messages already sitting in your Inbox, use the Run Now button at the top of the Rules and Alerts dialog box. When the Run Rules Now dialog box appears, check the rule you want to run and then click the Run Now button at the bottom of the dialog box.

Filtering Junk E-Mail

In 2003, a dubious milestone in the history of e-mail was achieved — more junk e-mail messages were sent over the Internet than legitimate ones. It's now safe to assume that if you get e-mail, you get junk e-mail, also known as *spam*. Outlook 2003 includes a filtering system that looks over all your incoming mail and automatically moves anything that looks like junk e-mail to a special folder. You can delete everything that gets moved to your Junk E-Mail folder now and again — after checking to make sure Outlook didn't mistakenly move real e-mail to your Junk E-Mail folder.

No machine is perfect, and no program that runs on a machine is perfect. I don't entirely know how Outlook figures out which messages are junk and which are real. I find that some junk e-mail still gets through, but Outlook catches more than half the junk messages I get. Once or twice I've seen it dump items from real people into the Junk E-Mail folder. (Outlook once sent a message from my father to the Junk E-Mail folder; I've been checking the Junk E-Mail folder regularly ever since.)

Fine-tuning the filter's sensitivity

You don't need to do anything to turn on Junk E-Mail filtering in Outlook 2003. The program already guards against junk e-mail the first time you start it up; however, the protection level is set at Low.

Whether you feel that Outlook moves too many incoming messages — or too few — to the Junk E-Mail folder, you can adjust Outlook's sensitivity to suit your taste by changing the Junk E-Mail settings.

To adjust Outlook's Junk E-Mail Settings, follow these steps:

1. **Choose Actions ⇨Junk E-Mail ⇨Junk E-Mail Options.**

   The Junk E-Mail Options dialog box appears (as in Figure 6-9) with the Options tab on top.

2. **Click the option you prefer.**

   The circle next to the option you click darkens to show what you've selected. The options that Outlook offers you include

   • **No protection:** At this setting, every sleazy message goes right to your Inbox, unchallenged. If that's your cup of tea, fine. Most people want a little more filtering.

- **Low:** The junkiest of the junk gets moved, but a lot of nasty stuff still gets through.

- **High:** This setting is aggressive enough that you can expect to see a certain amount of legitimate e-mail end up in the Junk E-Mail folder. If you choose this setting, be sure to check your Junk E-Mail folder from time to time to be sure that important messages don't get trashed by mistake.

- **Safe Lists only:** This setting moves all messages out of your Inbox except for the ones from people or companies that you've designated in your Safe Senders lists.

Also, the check box at the bottom of Options tab offers you a chance to permanently delete suspected junk e-mail. I think that might be a bit too aggressive, but it's your choice. I haven't seen a perfect Junk E-Mail filter yet, so it's probably better to push junk messages over to the Junk E-Mail folder and empty the folder occasionally. On the other hand, you may work in a company that limits the amount of e-mail you're allowed to store, and the messages in your Junk E-Mail folder count against your limit. So zapping junk e-mail may be the best option.

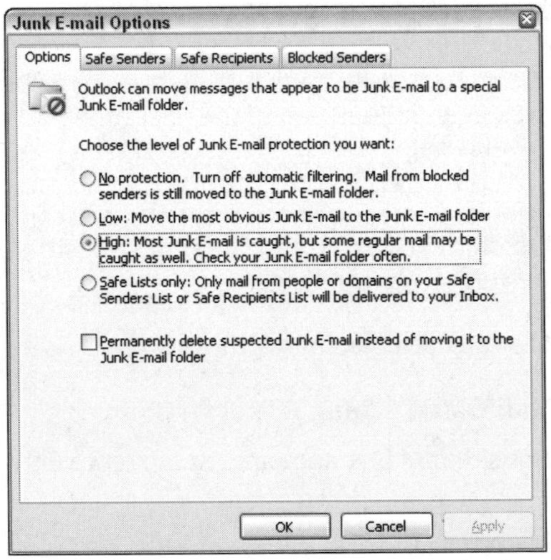

Figure 6-9:
Set your
Junk E-Mail
protection
as high or
low as
you like.

3. **Click OK.**

   The Junk E-Mail Options dialog box closes.

There you are! With any luck, you'll no longer need to wade through messages about get-rich-quick schemes or pills that enlarge body parts you don't even have.

Filtering your e-mail with sender and recipient lists

Outlook's Junk E-Mail handling feature includes an option that you can choose if you want to set up your own *safe lists* for handling where your e-mail comes from or goes to. You can make a list of people whose messages should *always* be moved to the Junk E-Mail folder (or people whose messages should *never* be moved there). Check out the other tabs of the Junk E-Mail Options dialog box for descriptions of the types of senders you can enter:

- **Safe Senders:** When a message arrives with an e-mail address or domain on this list in the From line of the message, Outlook makes sure not to treat the message as Junk E-Mail — no matter what else the message says.

- **Safe Recipients:** If you receive messages from an online mailing list, the messages often appear to come from many different people, but they're always addressed to the list. (For example, if you belong to any of the groups on yahoogroups.com, you'll see this.) In this case, you'd put the name of the list in your Safe Recipients list.

- **Blocked Senders:** This is the opposite of the two choices above; messages from the addresses on this list are always treated as Junk E-Mail.

Adding an individual to your Blocked Senders list is pretty simple: When you receive a message from someone you don't want to hear from anymore, select the message and choose Actions⇨Junk E-Mail⇨Add Sender to Blocked Senders List. This same method works for adding people to the Safe Senders and Safe Recipients lists. Just select the message, choose Actions⇨Junk E-Mail, and then choose the list to which you want the sender added.

Of course, if you want to be more precise, you can go directly to the appropriate tab in the Junk E-Mail Options dialog box and type in the addresses you want to filter.

Some other Junk E-Mail options that could save you time include these:

- **Contacts List:** A check box at the bottom of the Safe Senders tab is labeled "Also trust e-mail from my Contacts." If that box is checked, messages from anyone in your Contacts list automatically get treated as safe messages.

- **Import and Export:** If you have a particularly long list of people to add to your Safe Senders list or your Blocked Senders list, you can create a list in Notepad and then import that list to Outlook. Companies with lengthy client lists might make this feature available to all.

Filtering domains

Outlook gives you one rather powerful option among your junk e-mail choices that you need to be careful about. That option involves filtering domains. If you do business with people at a certain company, you can enter that entire company in your Safe Senders list by selecting the message and then choosing Actions⇨Junk E-Mail⇨Add Senders Domain (@example.com) to Safe Senders List.

However, if you accidentally add the domain of a friend who sends you e-mail via America Online to your Safe Senders list, you partly defeat the purpose of your Junk E-Mail filters (because so much junk e-mail comes from aol.com — or at least pretends to come from aol.com). So use the domain-filtering feature with care.

Archiving

It doesn't take long to accumulate more messages than you can deal with. Some people just delete messages as they read them. Others hold on to old messages for reference purposes. I hold onto all the messages I've ever sent or received in Outlook because I never know when I'll need to check back to see what someone said to me (or, for that matter, what I said).

The problem is, Outlook slows down when you store lots of e-mail messages. Besides, a huge collection of messages is cumbersome to manage. Also, if you're on a corporate e-mail system, your system administrators may not let you store more than a certain amount of e-mail because it clogs up the system.

Archiving is a feature built right into Outlook to help you store messages and other Outlook items you don't need to look at right now, but you still might want to refer to in the future. If you use Outlook on an Exchange network at work, Archiving makes it easy for you to get along with your system administrators by slimming down the number of messages you're storing in the e-mail system.

Even if you don't want to use the Archiving feature right now, you may want to understand how it works. Outlook sometimes archives items automatically — which may look to you as if your Outlook items are disappearing. In this section, I show you how to find the items that Outlook has archived for safekeeping.

If the AutoArchive feature seems scary and complicated to you, try not to worry. I agree that Microsoft hasn't done a good job of making the Archive feature understandable. When you get the hang of it, however, AutoArchiving could become valuable to you.

Although e-mail messages are what people archive most often, all Outlook items can be sent to the archive — appointments, tasks, everything. People don't usually archive Contacts and Notes, but you can even archive those if you want.

Setting up AutoArchive

You don't have to do anything to make Outlook archive your items; the program is set up to archive items automatically. If you want to see how Outlook is set up to archive your old items, or change the way Outlook does the job, follow these steps:

1. **Choose Tools⇨Options.**

   The Options dialog box appears.

2. **Click the Other tab.**

   The Other options page appears.

3. **Click the AutoArchive button.**

   The AutoArchive dialog box appears (as in Figure 6-10).

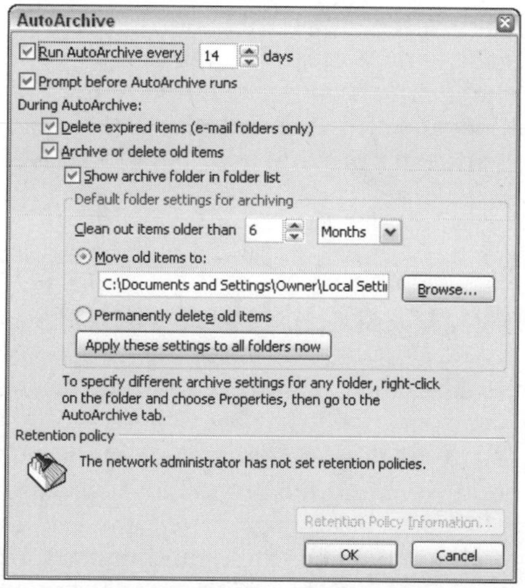

Figure 6-10:
The
AutoArchive
dialog box.

Don't go barging through the AutoArchive dialog box changing things willy-nilly — at least not until you look to see what's already set up. Four important tidbits that the AutoArchive dialog box normally tells you are as follows:

- How often Outlook archives items
- How old items have to be for Outlook to send them to the archive
- The name and location of the archive file
- Whether the AutoArchive feature is turned on

When you first install Outlook, the program automatically archives items every fourteen days, sending items over six months old to the archive file listed in the AutoArchive dialog box. For most people, those settings are just fine. Some people prefer to turn off the AutoArchive feature and run the Archive process manually, as I describe in the next section. You can turn off the AutoArchive process by clicking the check box labeled "Run AutoArchive Every 14 Days" at the top of the AutoArchive dialog box.

Activating the Archive process manually

You can archive messages any time you want by choosing File⇨Archive from the Outlook menu and following the prompts. The advantage of running the Archive process manually is that you get slightly better control of the process; you can give Outlook a cutoff date for archiving items, say the first of the year. You can also tell Outlook which folders to archive and where to send the archived items. You can even archive different Outlook folders to different archive files. The disadvantage to all this control is that it's possible to make an innocent mistake and send archived items to a place you can't find again easily. Try not to change the name or location of the files to which your archived items are sent, because it's surprisingly easy to lose track of what went where, and Outlook doesn't provide much help with keeping track of archived files.

Finding and viewing archived items

Sometimes AutoArchive seems like magic. Older items are mysteriously filed away without any action on your part. Isn't that easy? Sure — until you suddenly need to *find* one of those items that moved magically to your archive. Then you have to figure where it went and how to get at it again.

I usually like to talk up the good points of Outlook, but honestly, this is one place where the Outlook developers fell down on the job. Although it's easy to move items into your Archive, it's pretty confusing to get them back. What's the point of archiving items if you can't find them again?

Anyway, when you want to take another look at the items you've archived, open the archive folder, which Outlook also refers to as a *data file.*

To open a data file containing your archive items, follow these steps:

1. **Choose File ➪ Open ➪ Outlook Data File.**

   The Open Outlook Data File dialog box appears.

2. **Type the name of the file you want to open in the File Name box.**

   The name you enter appears in the File Name box.

3. **Click OK.**

   The name of the data file you opened appears in the Folder Banner in large letters. Your Folder List also appears, showing two sets of folders: Normal and Archive.

Simple enough, right? Yes, but there's a virtual fly in the virtual ointment. You probably don't know the name of the archive file you want to open, and it doesn't usually show up in the list in the Create or Open Outlook Data File dialog box.

 To find out the name of the archive file open, choose File ➪ Archive and look in the box labeled "Archive File." Be careful not to change anything about the information box; Otherwise Outlook may start sending your archived items someplace else. The information in the Archive File box is usually complex gobbledygook with colons and slashes and all sorts of stuff that normal people can't remember.

My favorite trick for capturing a long name in a dialog box is to copy the information. Here's what it looks like in fast-forward: Click the name once, press Tab, press Shift+Tab, press Ctrl+C, and then click Cancel. After you copy the file name, you can follow the steps given earlier in this section — pasting the name you want into the File Name box by pressing Ctrl+V, and rejoicing that you don't have to remember that long, crazy file name.

Closing the Archive file

You can keep your Archive file open in the Outlook Folder list as long as you want, but most people prefer to close it after they find what they need. Outlook runs a little faster when you close any unnecessary data files.

To close a data file, follow these steps:

1. **With the Folder List open, right-click the name of your Archive folder.**

   A shortcut menu appears.

2. **Choose Close Folder from the shortcut menu.**

   Your archive folder disappears from the Folder List.

The way folders are named in Outlook is odd. You may find "Personal Folders" appearing several times in your folder list. To make Outlook run as quickly as possible, close as many of them as you can. Your main set of folders — the set you use every day — won't close, so you don't have to worry about closing the folders you use every day.

Arranging Your Messages

Nobody gets a *little* bit of e-mail anymore. If you get one message, you get a ton of 'em. Fortunately, Outlook offers you a whole bunch of different ways to arrange that mess of messages so you have a fighting chance to figure out what's important and what can wait.

When Outlook is set up to display the Reading Pane on the right side of the screen, you'll see two buttons at the top of the list of messages. The left most button has a label that says something like "Arranged By: Date." The Arranged By button describes the system Outlook is using to organize your messages. To the right of the Arranged By button sits another button with a label that offers some detail about the arrangement Outlook is currently using. (For example, if your messages are currently arranged by date, the button on the right will say either "Newest on Top" or "Oldest on Top.")

To change the way Outlook is arranging your messages, simply click the Arranged By button to reveal a shortcut menu of all the arrangements you can use. These are the arrangements Outlook offers:

- ✔ **Date:** The most common way to organize messages is by date. When you first set up Outlook this is how your messages will be arranged. Click the button on the right to alternate between newest messages on top and oldest messages on top.

- ✔ **Conversation:** This arrangement groups messages of the same topic together. If you've been exchanging a series of messages with someone about a specific project or idea, you can choose the Conversation arrangement to follow the thread of the conversation.

✔ **From:** As you might guess, this arrangement organizes your message collection according to the person from whom the message was sent. Choosing the From arrangement is a little bit faster than setting up a Search Folder, but sometimes a Search Folder is still the best way to track messages from *specific* important people.

✔ **To:** Most messages you receive are addressed to you, but not always. Sometimes you receive messages addressed to a list of people, so your name doesn't appear on the To line of the message. This arrangement separates your messages according to whether your name is on the To line of each message.

✔ **Folder:** When you're viewing messages in a Search Folder, the messages you're viewing may actually be located in a variety of different folders. If you want to know exactly which folder contains each message, use the Folder arrangement. When you're viewing your Inbox, the Folder arrangement is not available; it's only for Search Folders.

✔ **Size:** Everyone knows that size doesn't matter; it's the sentiment that counts. Well, okay, not always. Size is important to certain system administrators — and it isn't *always* a personal problem. Some e-mail messages include photographs, music, and all sorts of heavyweight files that can really clog up your company's e-mail servers. So when your system administrator asks you to thin out your inbox, make some use of this feature: Identify and delete the messages that are the most overweight.

✔ **Subject:** This arrangement is similar to the Conversation arrangement, except it doesn't follow the thread of a conversation, it just lumps together messages that have the same subject.

✔ **Type:** Not every item that arrives in your Inbox is a simple message; you may also receive Meeting Invitations, Task Requests, and all sorts of other items. When you want to separate the messages from the Meeting Requests, switch to the Type arrangement so the most interesting messages rise to the top of the list.

✔ **Flag:** When you flag a message, you probably plan to get back to it. This arrangement puts flagged messages at the top of the list and unflagged messages at the bottom. If you use several different flag colors, this arrangement sorts according to flag color as well.

✔ **Attachment:** When you go to your Inbox, you may not be looking for a message, you may be hunting for an attachment. Arranging your messages by attachment enables you to examine the likely suspects first.

✔ **E-mail accounts:** You can set up Outlook to collect e-mail from several different e-mail addresses. Sometimes you want to know which message came from which of those addresses, or just to look at the messages sent to one of those addresses. If you want to see only the messages sent to a single address, choose the E-Mail Accounts arrangement and then click the minus (–) next to the names of accounts you don't want to see. With this arrangement, Outlook shows you only the messages from the accounts that interest you.

✔ **Importance:** First things first — you know the saying. When you need to see the messages marked with high importance first, this is the arrangement you want to use.

✔ **Categories:** You can assign categories to any message you send, and sometimes other people can assign categories to the messages they send you. To see which message falls into which category, use the Categories arrangement.

The Arrange By button appears at the top of your message list only when the Reading Pane is set to appear on the right side of the screen. You can turn the Reading Pane on by choosing View➪Reading Pane➪Right. If you want to arrange your messages when the Reading Pane is off, choose View➪Arrange By to see the list of arrangements and then pick the one you want.

Part III
Managing Contacts, Dates, Tasks, and More

The 5th Wave   By Rich Tennant

"I'm not sure that printing out my recurring task list was such a good idea."

In this part . . .

You can send messages to nearly anyone, anytime, but what are the messages about? Business — all those things that keep us off the streets, out of trouble, and (best of all) paid! Meetings and deadlines, schedule conflicts, and too many tasks — all crying out for your expert attention. In this part, you'll see how Outlook makes it easy to keep your business in line.

Chapter 7

Your Little Black Book: Creating Contact Lists

*H*ardly anybody works alone. Even if you work at home, you always have people to keep track of — people you sell things to, buy things from, have lunch with, or want to contact for any of several dozen reasons. All that personal information can be hard to store in a way you can find and use again quickly when you need it. And you need to know different things about people in different parts of your life. So you need a tool that's flexible enough to let you organize names, addresses, and all that other information in ways that make sense in different contexts.

For example, I work as a computer consultant and write for computer magazines. The information I need to keep about consulting clients (systems, software, hours, locations, and networks) differs from the information I need for dealing with people in the publishing business (editors, deadlines, topics, and so on). I'm also still active as a professional singer and actor, and my contacts in those businesses are two entirely different kettles of fish. But when someone calls on the phone, or when I want to do a mailing to a group from one world or another, I need to be able to look up the person right away, regardless of which category the person fits in.

Outlook is flexible enough to let you keep all your name and address information in a single place — but you can also sort, view, find, and print it differently, depending on what kind of work you're doing. You can also keep lists of family and friends stored in Outlook right alongside your business contacts and still distinguish them from one another quickly when the need arises.

Storing Names, Numbers, and Other Stuff

Storing lots of names, addresses, and phone numbers is no big trick, but finding them again can take magic unless you have a tool like Outlook. You may have used other programs for storing names and related numbers, but Outlook ties the name and number information together more tightly with the work you do that uses names, addresses, and phone numbers, such as scheduling and task management.

If you've ever used a little pocket address book, you pretty much know how to use the Outlook Contacts feature. Simply enter the name, address, phone number, a few juicy tidbits, and there you are!

The quick-and-dirty way to enter Contacts

Entering a new name to your Contact list is utterly simple. With the contact list open, click the New button on the toolbar to open the New Contact entry form, fill in the blanks on the form, and then click Save and Close. That's really all there is to it. If you don't enter every detail about a contact right away, it's okay — you can always add more information later.

The slow, complete way to enter Contacts

If you want, you can enter scads of details about every person you enter in your Contact list and choose from literally dozens of options, but if all you do is enter the essentials and move on, that's fine. If you're more detail-minded, here's the way to enter every jot and tittle for each contact record:

1. **Click the Contacts button in the Navigation Pane (or press Ctrl+3).**

   The Contact list appears (see Figure 7-1).

2. **Choose File⇨New⇨Contact.**

   The New Contact form appears.

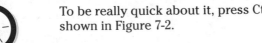

   To be really quick about it, press Ctrl+Shift+C instead to see the form shown in Figure 7-2.

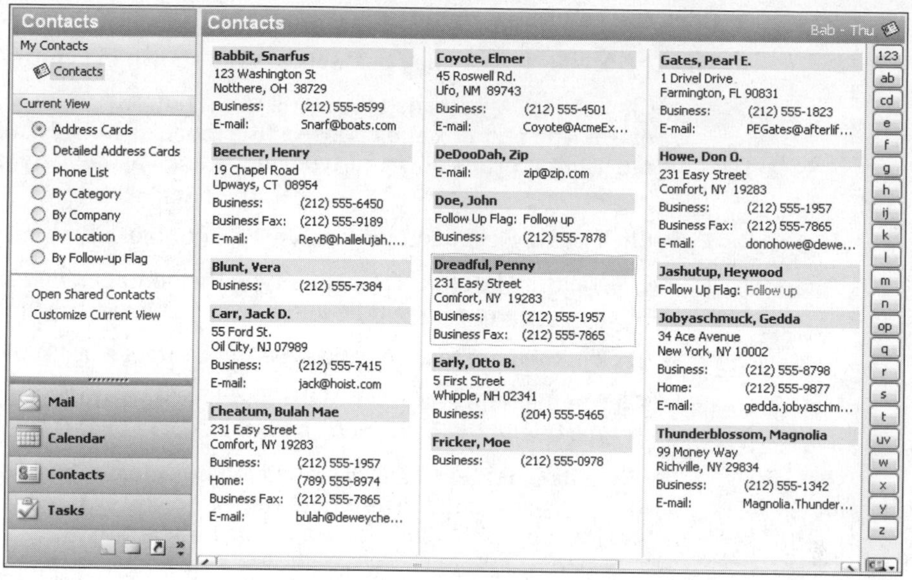

Figure 7-1:
The
Contacts
list.

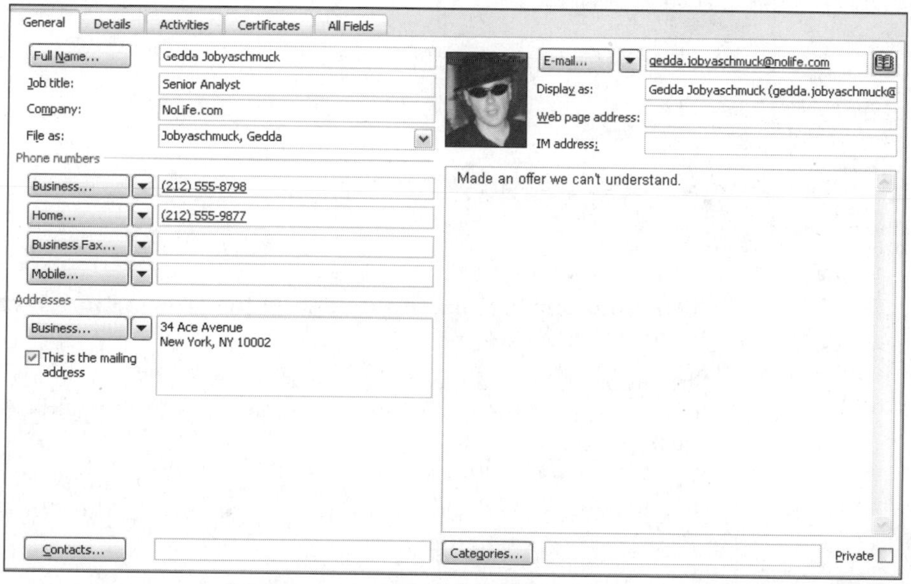

Figure 7-2:
The New
Contact
form.

3. Click the Full Name button.

The Check Full Name dialog box appears (as shown in Figure 7-3):

- Click the triangle (called the scroll-down button) on the right edge of the Title text box and choose a title (such as Mr., Ms., or Dr.) from the list that drops down, or type one — such as **Rev.**, **Ayatollah**, or whatever.

- Click in the First text box and type the contact's first name.

- Click in the Middle text box and type the contact's middle initial (if any). If there's no middle initial, you can leave this box blank.

- Click in the Last text box and type the contact's last name.

- Click in the Suffix drop-down list and choose a suffix, such as Jr., III, or type one in the box, such as **Ph.D.**, **D.D.S.**, or **B.P.O.E.**

- Click OK. The Check Full Name dialog box closes, and you're back in the New Contact form, where the name you entered is now shown in both the Full Name and File As text boxes.

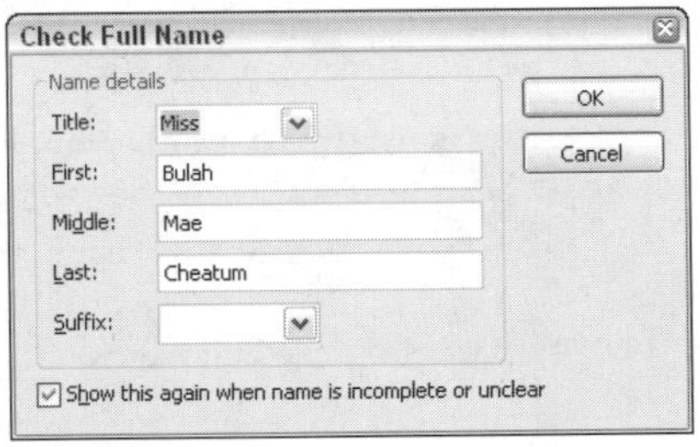

Figure 7-3:
The Check
Full Name
dialog box.

4. Click in the appropriate box and enter the information requested on the New Contact form.

If the information isn't available — for example, if the contact has no job title — leave the box blank. A triangle after the box indicates a drop-down list with choices you can select. If your choice isn't listed, type your choice in the box.

- If you've entered a name in the Full Name box, the File As box will already contain that name.

- If you want this person filed under something other than his or her name, click in the File As box and type in your preferred designation.

For example, you may want to file your dentist's name under the term *Dentist* rather than by name. If you put Dentist in the File As box, the name turns up under Dentist in the alphabetical listing rather than under the name itself. Both the Full Name and the File As designation exist in your Contact list. That way (for example), you can search for your dentist either by name or by the word *Dentist.*

5. **Click the triangle (called the scroll-down button) in the Address section to choose the type of address you want to enter.**

   You can choose to enter a Business address, Home address, or Other type of address.

6. **Click the button in the Address section to open the Check Address dialog box.**

   • Click the Street text box and type in the contact's street address.

   • Click the City text box and type in the contact's city.

   • Click the State/Province text box and type in the contact's state.

   • Click the ZIP/Postal Code box and type in the contact's postal code.

   • Click the triangle at the right end of the Country box and choose the contact's country if Outlook hasn't already chosen the correct one.

   See Figure 7-4 for a look at a completed Check Address dialog box.

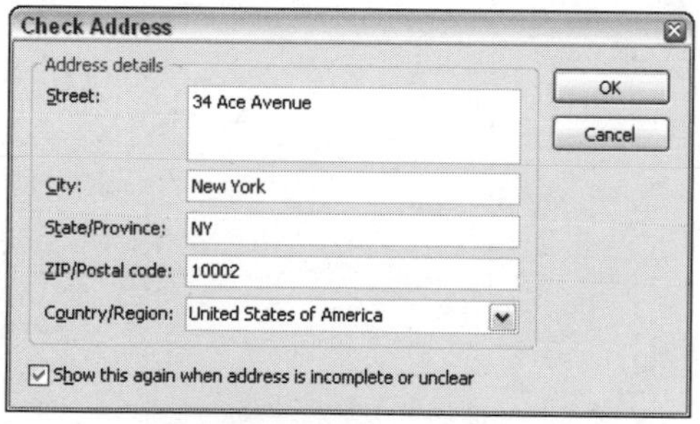

Figure 7-4:
The Check Address dialog box.

Check Address	⊠
Address details	
Street: 34 Ace Avenue	OK / Cancel
City: New York	
State/Province: NY	
ZIP/Postal code: 10002	
Country/Region: United States of America ▾	
☑ Show this again when address is incomplete or unclear	

7. **Click OK.**

   The Check Address dialog box closes.

8. **Click the check box on the New Contact form next to** This Is the Mailing Address **if the address you just entered is the address you plan to use for sending mail to the contact.**

9. **Click in the text box to the right of the Business phone box and type in the contact's business phone number.**

10. **Click in the text box to the right of the Home phone box and type in the contact's home phone number.**

    For numbers other than Business and Home phones, click the triangle to the right of the phone-number type block, choose the kind of number you're entering, and then enter the number.

    The New Contact form has four phone-number blocks. You can use any of them for any of the nineteen phone-number types available in the drop-down list. You can also add custom fields so you can include more than four phone numbers for a single contact. For the person who has everything, you can create custom fields for that person's Ski Phone, Submarine Phone, Gym Phone — as many as you want. For more about custom fields, see Chapter 13.

    You can choose any of nineteen phone number types to enter, depending on what types of phone numbers your contacts have (see Figure 7-5).

Figure 7-5:
You can always reach your contact at one of these phone numbers.

```
┌─ Phone numbers ──────────────────────────────┐
│ ┌───────────┬─┐  ┌──────────────────────────┐│
│ │ Business...│▼│  │ (212) 555-8798           ││
│ ├───────────┴─┤  └──────────────────────────┘│
│ │  Assistant  │  ┌──────────────────────────┐│
│ │ ✓ Business  │  │ (212) 555-9877           ││
│ │  Business 2 │  └──────────────────────────┘│
│ │  Business Fax│  ┌─────────────────────────┐│
│ │  Callback   │  └──────────────────────────┘│
│ │  Car        │                               │
│ │  Company    │  ┌──────────────────────────┐│
│ │ ✓ Home      │  │ 34 Ace Avenue            ││
│ │  Home 2     │  │ New York, NY 10002       ││
│ │  Home Fax   │  │                          ││
│ │  ISDN       │  └──────────────────────────┘│
│ │  Mobile     │                               │
│ │  Other      │                               │
│ │  Other Fax  │                               │
│ │  Pager      │                               │
│ │  Primary    │                               │
│ │  Radio      │                               │
│ │  Telex      │                               │
│ │  TTY/TDD    │                               │
│ ├─────────────┤  ┌──────────────────────────┐│
│ │  Contacts...│  │                          ││
│ └─────────────┘  └──────────────────────────┘│
└───────────────────────────────────────────────┘
```

11. **Click in the E-mail text box and enter your contact's e-mail address.**

    If your contact has more than one e-mail address, click the triangle at the left edge of the E-mail box (shown in Figure 7-6), select E-mail 2, click in the text box, and then enter the second address.

12. **Click in the Web Page text box if the contact has a Web page, and type the URL address for that page if you want to link to that page directly from the Address Card.**

    URL is a fancy name for the address of a page on the World Wide Web. When you see ads on TV that refer to www.discovery.com or www.dummies.com, what you're seeing is a *Uniform Resource Locator* (the even fancier term that URL stands for — essentially an Internet address).

You can view a Web page by entering the URL for the page in the Address box of your Web browser. If a person or company in your Outlook Contact list has a Web page, you can enter the URL for that page in the Web Page box. To view the Web page for a contact, open the contact record and choose Actions⇨Explore Web Page (or press Ctrl+Shift+X); your Web browser opens and loads the contact's Web page.

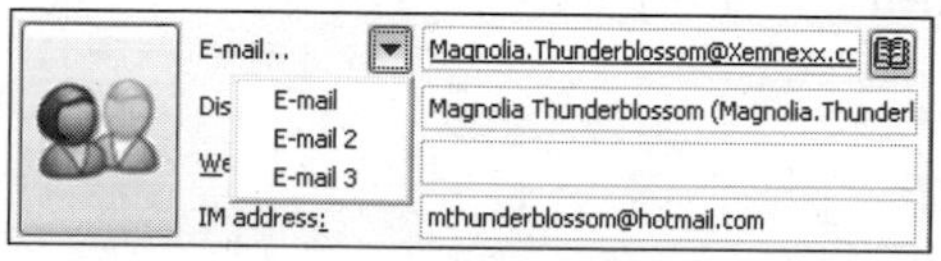

Figure 7-6:
You can enter more than one e-mail address for each person in your Contact list.

E-mail...		Magnolia.Thunderblossom@Xemnexx.cc
Dis	E-mail	Magnolia Thunderblossom (Magnolia.Thunderl
	E-mail 2	
We	E-mail 3	
IM address:		mthunderblossom@hotmail.com

13. Click in the large text box at the bottom of the form and type in anything you want.

You can enter directions, details about meetings, the Declaration of Independence — anything you want (preferably something that can help you in your dealings with the contact).

TIP

Format the text in the big text box (see Figure 7-7) by using the buttons on the formatting toolbar, if you want. The tools on the formatting toolbar are just like the ones that all other word-processing programs use: font, point size, bold, italic, justification, and color. Select the text you want to format and change the formatting. You can change the formatting of a single letter or the whole text box. You can't format the text in the smaller data text boxes in the other parts of the Contact form — only that in the big text box at the bottom of the form. If your formatting toolbar isn't showing, choose View⇨Toolbars⇨Formatting from the Contact form menu.

14. Click the Categories button at the bottom center of the screen to assign a category to the contact, if you want.

Assigning categories is another trick to help you find items easily. For an example of how to use categories with any Calendar item, see Chapter 8. After you assign categories to Outlook items, you can easily sort or group the items according to a category you've assigned.

Choose one of the existing categories if one suits you, and then click OK (as in Figure 7-8).

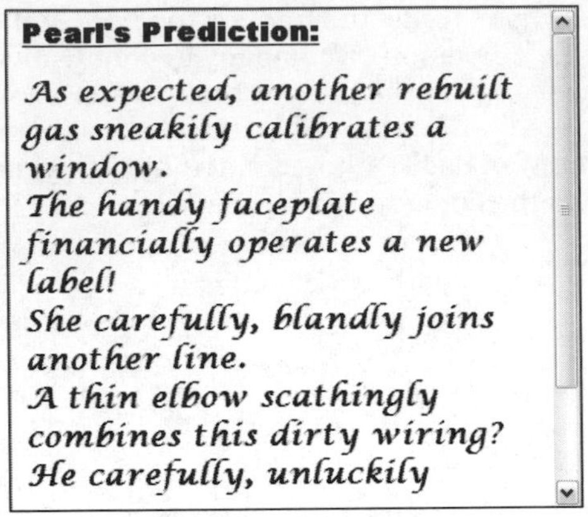

Pearl's Prediction:

As expected, another rebuilt gas sneakily calibrates a window.
The handy faceplate financially operates a new label!
She carefully, blandly joins another line.
A thin elbow scathingly combines this dirty wiring?
He carefully, unluckily

Figure 7-7: Have fun with formatting in the Contact text box.

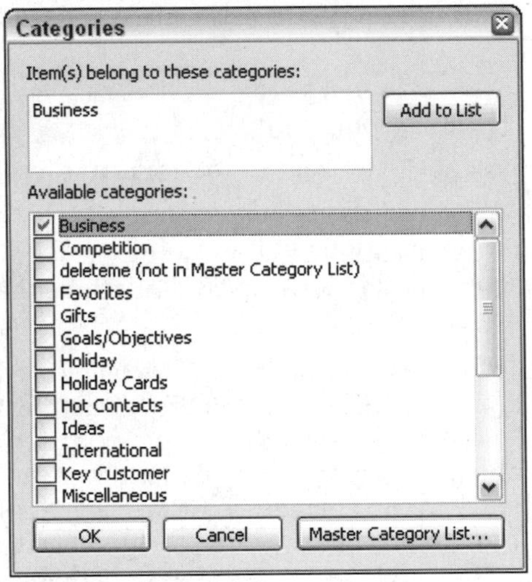

Categories

Item(s) belong to these categories:

Business   [Add to List]

Available categories:

- [x] Business
- [ ] Competition
- [ ] deleteme (not in Master Category List)
- [ ] Favorites
- [ ] Gifts
- [ ] Goals/Objectives
- [ ] Holiday
- [ ] Holiday Cards
- [ ] Hot Contacts
- [ ] Ideas
- [ ] International
- [ ] Key Customer
- [ ] Miscellaneous

[OK]   [Cancel]   [Master Category List...]

Figure 7-8: Put your contact in a category for easy reference.

15. **If none of the existing categories suits you, click Master Category List in the lower-right corner to see the Master Category List box.**

    Type a category of your choice in the New Category box (as shown in Figure 7-9). Be sure not to add too many new categories; doing so could make it hard to find things.

16. **Click Add and then click OK to return to the Categories list.**

    Choose the new category from the list if you want. You can choose more than one category at a time.

Figure 7-9:
Create your
own
category in
the Master
Category
List.

17. **Click the Private box in the lower-right corner of the New Contact form if you're on a network and you don't want others to know about this contact.**

    I'm not suggesting that you get all paranoid and secretive here, but you may want to keep contact information confidential.

18. **When you're done, click Save and Close.**

After you enter anything you want or need (or may need) to know about people you deal with at work, you're ready to start dealing.

Viewing Contacts

After you enter your contact information, Outlook lets you see the information arranged in many different and useful ways, called *views*. Viewing your contact information and sorting the views are quick ways to get the big picture of the data you've entered (see Chapter 12 for more information on views). Outlook comes with anywhere from five to twelve predefined views in each module. You can easily alter any predefined view. Then you can name and save your altered view and use it just as you would the predefined views that come with Outlook.

To change the view of your Contact list, follow these steps:

1. **Click the Contacts button in the Navigation Pane (or press Ctrl+3).**

   The Contact list appears in the main part of the Outlook screen; a list of views appears in the top part of the Navigation Pane.

2. **Pick the view you want from the Current View menu on the Navigation Pane.**

   You can shift between views as you can switch television stations, so don't worry about changing views and changing back. Figure 7-10 shows the Current View menu and its list of views for Contacts with the Detailed Address Cards view selected.

3. **Choose By Location from the list (or whatever other view you want).**

   The view you picked appears, as shown in Figure 7-11. You can also choose Address Cards, Detailed Address Cards, Phone List, By Category, By Company, By Location, or whatever other views are listed. To use one of the other views, repeat the preceding steps and choose the view you want.

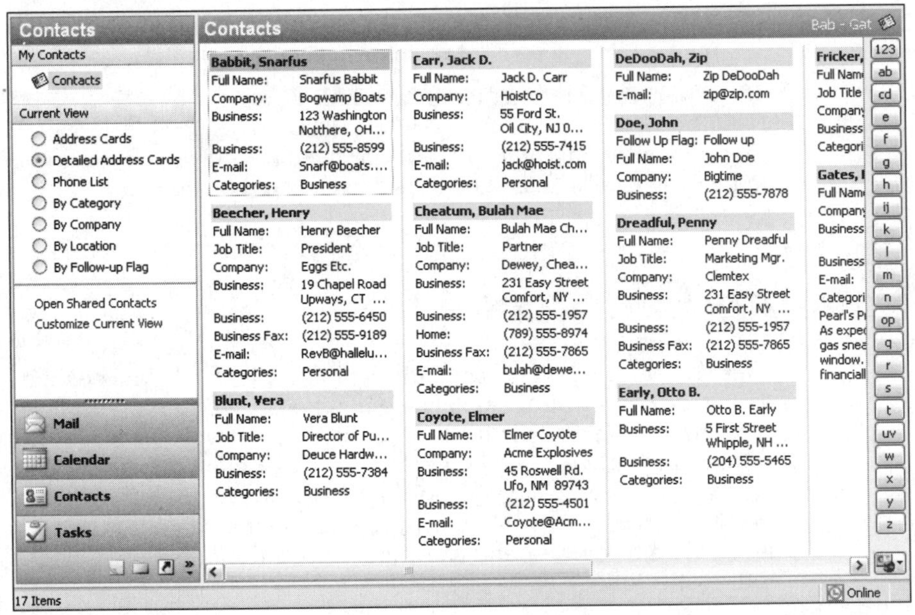

Figure 7-10:
The Detailed
Address
Cards view.

Figure 7-11:
Your
contacts in
the By
Location
view.

Sorting a view

Some views are organized as simple lists, such as the Phone List view of the Contacts module. Figure 7-12 shows the Phone List: a column of names on the left, followed by a column of company names, and so on.

If you're unable to find a certain contact in a view that is arranged in columns, all you have to do to sort that column is click once on the title of the column. For example, suppose you want to see the names of the people who work for IBM who are entered in your Contact list. One easy way to see all their names simultaneously is to run a sort on the Company column, like this:

1. **Click the Contacts button in the Navigation Pane (or press Ctrl+3).**

    The Contact list appears in the main part of the Outlook screen and a list of views appears in the top part of the Navigation Pane.

2. **Choose the Phone List view.**

    Your list of contacts appears in the Phone List view.

3. **Click the heading at the top of the Company column.**

    Your contacts appear in alphabetical order according to the name in the Company column. If you click the heading a second time, your contacts appear in reverse alphabetical order.

			Full Name	Company	File As	Business Phone	Business Fax
			Click here to add a new C...				
			Snarfus Babbit	Bogwamp Boats	Babbit, Snarfus	(212) 555-8599	
			Henry Beecher	Eggs Etc.	Beecher, Henry	(212) 555-6450	(212) 555-9189
			Vera Blunt	Deuce Hardware	Blunt, Vera	(212) 555-7384	
			Jack D. Carr	HoistCo	Carr, Jack D.	(212) 555-7415	
			Bulah Mae Cheatum	Dewey, Cheatum...	Cheatum, Bulah Mae	(212) 555-1957	(212) 555-7865
			Elmer Coyote	Acme Explosives	Coyote, Elmer	(212) 555-4501	
			Zip DeDooDah		DeDooDah, Zip		
			John Doe	Bigtime	Doe, John	(212) 555-7878	
			Penny Dreadful	Clemtex	Dreadful, Penny	(212) 555-1957	(212) 555-7865
			Otto B. Early		Early, Otto B.	(204) 555-5465	
			Moe Fricker	Salt Mines, Inc	Fricker, Moe	(212) 555-0978	
			Pearl E. Gates	Celestial Security	Gates, Pearl E.	(212) 555-1823	
			Don O. Howe	Dewey, Cheatum...	Howe, Don O.	(212) 555-1957	(212) 555-7865
			Heywood Jashutup	NoLife.com	Jashutup, Heywood		
			Gedda Jobyaschmuck	NoLife.com	Jobyaschmuck, Gedda	(212) 555-8798	
			Magnolia Thunderblossom	Xemnexx	Thunderblossom, Magnolia	(212) 555-1342	
			Targus Toadslinger	Warts 'n All	Toadslinger, Targus	(212) 555-1484	

Figure 7-12:
The Phone
List view.

After you sort your list, it's easier to find someone's name by scrolling down to that part of the alphabet. If you sort by company, all the contacts line up in order of company name, so you can scroll down to the section of your list where all the people from a certain company are listed.

Rearranging views

You can rearrange views simply by dragging the column title and dropping the title where you want it. For example, to move the Business Phone column in the Phone List view, follow these steps:

1. **Choose the Phone List view from the list in the Navigation Pane.**

   The Phone List view of your contacts appears.

2. **Click the Business Phone heading and drag it on top of the column to its left.**

   You see a pair of red arrows pointing to the border between the two columns to the left of the Business Phone column. The red arrows tell you where Outlook will drop the column when you release the mouse button (as in Figure 7-13).

Figure 7-13:
You can rearrange the columns in an Outlook Table view by dragging the column heading to the location you desire.

3. **Release the mouse button.**

   The Business Phone column is now to the left of the File As column (instead of to the right. If it makes more sense to you to have File As to the right of Business Phone, you can set up your view in Outlook to put it there.

You can use the same process to move any column in any Outlook view. Because the screen is not as wide as the list, you may need to move columns around at times to see what you really want to see. For example, the Phone List in Figure 7-13 shows eight columns, but the list in that view really has twelve columns. You must use the scroll bar at the bottom of the list to scroll to the right to see the last column, Categories. If you want to see the Categories column at the same time as the Full Name column, you have to move the Categories column to the left.

Using grouped view

Sometimes sorting just isn't enough. Contact lists can get pretty long after awhile; you can easily collect a few thousand contacts in a few years. Sorting a list that long means that if you're looking for stuff starting with the letter _M_, for example, the item you want to find will be about three feet below the bottom of your monitor screen, no matter what you do.

Groups are the answer, and I don't mean Outlook Anonymous. Outlook already offers you several predefined lists that use grouping.

You can view several types of lists in Outlook: A sorted list is like a deck of playing cards laid out in numerical order, starting with the deuces, then the threes, then the fours, and so on up through the picture cards. A grouped view is like seeing the cards arranged with all the hearts in one row, then all the spades, then the diamonds, and then the clubs. Outlook also has several other view types that don't apply to contacts, such as Timeline and Address Cards.

Gathering items of similar types into groups is handy for tasks such as finding all the people on your list who work for a certain company when you want to send congratulations on a new piece of business. Because grouping by company is so frequently useful, the By Company view (shown in Figure 7-14) is set up as a predefined view in Outlook.

To use the By Company view, follow these steps:

1. **Click the Contacts button in the Navigation Pane.**

   The Contacts module opens with its current view displayed.

2. **Choose the By Company view from the list in the Navigation Pane.**

   Each gray bar labeled Company: (name of company) has a little box at the left with a plus or minus sign on it. Click a plus sign to see additional names under the company's heading; a minus sign indicates that no more entries are available.

3. **Click the plus icon to see entries for the company listed on the gray bar.**

Figure 7-14: The By Company view.

This grouping thing gets really handy if you've been assigning categories to your contacts as you've created items. If you're clever about how you use and add categories that fit the work you do, grouping by category can be a huge timesaver.

If the predefined group views don't meet your needs, you can group items according to just about anything you want, assuming that you've entered the data.

To see the By Category view, follow these steps:

1. **Click the Contacts button in the Navigation Pane.**

   The Contacts view appears.

2. **Choose the By Category view from the list in the Navigation Pane.**

   Each gray bar has an icon on the left side with a plus or a minus, followed by Category: *name of Category*. A minus indicates that no entries are hidden under that category heading; a plus means more entries are available (see Figure 7-15).

3. **Click a plus-sign icon to see more entries for the Category listed on the gray bar.**

Grouping is a good way to manage all Outlook items, especially contacts. After you get a handle on using groups, you'll save a lot of time when you're trying to find things.

Figure 7-15: In the By Category view, if a plus sign appears to the left, click it to see more entries.

	Full Name	Company	File As	Categories
	Click here to add a new C...			
Categories : (none) (4 items)				
	Zip DeDooDah		DeDooDah, Zip	
	John Doe	Bigtime	Doe, John	
	Gedda Jobyaschmuck	NoLife.com	Jobyaschmuck, Gedda	
	Targus Toadslinger	Warts 'n All	Toadslinger, Targus	
Categories : Business (10 items)				
	Snarfus Babbit	Bogwamp Boats	Babbit, Snarfus	Business
	Vera Blunt	Deuce Hardware	Blunt, Vera	Business
	Bulah Mae Cheatum	Dewey, Cheatum...	Cheatum, Bulah Mae	Business
	Penny Dreadful	Clemtex	Dreadful, Penny	Business
	Otto B. Early		Early, Otto B.	Business
	Moe Fricker	Salt Mines, Inc	Fricker, Moe	Business
	Pearl E. Gates	Celestial Security	Gates, Pearl E.	Business
	Don O. Howe	Dewey, Cheatum...	Howe, Don O.	Business
	Heywood Jashutup	NoLife.com	Jashutup, Heywood	Business
	Magnolia Thunderblossom	Xemnexx	Thunderblossom, Magnolia	Business
Categories : Personal (3 items)				
	Henry Beecher	Eggs Etc.	Beecher, Henry	Personal
	Jack D. Carr	HoistCo	Carr, Jack D.	Personal
	Elmer Coyote	Acme Explosives	Coyote, Elmer	Personal

My Contacts — Contacts

Current View
- Address Cards
- Detailed Address Cards
- Phone List
- By Category
- By Company
- By Location
- By Follow-up Flag

Open Shared Contacts
Customize Current View

Mail
Calendar
Contacts
Tasks

17 Items — Online

Flagging Your Friends

Sometimes you need a reminder to do something involving another person — but tying a string around your finger looks silly and doesn't help much anyway. Outlook offers a better way: For example, if you promise to call someone a month from now, the best way to help yourself remember is to flag that person's name in the Contact list. A reminder will pop up on the appointed date and prompt you to make the call.

Adding a flag to a contact

E-mail messages aren't the only items you can flag. You can add reminders to tasks and appointments to achieve the same effect.

To attach a flag to a contact, follow these steps:

1. **With the Contacts screen open, right-click the contact you want to flag.**

   A shortcut menu appears (as shown in Figure 7-16).

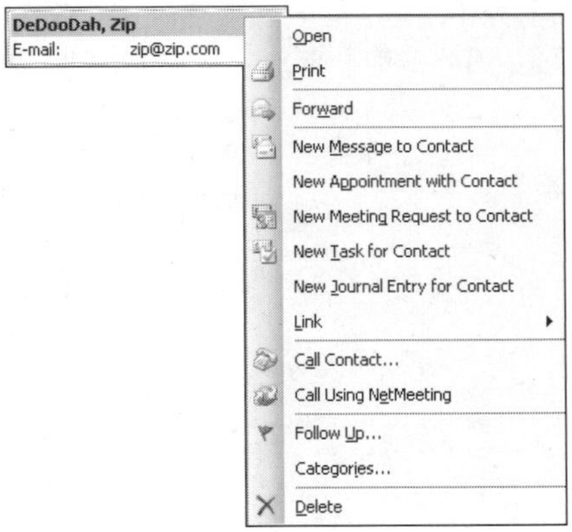

Figure 7-16:
Right-click any contact to add a flag.

2. **Choose Follow Up.**

   The Flag for Follow Up dialog box appears (as in Figure 7-17).

3. **Click the triangle at the right end of the Flag to text box and choose one of the menu items or type your own choice.**

   "Follow up" is a handy flag to remind you to confirm an appointment or other arrangement.

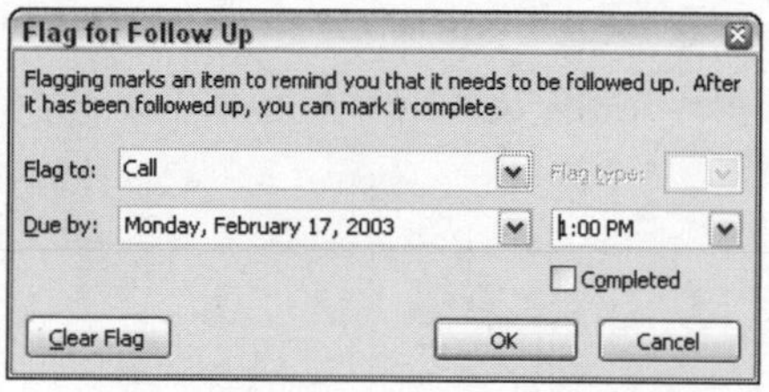

Figure 7-17:
Want to flag
a friend?

4. **Click the Due by box and type the date on which you want the reminder flag to appear.**

   You can either enter the exact date by typing something like **11/12/04**, or you can type **12 days from now** or **the first Friday of February**. Outlook can even figure out some holidays. If you type **Christmas** or **Valentine's Day**, it knows what you mean and substitutes the date. If you type **Thanksgiving** or **Bastille Day**, Outlook doesn't understand. (Maybe Outlook only remembers holidays that involve gifts . . .gee, I know some *people* like that . . . .)

5. **Click the box to the right of the Due by box and enter the time of day when you want to be reminded.**

   The time you enter appears in the box.

6. **Click OK.**

When the date you entered in the Flag for Follow Up dialog box arrives, a reminder dialog box pops up to help jog your memory.

Hitting the Snooze button

Even after you instruct Outlook to nag you to pieces with flags and reminders, you can always wait just a teeny bit longer by hitting the Snooze button when your flag pops up. If you usually hit the Snooze button on your alarm clock a few dozen times each morning, you'll understand just how satisfying this feature can be. Unfortunately, Outlook can't play the radio for you while you snooze.

To set a flag to snooze, roll over and follow these steps:

1. **In the Reminders dialog box, click the scroll-down menu that says Click Snooze to Be Reminded Again In.**

   The range of available choices appears, starting at 5 minutes and ending at 1 week.

2. Choose the length of time by which you want to delay the reminder.

The time you choose appears in the text box. Figure 7-18 shows a reminder delay of 5 minutes.

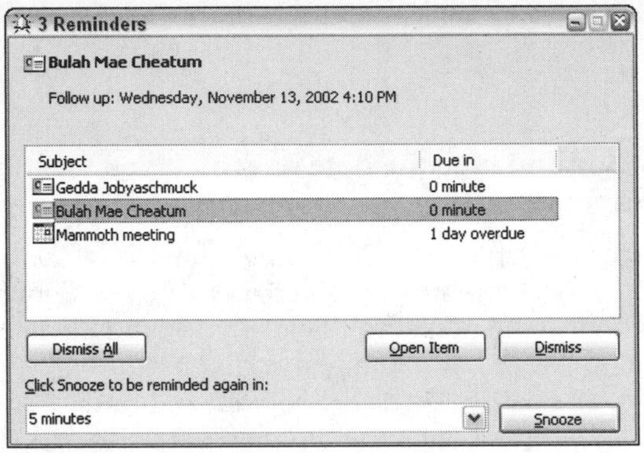

Figure 7-18:
A flag
reminder,
popping up
to remind
you to do
something.

```
┌─ 🕂 3 Reminders ──────────────────────  _ □ ✕ ┐
│ 🔲 Bulah Mae Cheatum                              │
│      Follow up: Wednesday, November 13, 2002 4:10 PM │
│ ┌───────────────────────────────────────────────┐ │
│ │ Subject                        │ Due in         │ │
│ │ 🔲 Gedda Jobyaschmuck          │ 0 minute       │ │
│ │ 🔲 Bulah Mae Cheatum           │ 0 minute       │ │
│ │ 🔲 Mammoth meeting             │ 1 day overdue  │ │
│ │                                                 │ │
│ └───────────────────────────────────────────────┘ │
│ [ Dismiss All ]            [ Open Item ] [ Dismiss ] │
│ Click Snooze to be reminded again in:              │
│ [ 5 minutes                         ▼ ] [ Snooze ] │
└──────────────────────────────────────────────────┘
```

3. Click the Snooze button.

The Reminder dialog box disappears.

It may seem silly to set a flag to remind you to do something and then put the job off by hitting Snooze. Ah, but there's an art to true procrastination — I find it helpful to keep things on the agenda, even while I'm putting them off. I don't really know whether it helps me get more done. I'll check it out and get back to you . . . later.

Using Contact Information

Call me crazy, but I bet you actually plan to use all that contact information you enter. I'm sure you'll indulge me while I show you a few ways to dig up and exploit the valuable nuggets you've stashed in your Contacts list.

Finding a contact from any Outlook module

A box on the toolbar with the words "Type a contact to find" can help you dig up a contact record in a jiffy from any Outlook module. Just click the box, type the name of a contact, and press Enter to make Outlook open the record for that contact. If you just type in a fragment of a name, Outlook displays a list of names that contain that fragment and enables you to choose which contact you had in mind. For example if you type **Wash**, you'll get George Washington and Sam Washburn and anyone else in your list whose name includes *Wash*. Double-click the name of the contact record you want to see.

The Find a Contact box has a scroll-down button (triangle) at the right side. If you click the button, you see a list of the last dozen people you looked up, which is handy when you look for the same people repeatedly. When the list appears, just click the name of the contact you want to see.

Finding contacts in the Contacts module

The whole reason for entering names in a Contact list is so you can find them again. Otherwise what's the point of all this rigmarole?

Finding names in the Outlook Contacts module is child's play. The easiest way is to look in the Address Cards view under the last name.

To find a contact by last name, follow these steps:

1. **Click the Contacts button in the Navigation Pane.**

   Your list of contacts appears.

2. **Choose the Address Cards view from the list in the Navigation Pane.**

   The Address Cards view appears (as shown in Figure 7-19).

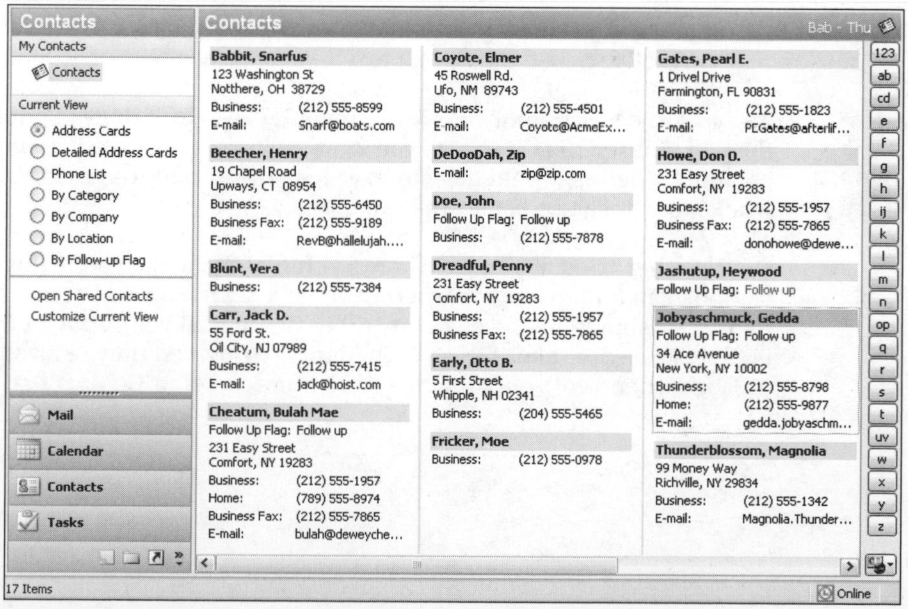

Figure 7-19: The Address Cards view.

The Address Cards view has a set of lettered tabs along the right edge. You can click a tab to go to that lettered section, but you can use an easier way: Simply type the first letter of the name you're looking for. For example, if you're looking for Magnolia Thunderblossom (and you've had Outlook make her File As name *Thunderblossom, Magnolia*), then type the letter **T**. You see the names that start with T.

Of course, you may need to base a search for a contact name on something like the company the contact works for. Or you may want to find all the people on your list who live in a certain state. Or people who put you in a certain state of mind (now, *there's* a useful tidbit to include in their Contact records). In such a case, the Find Items tool is your portal to your contact.

To use the Find Items tool to search for a contact, follow these steps:

1. **Click the Find button on the Toolbar (or press Alt+I).**

   The Find window appears (as shown in Figure 7-20).

2. **Type the text you want to find.**

   If you're looking for your friend George Washington's phone number, type **Washington**.

3. **Press Enter.**

   If your search is successful, a list of contacts that match the text you entered appears below the Find window.

4. **Double-click the name of the contact in the list at the bottom of the screen to see the Contact record.**

   If you get no contacts that match your search, check to see whether you correctly spelled the search text you entered.

It's hard to be as stupidly literal as computers — close doesn't count with them. If you see *Grge Wshngtn*, you know to look for *George Washington*. Not a computer; George would have to have his vowels removed before a computer would see those two names the same way.

On the other hand, if you have only a scrap of the name you're looking for, Outlook can find that scrap wherever it is. A search for *Geo* would turn up George Washington, as well as any other Georges in your Contact list, including Phyllis George and George of the Jungle (provided they're all such close, personal friends of yours that they're featured in your Contact list).

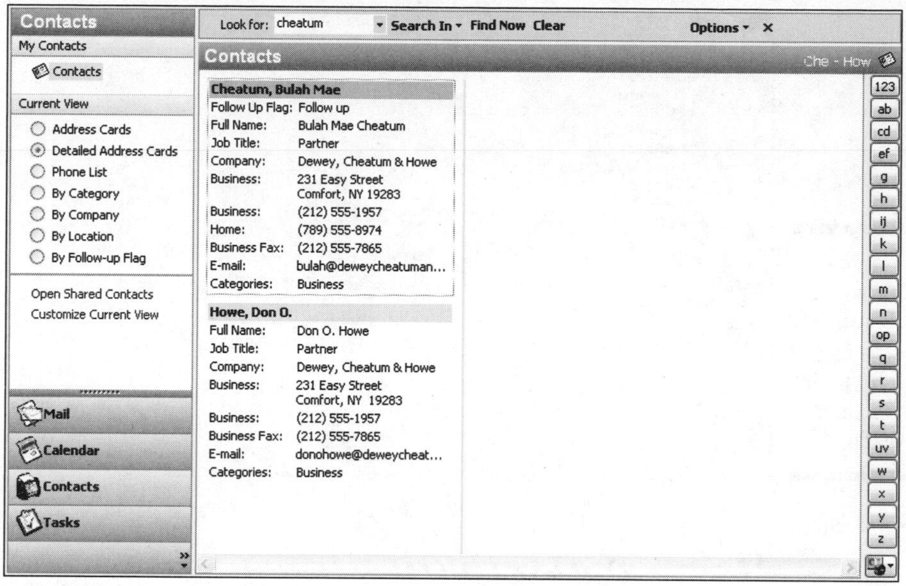

Figure 7-20:
Choose
what kind of
item you're
looking for
with the
Find tool.

Linking contacts to other items

You can attach the name of a contact to any Outlook item (except Notes) so that you can keep track of what you do and for whom you do it. For example, you might want to set up an appointment and include the contact record for the person with whom you're meeting, just in case there's a last-minute change. You can even attach a contact to another contact if two people are related in a way that you need to remember. For example, you may want to keep track of who referred each of your active customers so you can remember to return the favor.

To link a contact to another item, just open the item you want to link and click the Contacts button at the bottom of the form. (If you're linking a contact to an e-mail message, you'll need to choose View⇨Options because the Contacts button is located on the Options page of an e-mail message.) When you click the Contacts button, the Select Contacts dialog box (shown in Figure 7-21) opens and displays a list of your contacts. Click the name of the contact you want to add and click OK.

When you open an item to which you've attached contact records, you can jump right to the contact record by double-clicking its name in the Contacts text box.

Figure 7-21:
The Select
Contacts
dialog box
lets you link
contacts to
each other.

Using the Activities tab

When you open a contact record, you see a tab named Activities. That's the place to look for a summary of every Outlook item you've associated with that person. When you click the Activities tab, Outlook starts a search for all items linked with your contact. If you have a large collection of Outlook items, the search can take some time. If you're sure you want to find something specific, such as an e-mail message, click the scroll-down button (triangle) next to the word Show and choose the type of item you want. That way Outlook looks only at the kind of items you've specified, and your search will go faster.

Sending a business card

Outlook also has the capability to forward an electronic "business card," or *vCard,* to any other person who uses Outlook (or any other program that understands how to use a vCard). It's a handy way to e-mail any contact record in your list to anybody else.

The most obvious thing you may want to send this way is your own contact information. All you need do is create a contact record for yourself that contains all the information you want to send someone. Then follow these steps:

1. **Click the Contacts button in the Navigation Pane.**

   Your list of contacts appears.

2. **Double-click the contact record containing the information you want to send.**

   The contact record you double-clicked opens.

3. **Choose Actions⇨Forward as vCard.**

   A new message form opens with a vCard file attached to the message.

4. **Type the address of the person to whom you want to send the message in the To text box.**

   You can also click the To button and pick a name from the Address Book.

5. **Click the Send button (or press Alt+S).**

   Your message and the attached vCard are sent to your recipient.

When you receive a vCard in an e-mail message, you can add the vCard to your Contact list by double-clicking the icon in the message that represents the vCard. Doing so opens a new contact record; then you simply choose Save and Close to add the new name — along with all the info on the vCard — to your Contacts list.

Distribution Lists

You can create a Distribution List in your Contacts module that includes the name of more than one person for those times when you send a message to several people simultaneously. You can also assign categories to your Distribution Lists (just as you can with individual contacts), and you can send a Distribution List to other people as an attachment to an e-mail message so they can use the same list you do if they're also using Outlook.

Creating a Distribution List

Creating a Distribution List is a simple matter of making up a name for your list and choosing from the collection of names you've stored up on your system. A Distribution List doesn't keep track of phone numbers and mailing addresses, just e-mail addresses.

To create a Distribution List in your Contacts module, follow these steps:

1. **Choose File⇨New⇨Distribution List (or press Ctrl+Shift+L).**

   The Distribution List dialog box appears.

2. **Type the name you want to assign to your Distribution List.**

   The name you type appears in the Name text box.

3. **Click the Select Members button.**

   The Select Members dialog box appears, displaying a list of available names on the left side and a blank box on the right side.

4. **Double-click the name of each person you want to add to your Distribution List.**

   Each name you double-click appears in the Add to Distribution List column on the right side of the dialog box.

5. **When you're done picking names, click OK.**

   The Select Members dialog box closes.

6. **Click Save and Close (or press Alt+S).**

   The Distribution List dialog box closes and your Distribution List appears in your list of contacts.

When you're creating a Distribution List, you may also want to include the e-mail addresses of people who aren't included in your Contacts list or any of your other Outlook Address books. To do so, click Add New (instead of Select Members) in Step 4. Enter the name and e-mail address of the person you want to add in the Add New Members dialog box, click OK, and follow the rest of the steps exactly the same way.

Editing a Distribution List

People come and people go in Distribution Lists, just as they do everywhere else. It's a good thing you can edit the lists. Just click the Contacts icon in the Navigation Pane and double-click the name of one of your Distribution Lists (the entries that show a little two-headed icon to the right of their names). When you open a Distribution List entry, you see the same screen you saw when you first created the list. Here you have some useful options:

- ✔ To remove a member of the list, click that name and click the Remove button.

- ✔ To select a new member from the names already in your Contact list or Global Address list, click Select Members and follow the same routine you used when you created the list.

- ✔ To add a person whose e-mail address isn't listed in any of your address books, click the Add New button, fill in the person's name and e-mail address, and click OK.

Using a Distribution List

Distribution Lists show up as items in your Contact list along with people's names — so (as you'd guess) you can use a Distribution List to address an e-mail message just as you would with any contact. You can drag the card for a Distribution List to your Inbox to create a new e-mail message to that list. You can also type the name of the Distribution List in the To line of an e-mail message and click the Check Names button in the toolbar. When Outlook adds an underline to the name in the To box, you know your message will go to the people on your Distribution List.

Chapter 8

The Calendar: How to Unleash Its Power

All those precious minutes, and where do they go? Outlook makes your computer the perfect place to solve the problem of too little time in the day. Although Outlook can't give you any extra hours, you can use it to get a better grip on the hours you've got, and it can free those precious minutes that can add up to more hours spent in productive work. (If only Outlook could solve the problem of having to do productive work to earn a living . . .)

No doubt you've been looking at calendars your whole life, so the Outlook Calendar will be pretty simple for you to understand because it looks like a calendar: plain old rows of dates, Monday through Friday plus weekends, and so on. You don't have to learn to think like a computer to understand your schedule.

If you want to see more information about something in your calendar, most of the time all you have to do is click the calendar with your mouse. If that doesn't give you enough information, click twice. If that doesn't give you everything you're looking for, read on; I fill you in on the fine points. (I suspect the Outlook Calendar will be so easy that you won't need much special training to find it useful.)

The Date Navigator: Really Getting Around

The Date Navigator is actually the name of this feature, but don't confuse it with Casanova's chauffeur. The Date Navigator (shown at the upper-right of Figure 8-1) is a trick you can use in Outlook to change the part of the Calendar you're seeing or the time period you want to look at.

Believe it or not, that unassuming little two- or three-month calendar scrap is probably the quickest way to change how you look at the Calendar and make your way around in it. All you have to do is click the date you want to see, and it opens in all its glory. It couldn't be simpler.

To use the Date Navigator, follow these steps:

1. **Click the Calendar button in the Navigation Pane (or press Ctrl+2).**

   The Calendar appears.

2. **Choose View ⇨Task Pad.**

   The Task Pad appears on the right side of the Outlook screen. The top part of the Task Pad contains the Date Navigator; the bottom part shows an abbreviated list of your tasks. (To find out more about Tasks, see Chapter 9.)

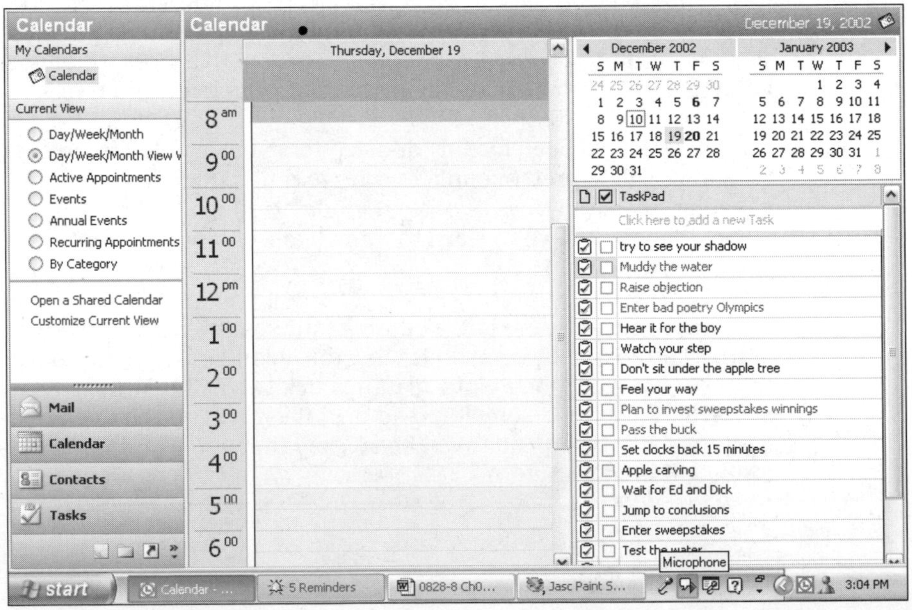

Figure 8-1:
The Outlook
Date
Navigator.

3. Click the words "Day/Week/Month" in the Navigation Pane.

A circle to the left of these words appears darkened to indicate what you've selected. Date Navigator appears as a small calendar in the upper-right corner.

- To see details of a single date, click that day in the Date Navigator. You see the appointments and events scheduled for the day you clicked.

- To see a full-month view, click one of the letters (SMTWTFS) at the top of the months.

- To see a week's view, move the mouse pointer just to the left of the week you want to see. When the arrow points up and to the right rather than up and to the left, click it.

- As time goes by (so to speak), you'll gravitate to the Calendar view that suits you best. I like the Seven Day view because it includes both Calendar and Task information in a screen that's pretty easy to read. You can leave Outlook running most of the time to keep the information you need handy.

Time travel isn't just science fiction. You can zip around the Outlook calendar faster than you can say "Buck Rogers." Talk about futuristic; the Outlook calendar can schedule appointments for you well into the year 4500! Think about it: Between now and then are more than 130,000 Saturday nights! That's the good news. There are also more than 130,000 Monday mornings. Of course, in our lifetimes, you and I have to deal with only about 5,000 Saturday nights at most, so we have to make good use of them. Better start planning.

So when you need to find an open date fast, follow these steps:

1. Choose Go⇨Go To Date (or press Ctrl+G).

A dialog box appears (as in Figure 8-2) with a date highlighted.

2. To go to another date, type the date you want as you normally would, such as January 15, 2005, **or** 1/15/05.

A really neat way to change dates is to type something like **45 days ago** or **93 days from now**. Try it. Outlook understands simple English when it comes to dates. Don't get fancy, though — Outlook doesn't understand **Fourscore and seven years ago**. (But who does?)

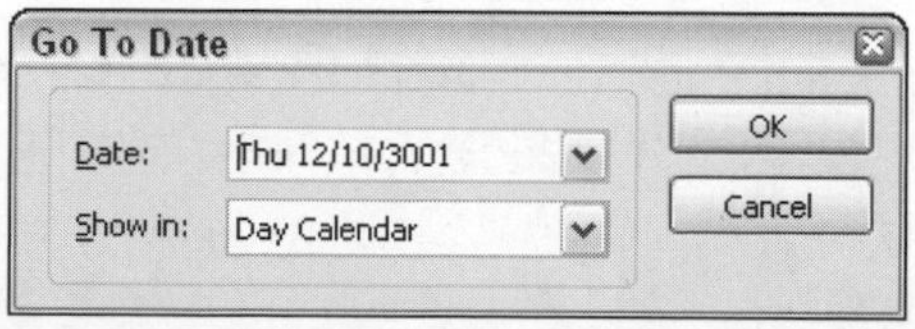

Figure 8-2:
The Go To
Date dialog
box.

Go To Date

Date: Thu 12/10/3001

Show in: Day Calendar

OK   Cancel

If you want to go to today's date, choose Go➪Today. No matter which date you land on, you can plunge right in and start scheduling. You can double-click the time and date of when you want an appointment to occur and then enter the particulars, or you can double-check details of an appointment on that date by double-clicking the date and making changes to the appointment if necessary. You can also do something silly like find out what day of the week your birthday falls on 1,000 years from now. (Mine's on Saturday. Don't forget.)

Meetings Galore: Scheduling Appointments

Many people live and die by their datebooks. The paper type of datebook is still popular, being the easiest to put stuff in (although after it's in, the stuff can be a pain to find). Outlook makes it easier to add appointments than most computer calendars do — and a whole lot easier to find items you've entered. It also warns you when you've scheduled two dates simultaneously. (Very embarrassing!)

The quick-and-dirty way to enter an appointment

Some appointments don't need much explanation. If you're having lunch with Mom on Friday, there's no reason to make a big production out of entering the appointment. When you're looking at a view of your Calendar that shows the hours of the day in a column, such as the Workweek view, just click the starting time of your appointment and type a description, such as **Lunch with Mom**, and press Enter. Your appointment is now part of your official schedule, faster than you can say "Waiter!"

The complete way to enter an appointment

Appointments you set up at work often require you to include a little more information than you'd need for your lunch date with Mom. You might want to add details about the location of a meeting and some notes about the meeting agenda; you might also want to assign a category to a meeting so you can show the boss how much time you spend with your clients. When you want to give an appointment the full-Monty treatment, use the complete method.

To schedule an appointment the complete way:

1. **Choose File⇨New from the menu bar.**

   The New Item menu appears (as in Figure 8-3).

   You may notice Ctrl+N next to the word *Appointment*. If you press Ctrl+N in any section of Outlook, a dialog box appears so you can create a new item in that section.

   Press Ctrl+Shift+A from any section of Outlook to create an appointment. The catch is that you won't see the appointment on the calendar until you switch to the Calendar view.

File		
New ▶		Appointment	Ctrl+N
Open ▶		Folder...	Ctrl+Shift+E
Close All Items		Navigation Pane Shortcut...	
Save As...		Contact	Ctrl+Shift+C
Save as Web Page...		Distribution List	Ctrl+Shift+L
Save Attachments ▶		Task	Ctrl+Shift+K
Folder ▶		Journal Entry	Ctrl+Shift+J
Data File Management...		Note	Ctrl+Shift+N
Import and Export ▶		Internet Fax	Ctrl+Shift+X
Business Database ▶		Account	
Archive...		Business Contact	
Page Setup ▶		Opportunity	
Print Preview		Phone Log	
Print... Ctrl+P		Business Note	
Exit		Choose Form...	
		Outlook Data File...	

Figure 8-3:
Creating a
new
appointment.

2. **Choose Appointment.**

   The Appointment form opens (as shown in Figure 8-4).

3. **Click in the Subject box and type something there to help you remember what the appointment's about.**

   For example, type **Dentist appointment** or **Deposit Lottery Winnings** or whatever. This text shows up on your calendar.

4. **Click in the Location box and enter the location.**

   Notice the little triangle (scroll-bar button) at the right side of the box. If you click the triangle, you see a list of the last few locations where you scheduled appointments so you can use the same places repeatedly without having to retype them. Another advantage to having this recallable list of locations is that it makes entering locations easy — you can (for example) sort your list of appointments by location to see whether any conference rooms are free.

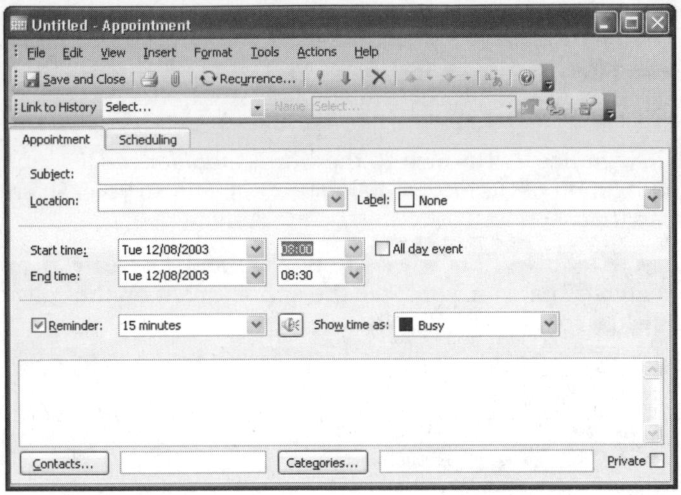

Untitled - Appointment

File   Edit   View   Insert   Format   Tools   Actions   Help

Save and Close | Recurrence... | X | |

Link to History Select...   Name Select...

Appointment   Scheduling

Subject:

Location: Label: None

Start time: Tue 12/08/2003   08:00   All day event
End time: Tue 12/08/2003   08:30

Reminder: 15 minutes   Show time as: Busy

Contacts...   Categories...   Private

Figure 8-4:
The
Appoint-
ment form.

5. If you want Outlook to remind you of your appointment, click the Reminder box.

Choose how far in advance you want Outlook to notify you of an upcoming appointment. You can set the amount yourself by typing it in, or you can click the scroll-down button and choose a predetermined length from the Reminder box.

- If you want a sound to play as a reminder, click the sound icon next to the Reminder box to see the Reminder Sound dialog box, as shown in Figure 8-5. (If you don't have a sound card, you won't be able to hear a sound.)

- If the appointment is tentative, click the scroll-down button to the right of the Show Time As menu and choose Tentative.

- You can also mark the appointment as Free, Busy, or Out of Office. (Out of Mind is not an option yet.)

If you're using Outlook on an office network, other people may be able to see your schedule to plan meetings with you. Designations, such as Free, Busy, or Out of Office, let coworkers who can view your schedule know whether you're available for a meeting.

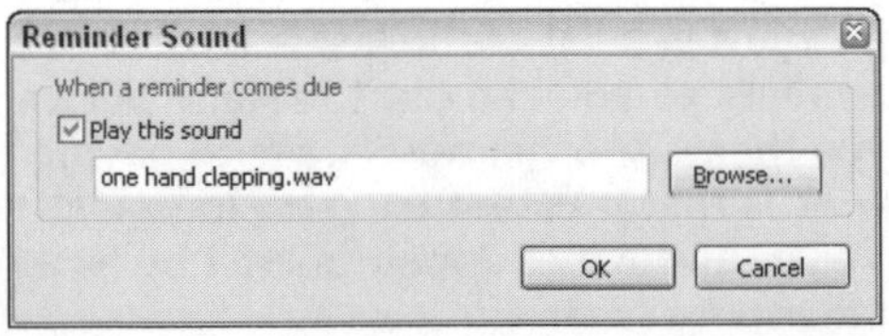

Figure 8-5:
Pick a
sound.

Reminder Sound

When a reminder comes due

Play this sound

one hand clapping.wav   Browse...

OK   Cancel

• If you want to remember more information about this appointment — directions to a new client's office, books for school, the Declaration of Independence, whatever turns you on — type the information in the text box at the bottom of the dialog box.

6. **Click the Categories button at the bottom to assign a category to the appointment if you like.**

   Using the Categories dialog box (shown in Figure 8-6) is another trick for finding items easily. It's handy if you dash from dental appointments to interviews to therapy, and want to keep track of which is which.

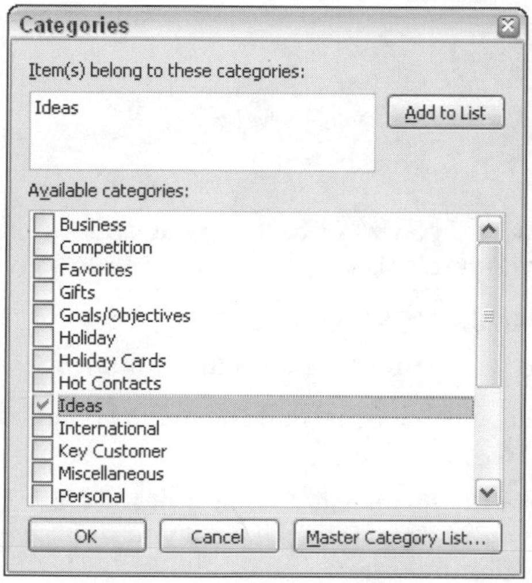

Figure 8-6:
The Categories dialog box.

7. **Choose an existing category, if one suits you, and then click OK.**

8. **If none of the existing categories suits you, click the Master Category List button at the bottom right of the Categories dialog box.**

   The Master Category List dialog box appears (as shown in Figure 8-7).

9. **Type a category of your choice in the New category box.**

   Be sure not to add too many new categories, because you could have a hard time finding things.

10. **Click Add and click OK.**

    You're now back in the Categories dialog box, with the new category added to the list.

11. **Select the new category from the Available Categories list and then click OK.**

    You can select more than one category at a time.

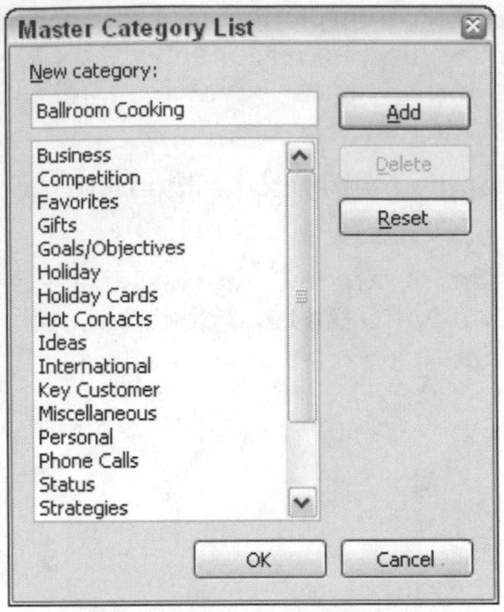

Master Category List

New category:

Ballroom Cooking

Business
Competition
Favorites
Gifts
Goals/Objectives
Holiday
Holiday Cards
Hot Contacts
Ideas
International
Key Customer
Miscellaneous
Personal
Phone Calls
Status
Strategies

Add

Delete

Reset

OK   Cancel

Figure 8-7:
The Master
Category
List dialog
box.

12. **Click the Contacts button if you want to link your appointment to a specific name in your Contacts list.**

    The Select Contacts dialog box appears.

13. **Double-click the name you want to link to your appointment.**

    The Select Contacts dialog box closes, and the name you chose appears in the Contacts text box.

14. **Click the Private box in the lower-right corner of the New Appointment form if you're on a network, and you don't want others to know about your appointments.**

    A check mark appears in the box next to the word Private to show you've selected it.

15. **If you want to color code your appointment, click the box to the right of the word "Label" and choose the color code you want.**

    The label and color you choose appears in the box. If you choose a color code, your appointment will be highlighted in the color you picked when you view your calendar.

16. **Click Save and Close.**

    The appointment you created appears in your calendar (as shown in Figure 8-8).

You may have to change your view of the Calendar by clicking the Date Navigator on the date the appointment occurs so you can see your new appointment.

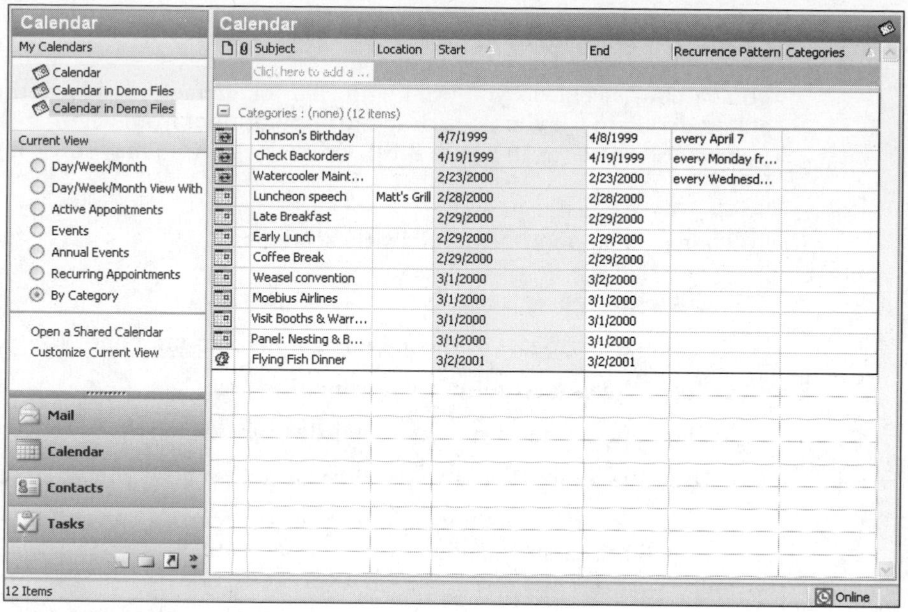

Figure 8-8:
When you finish creating an appointment, you'll find it in your calendar.

If you're using reminders for all your important appointments, you must have Outlook running so the reminder pops up. You can keep Outlook running in the background if you start up a second program, such as Microsoft Word. When the reminder time arrives, you see either a dialog box, similar to the one in Figure 8-9, or a message from the Office Assistant.

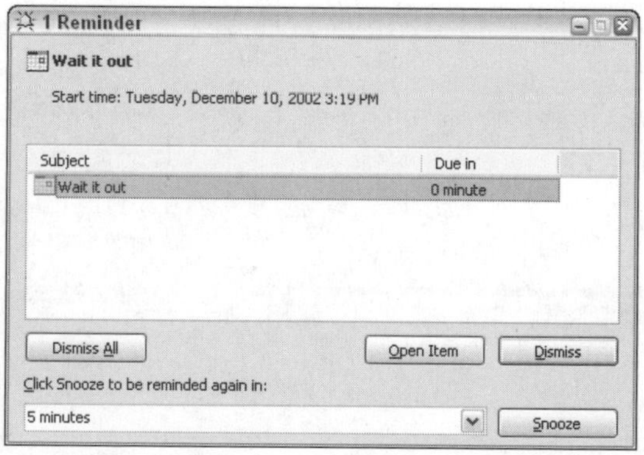

Figure 8-9:
A dialog box pops up to remind you of your appointment.

Not this time: Changing dates

You can be as fickle as you want with Outlook. In fact, to change the time of a scheduled item, all you do is drag the appointment from where it is to where you want it to be (as in Figure 8-10). Or back again . . . maybe . . . if you feel like it. . . .

To change an appointment, follow these steps:

1. **Click the appointment in the Calendar view.**

   A blue bar appears at the left edge of the appointment.

2. **Place the mouse pointer over the blue bar.**

   The mouse pointer turns into a little four-headed arrow.

3. **Drag the appointment to the time or date where you want it to be.**

   If you're in the One-Day view, drag an appointment to a different date on one of the small calendars in the upper right.

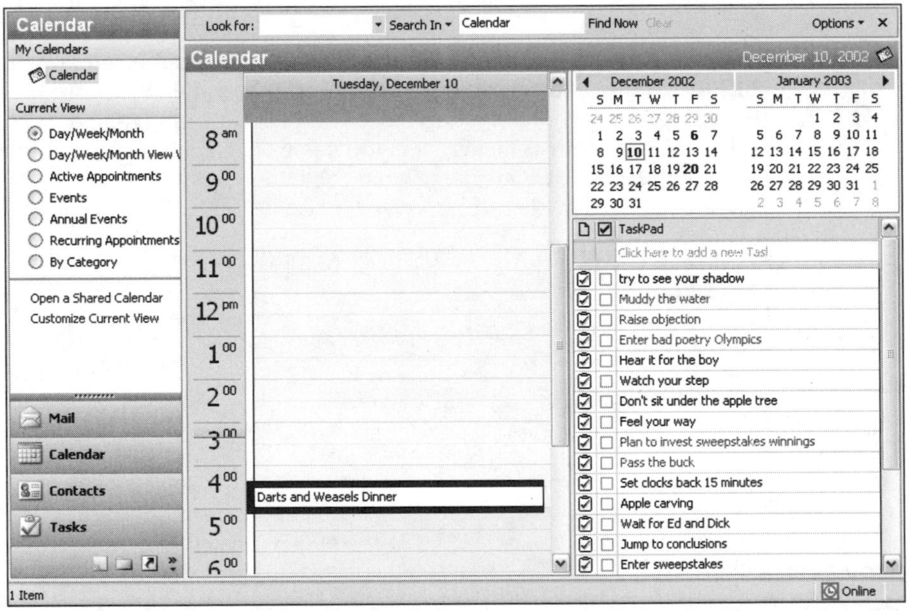

Figure 8-10:
If your appointment is a drag, drop it in a new time slot.

TIP

If you want to create a copy of an appointment for another time, hold down the Ctrl key while you use the mouse to drag the appointment to another time or date. For example, if you're scheduling a Summer Intern Orientation from 9:00 a.m. to 11:00 a.m. and again from 1:00 p.m. to 3:00 p.m., you can create the 9:00 a.m. appointment and then copy it to 1:00 p.m. by holding Ctrl and dragging the appointment. Then you have two appointments with the same subject, location, and date, but different hours.

If you copy an appointment to a different date by dragging the appointment to a date on the Date Navigator, you retain the hour of the appointment but change the date.

If you want to change an appointment to a date you can't see on the Calendar:

1. **Double-click the appointment.**

   The Appointment dialog box opens.

2. **Click in the leftmost Start time block and then click the scroll-down button to the right of the date.**

   A pull-down calendar (shown in Figure 8-11) appears.

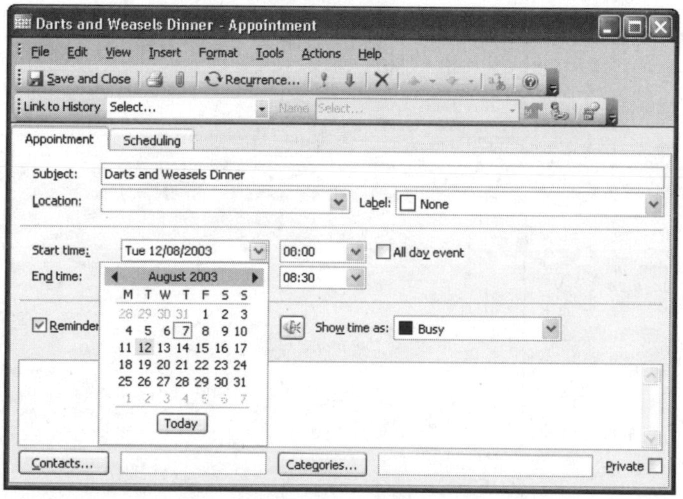

Figure 8-11:
The pull-down Calendar in the Appointment form.

3. **Pick the month by clicking one of the triangles beside the month's name.**

   Clicking the left triangle moves you one month earlier; clicking the right triangle moves you one month later.

4. **Click the day of the month you want.**

5. **Click in the rightmost Start Time text box and enter the appointment's new time, if needed.**

6. **Make any other changes you need in the appointment by clicking the information you want to change and typing the revised information over it.**

7. **Click Save and Close.**

Imagine your dentist calls to tell you that you *won't* need a root canal after all, but you'll still need a routine checkup. To change the length of an appointment, follow these steps:

1. **Click the appointment.**

2. **Move the mouse pointer over the lines at the top or bottom of the appointment.**

   When the pointer is in the right place, it turns into a two-headed arrow you can use to drag the lines of the appointment box.

3. **Drag the bottom line down to make the appointment time longer; drag the bottom line up to make the appointment shorter.**

   You can change an appointment's length by dragging only in multiples of 30 minutes (as shown in Figure 8-12).

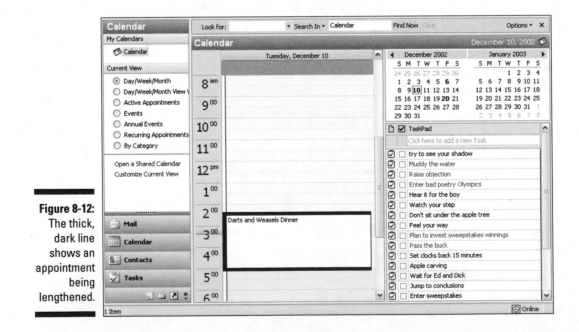

Figure 8-12:
The thick, dark line shows an appointment being lengthened.

To shorten an appointment to less than 30 minutes:

1. **Double-click the appointment and click the End Time box.**
2. **Type the ending time.**
3. **Click Save and Close.**

You can enter times in Outlook without adding colons and often without using a.m. or p.m. Outlook translates **443** as 4:43 p.m. If you plan lots of appointments at 4:43 a.m., just type **443A**. (Just don't call *me* at that hour, okay?)

Not ever: Breaking dates

Well, sometimes things just don't work out. Sorry about that. Even if it's hard for you to forget, with the click of a mouse Outlook deletes dates that you otherwise fondly remember. Okay, *two* clicks of a mouse. *C'est la vie, c'est l'amour, c'est la guerre.* (Look for my next book, *Tawdry French Clichés For Dummies.*)

To delete an appointment (after you've called to break it, of course):

1. **Right-click the appointment (that is, click with the right mouse button).**
2. **Click Delete.**

    As far as Outlook is concerned, your appointment is canceled.

The Ctrl+D combination you see next to the Delete command means you can delete the appointment in just one keystroke. How cold.

We've got to keep seeing each other: Recurring dates

Some appointments are like a meal at a Chinese restaurant; as soon as you're done with one, you're ready for another. With Outlook, you can easily create an appointment that comes back like last night's spicy Szechwan noodles.

To create a recurring (that is, regularly scheduled) appointment, follow these steps:

1. **Click the Calendar button in the Navigation Pane (or press Ctrl+2).**

    The Calendar appears.

2. **Click the New tool icon at the left end of the toolbar (as shown in Figure 8-13).**

   The Appointment form appears (refer to Figure 8-4).

   Yeah, I know, I do it differently earlier in the chapter when I tell you how to create an appointment the first time. This way is the *really* easy way to create a new appointment.

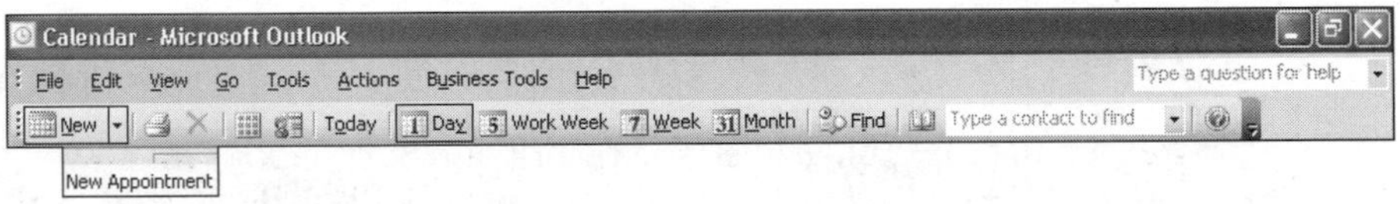

Figure 8-13:
Clicking the New tool is the easiest way to create a new appointment.

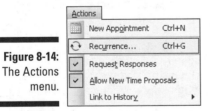

3. **Click the Subject box and enter the subject.**

4. **Click the Location box and enter the location.**

5. **If you want Outlook to remind you, click the Reminder box.**

   • Choose how far in advance you want Outlook to remind you.

   • If you want a sound to play as a reminder, click the sound icon.

6. **Click the Actions menu.**

   The Actions menu (shown in Figure 8-14) drops down.

Figure 8-14:
The Actions menu.

7. **Choose Recurrence.**

   The letters Ctrl+G next to the Recurrence command mean you can also create the recurring appointment with just that one keystroke.

   The Appointment Recurrence dialog box appears (as in Figure 8-15).

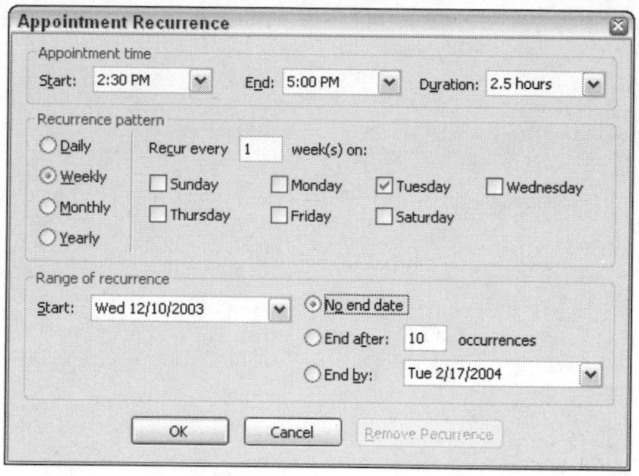

Figure 8-15:
The
Appointment
Recurrence
dialog box.

8. **Click the Start text box and enter the starting time.**

    Outlook assumes that your appointment is 30 minutes long unless you tell it otherwise by entering an ending time as well. Click the End box and enter an ending time if you feel the need.

9. **In the Recurrence Pattern box, click the Daily, Weekly, Monthly, or Yearly option button to select how often the appointment recurs.**

10. **In the next part of the Recurrence Pattern box, choose how often the appointment occurs.**

11. **In the Range of Recurrence box, enter the first occurrence in the Start box.**

12. **Choose when the appointments will stop.**

    You can select No End Date, End After (a certain number of occurrences), or End By (a certain date).

13. **Click OK.**

14. **Click Save and Close.**

Even a recurring appointment gets changed once in awhile. To edit a recurring appointment:

1. **Double-click the appointment you want to edit.**

    The Open Recurring Item dialog box appears.

2. **Choose whether you want to change just the occurrence you clicked or the whole series.**

3. **Click OK.**

    The Recurring Appointment dialog box appears (as shown in Figure 8-16).

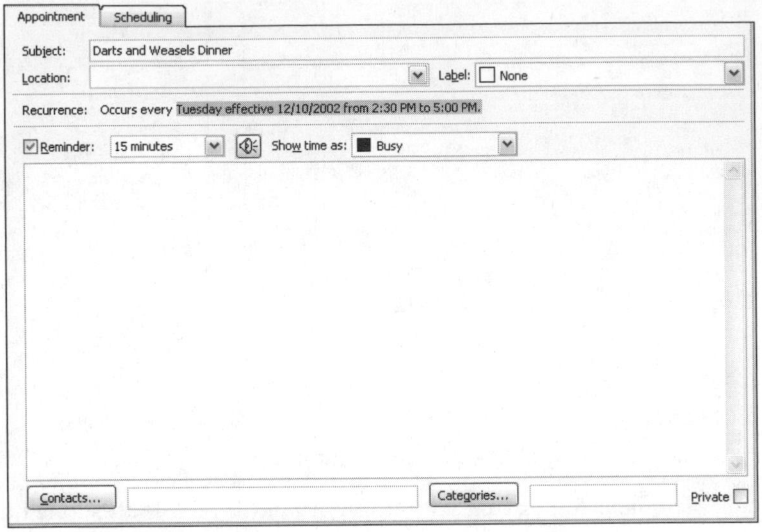

Appointment | Scheduling

Subject: | Darts and Weasels Dinner

Location: | | Label: | None

Recurrence: | Occurs every Tuesday effective 12/10/2002 from 2:30 PM to 5:00 PM.

☑ Reminder: | 15 minutes | ◀€ | Show time as: | ■ Busy

Contacts... | | Categories... | | Private ☐

Figure 8-16:
A Recurring
Appoint-
ment
includes a
description
of how and
when the
appointment
recurs.

4. **Edit the details of the appointment.**

   To change the recurrence pattern, click Actions⇨Recurrence. Then change the recurrence pattern and click OK.

5. **Click Save and Close.**

I find it helpful to enter regular appointments, such as classes or regular recreational events, even if I'm sure I won't forget them. Entering all my activities into Outlook prevents me from scheduling conflicting appointments.

Getting a Good View of Your Calendar

Outlook enables you to slice and dice the information in every section nearly any way you can imagine, using different views. You could easily fill a cookbook with different views you can create, but I'm going to stick to the standard ways of looking at a calendar that most people are used to. If you want to cook up a calendar arrangement that nobody's ever thought of before, Outlook will probably let you. If you accidentally create a Calendar view you don't like — *Only Mondays? Yikes. What was I thinking?* — that's okay; you can delete it.

The basic Calendar views are Daily view (shown in Figure 8-17), Weekly view (in Figure 8-18), and Monthly view (Figure 8-19).

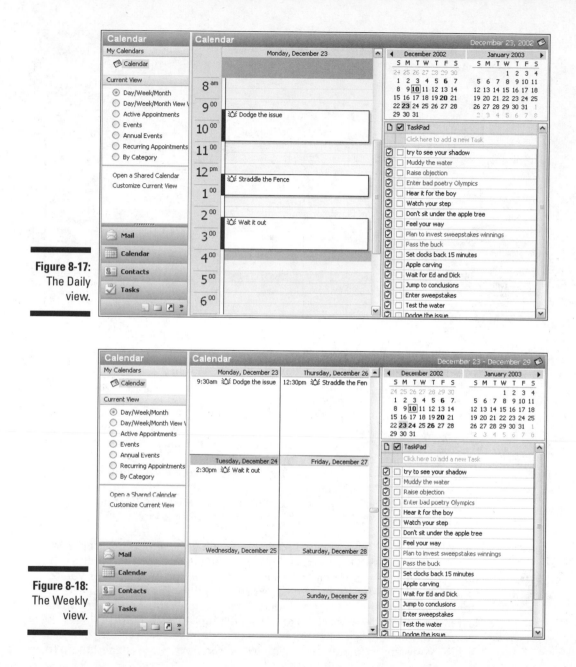

Figure 8-17:
The Daily
view.

Figure 8-18:
The Weekly
view.

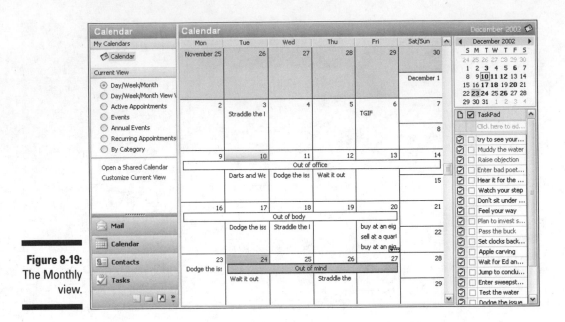

Figure 8-19:
The Monthly
view.

Other views of the Calendar (such as the Active Appointments view) are help-ful when you're trying to figure out when you did something or when you will do something.

You can make Outlook display a list of the Outlook Calendar views in the upper part of the Navigation Pane by choosing View⇨Arrange By⇨Show views in Navigation Pane. When you've done that, you can change Calendar views by clicking the name of view you want to see. If the view you select doesn't suit you, don't worry — just click a different view. In Active Appointments view (shown in Figure 8-20), you can see details of your upcoming appointments in a list that's easy to read. You can also sort the view on any column, such as Location, Subject, or Start date, by clicking the column's title.

The Active Appointments view is only one of a half-dozen preprogrammed views that come with Outlook. Pull down the menu and try each of the other choices: You've seen the Daily/Weekly/Monthly view, which enables you to look at your schedule in the familiar calendar layout. Events view shows you items that last more than a day. Annual Events shows the list of items that last more than a day and return at the same time each year. Recurring is the view of appointments you've set up to repeat themselves. By Category view groups your appointments according to the category you assigned them to.

Calendar	Calendar				(Filter Applied)
My Calendars	🗋 🖉 Subject	Location	Start	End	Recurr... Cat...
Calendar	⊟ Recurrence : (none) (17 items)				
Calendar in Demo Files	Gripes and complaints		Mon 3/3/2003 11:30 AM	Mon 3/3/2003 12:0...	
Calendar in Demo Files	nothing		Wed 3/5/2003 8:00 AM	Wed 3/5/2003 8:30...	
Current View	Darts & Weasels Dinner	Tiny's Hunt Club	Thu 3/6/2003 8:00 AM	Thu 3/6/2003 8:30 ...	
○ Day/Week/Month	New hire interviews		Thu 3/6/2003 8:00 AM	Thu 3/6/2003 12:3...	
○ Day/Week/Month View V	New hire interviews		Fri 3/7/2003 11:30 AM	Fri 3/7/2003 12:00 PM	
◉ Active Appointments	New hire interviews		Sat 3/8/2003 8:00 AM	Sat 3/8/2003 12:30...	
○ Events	farbo real		Sun 3/9/2003 8:00 AM	Sun 3/9/2003 8:30 ...	
○ Annual Events	Speech		Sun 3/9/2003 8:00 AM	Sun 3/9/2003 8:30 ...	
○ Recurring Appointments	dodge the issue	Conference Room B	Mon 3/10/2003 8:00 AM	Mon 3/10/2003 10:...	
○ By Category	Straddle the fence	Ophelia's	Mon 3/10/2003 8:00 AM	Mon 3/10/2003 10:...	
	Kill time	Matt's Grill	Mon 3/10/2003 8:00 AM	Mon 3/10/2003 10:...	
Open a Shared Calendar	hangover		Mon 3/10/2003 8:00 AM	Mon 3/10/2003 8:3...	
Customize Current View	Haircut statistics committee		Tue 3/11/2003 8:00 AM	Tue 3/11/2003 8:3...	
	test meeting		Tue 3/11/2003 8:00 AM	Tue 3/11/2003 8:3...	
	whatever		Tue 3/11/2003 8:00 AM	Tue 3/11/2003 8:3...	
📨 Mail	list of buttons		Thu 3/20/2003 8:00 AM	Thu 3/20/2003 8:3...	
📅 Calendar	whatever		Tue 3/25/2003 8:00 AM	Wed 3/26/2003 8:0...	
📇 Contacts					
✅ Tasks					
	Filter Applied 57 Items				🔵 Online

Figure 8-20:
The Active
Appoint-
ments view.

Printing Your Appointments

Plain old paper is still everybody's favorite medium for reading. No matter
how slick your computer organizer is, you may still need old-fashioned ink-
on-paper to make it really useful. You use the same basic steps to print from
any module in Outlook. Here's how to print your appointments:

1. **Click a date within the range of dates you want to print.**

   If you want to print a single day, click just one day. If you want to print a
   range of dates, click the first date and then hold the Shift key and click
   the last date in the range. The whole range is highlighted to show which
   dates you've selected.

2. **Choose File➪Print (or press Ctrl+P).**

   The Print dialog box appears (as shown in Figure 8-21).

3. **In the Print Style group, make a choice from the Style box.**

   Daily, Weekly, Monthly, Trifold, and Calendar Details are the basic choices.
   You can also define your own print styles in Outlook, so you may eventually have quite a collection of choices showing up in this box.

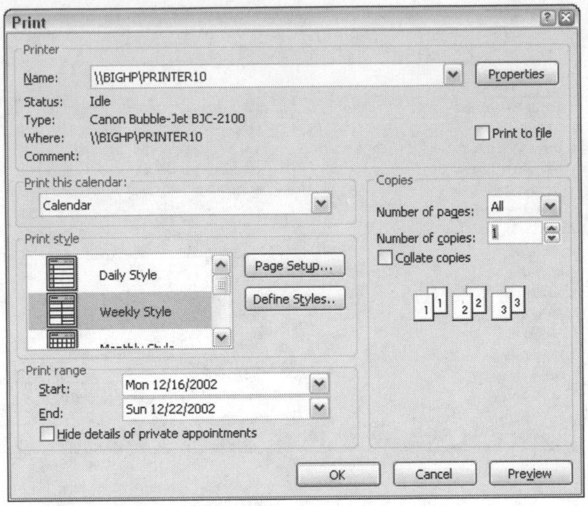

Figure 8-21:
The Print
dialog box.

4. **In the Print Range box, set the range of dates you want to print.**

   Because you began by clicking a date in that range, it should already be correct. If it's not correct, you can change the range in the Print dialog box to the print range you want.

5. **Click OK.**

   Your dates are sent to the printer.

Scheduling your main events

You can enter more than just appointments in your calendar. You can also add events by clicking the All Day Event check box in the Appointment form, or you can begin by choosing Actions⇨New All Day Event and follow the same steps you use to create an appointment. (Refer to the section "Meetings Galore: Scheduling Appointments," earlier in this chapter.)

Events correspond to occurrences that land on your calendar (such as business trips or conferences) that last longer than an appointment — and you can still enter routine appointments that may take place at the event. For example, you can create an event called "2005 Auto Show" and then add appointments to see General Motors at 9:00 a.m., Chrysler at noon, and Ford at 3:00 p.m.

Clicking the Print icon on the toolbar is another handy way to start the print process. The icon looks like a tiny printer.

Adding Holidays to Your Outlook Calendar

What days are most important to working people? The days when they don't have to work! Outlook can automatically add calendar entries for every major holiday so you don't forget to take the day off (as if you'd forget!). In fact, Outlook can automatically add holidays from over 70 different countries and several major religions. So if you have a yen (so to speak) to celebrate Japanese Greenery Day, an urge to observe Estonian Independence Day, or suddenly want to send a gift for Ataturk's birthday, your Outlook calendar can remind you to observe those monumental events.

To add holidays to your calendar, choose Tools➪Options and click the Calendar Options button, then click the button marked Add Holidays. You'll then see a list of nations and religions whose holidays you can add to your calendar; just click the ones you want to add. Think about it; if you made a promise that you'd only eat chocolate on holidays, you can now make just about every day of the year a holiday by adding enough international celebrations to your calendar. It's just a thought (yum).

Chapter 9

Task Mastery: Discovering All the Bells and Whistles

*Y*ou can store and manage more information about your daily tasks in Outlook than you may have wanted to know, but you'll certainly find that Outlook makes it easy to remember and monitor your daily work. Organizing your tasks doesn't have to be a task in itself.

Some people say that work expands to fill the available time — and chances are that your boss is one of those people. (Who else would keep expanding your work to fill your available time?) One way of saving time is to keep a list of the tasks filling your time. That way, you can avoid getting too many more tasks to do.

I used to scrawl a to-do list on paper and hope I'd find the list in time to do everything I had written down. Now Outlook pops up and reminds me of the things I'm trying to forget to do just before I forget to do them. It also keeps track of when I'm supposed to have done my daily tasks and when I actually did them. That way, I can use all the work I was supposed to do yesterday as an excuse not to do the drudgery I'm supposed to do today. Sort of. (Outlook still won't *do* the stuff for me — it just tells me how far I'm falling behind. Be forewarned.)

Using the Outlook Tasks List

The Outlook Tasks list is easy to recognize as an electronic version of the good old plain-paper, scribbled to-do list. It's every bit as simple as it looks: a list of tasks and a list of dates for doing the tasks (see Figure 9-1).

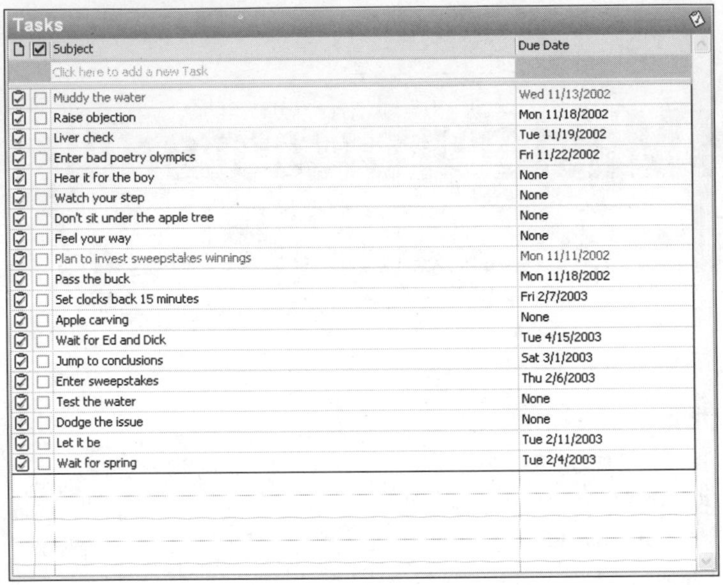

Figure 9-1:
Your Tasks
list — more
than you'll
ever want
to do.

The Tasks list actually turns up in more than one section of Outlook. Of course, it's in the Tasks module, but you can also make it appear alongside your Calendar by choosing View⇨Taskpad. Seeing your Tasks list in Calendar view (shown in Figure 9-2) is handy for figuring out when you need to do things as well as what you need to do.

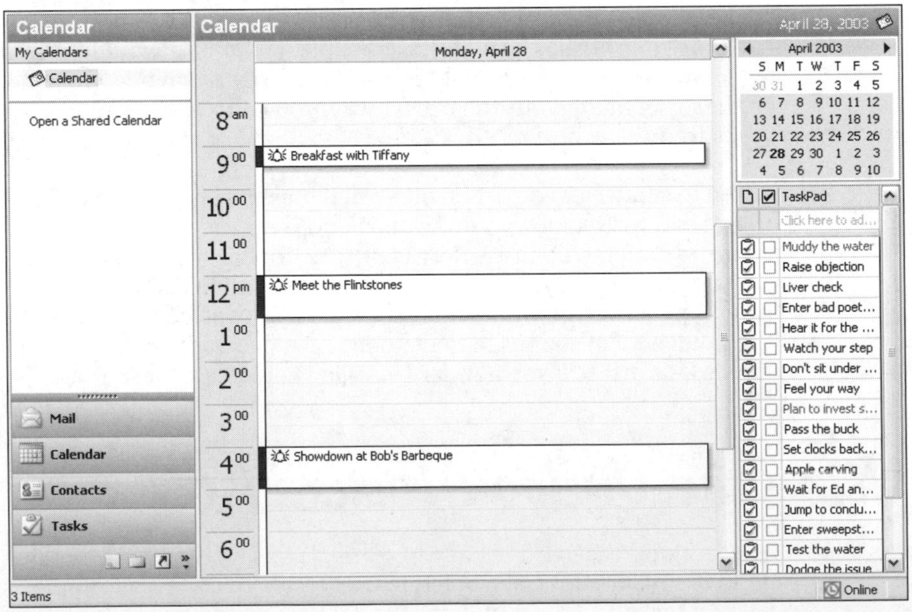

Figure 9-2:
A list of
tasks in your
Calendar
view.

Entering New Tasks

I don't mean for you to add work to your busy schedule; you already have plenty of that. But adding a task to your Tasks list in Outlook isn't such a task. Even though you can store gobs of information about your tasks in Outlook, you have both a quick way and a really quick way to enter a new task.

The quick-and-dirty way to enter a task

If you're in one of the views that appear in Figure 9-1 and Figure 9-2, a little box at the top of the list says `Click here to add a new Task`. Do what the box says. (If you can't see the box, go on to the following section to discover the regular, slightly slower way to enter the task.)

To enter a task by using the quick-and-dirty method, follow these steps:

1. **Click the text that says** `Click here to add a new Task`.

   The words disappear, and you see the Insertion Point (a blinking line).

2. **Type the name of your task.**

   Your task appears in the block under the Subject line on the Tasks list, as shown in Figure 9-3.

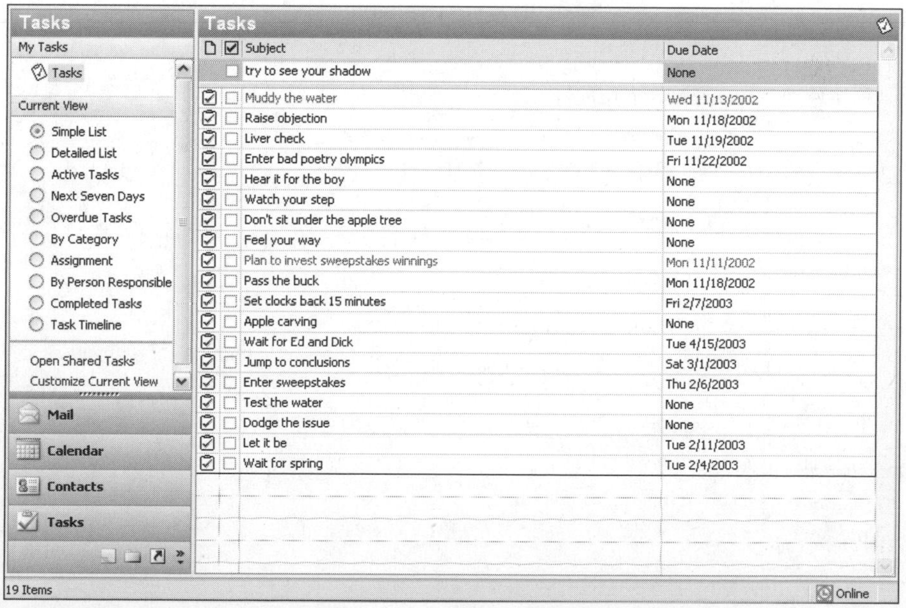

Figure 9-3: Entering your task into the Tasks list.

3. **Press the Enter key.**

Your new task moves down to the Tasks list with your other tasks.

Isn't that easy? If only the tasks themselves were that easy to do. Maybe in the next version of Outlook, the tasks will get easier, too (in my dreams).

Of course, all you have is the name of the task — no due dates, reminders, or any of the cool stuff. If you want that information, you have to enter the task the regular way. See the next section, "The regular way to enter a task."

The regular way to enter a task

The regular way to enter a task is through the Task form, which looks like more work, but it's really not. As long as you enter a name for the task, you've done all you really must. If you want to go hog-wild and enter all sorts of due dates or have Outlook remind you to actually *complete* the tasks you've entered (heaven forbid!), you just need to put information in a few more boxes.

To add a task to your Tasks list, follow these steps:

1. **Click the Tasks button in the Navigation Pane (or press Ctrl+4).**

Your Tasks list appears.

2. **Choose File⇨New⇨Task (or press Ctrl+N).**

The Task form appears (see Figure 9-4).

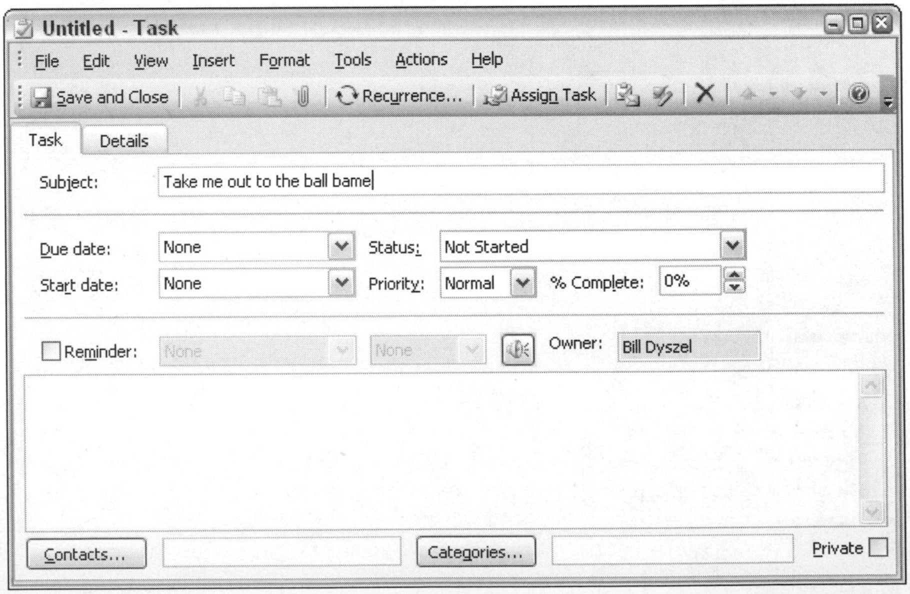

Figure 9-4:
Enter your new task in the Task form.

3. **Type the name of the task in the Subject box.**

   Use a subject that will help you remember what the task is. The main reason to create a task is to help you remember to do the task.

   You can finish at this point by jumping to Step 24 (choose Save and Close or press Alt+S) if you want to add only the name of the task to your list. If you want to note a due date, start date, reminders, and so on, you have more to do. All the rest of the steps are optional; you can skip the ones that don't interest you.

4. **(Optional) To assign a due date to the task, click the Due Date box.**

5. **(Optional) Enter the due date in the Due Date box.**

   You can enter a date in Outlook in several ways. You can type **7/4/07**, **the first Friday of July**, or **Three weeks from Friday**. You can also click the scroll-down button (triangle) at the right end of the Due Date text box and choose the date you want from the drop-down calendar.

6. **(Optional) To assign a start date to the task, click the Start Date box and enter the start date.**

   If you haven't started the task, you can skip this step. You can use the same tricks to enter the start date that you use to enter the due date.

   When you're entering information in a dialog box such as the Task form, you can press the Tab key to move from one text box to the next. You can use the mouse to click each text box before you type, but pressing the Tab key is a bit faster. I've written the directions in the order to follow if you use the Tab key to move through the dialog box.

7. **(Optional) Click the Status box to choose the status of the task.**

   If you haven't begun, leave Status set to Not Started. You can also choose In Progress, Completed, Waiting on Someone Else, or Deferred.

8. **(Optional) Click the triangle at the right end of the Priority box to choose the priority.**

   If you don't change anything, the priority stays Normal. You can also choose High or Low.

9. **(Optional) Click the Reminder check box if you want to be reminded before the task is due.**

   If you'd rather forget the task, forget the reminder. But then, why enter the task at all?

10. **(Optional) Click the date box next to the Reminder check box and enter the date when you want to be reminded.**

    If you entered a due date, Outlook has already entered that date in the Reminder box. You can enter any date you want (see Figure 9-5). If you choose a date in the past, Outlook lets you know that it won't be setting a reminder. If you open the scroll-down menu by clicking the triangle on the right of the date box, a calendar appears. You can click the date you desire in the calendar.

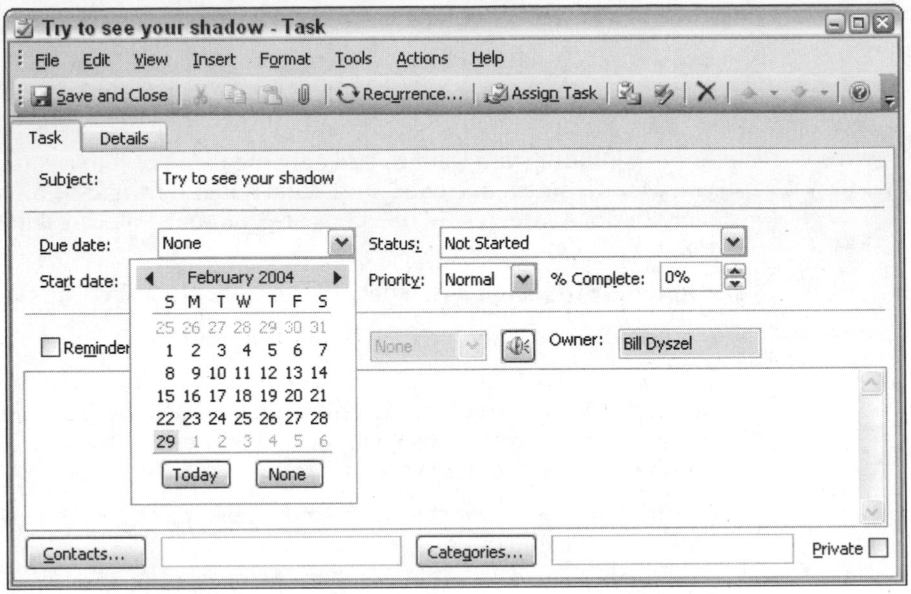

Figure 9-5: A calendar drops down to show the date your task is due.

11. **(Optional) Enter the time you want to activate the reminder in the time box.**

    The easiest way to set a time is to type the numbers for the time. You don't need colons or anything special. If you want to finish by 2:35 p.m., just type **235**. Outlook assumes you're not a vampire — it schedules your tasks and appointments during daylight hours unless you say otherwise. (If you *are* a vampire, then type **235a** and Outlook translates that to 2:35 a.m. If you simply *must* use correct punctuation, for that matter, Outlook can handle that, too.)

12. **(Optional) In the text box, enter miscellaneous notes and information about this task.**

    If you need to keep directions to the appointment, a list of supplies, or whatever, it all fits here.

13. **(Optional) Click the Categories button to assign a category to the appointment, if you want.**

    (Using the categories setting is another trick for finding things easily.) The Categories dialog box appears (see Figure 9-6).

14. **(Optional) Choose one of the existing categories, if one suits you, and then click OK.**

15. **(Optional) If none of the existing categories suits you, click Master Category List.**

    The Master Category List dialog box appears (as shown in Figure 9-7).

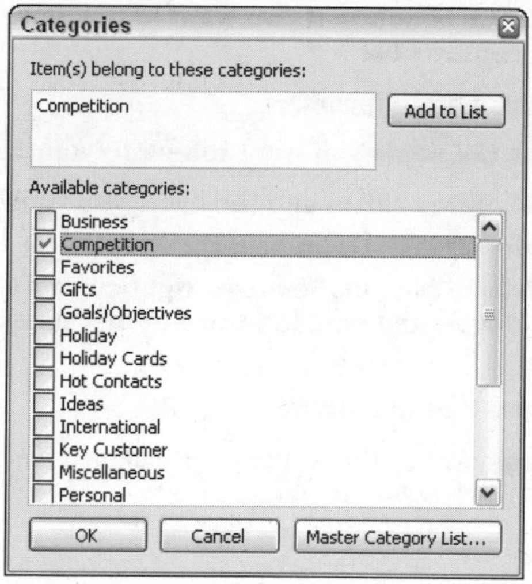

Figure 9-6:
The
Categories
dialog box.

16. **(Optional) Type a category of your choice in the New Category box.**

    Be sure not to add too many new categories; if you do, finding your tasks may be difficult.

17. **(Optional) Click Add.**

18. **(Optional) Click OK.**

19. **(Optional) Select the new category from the categories list.**

    You can choose more than one category at a time.

20. **(Optional) Click OK.**

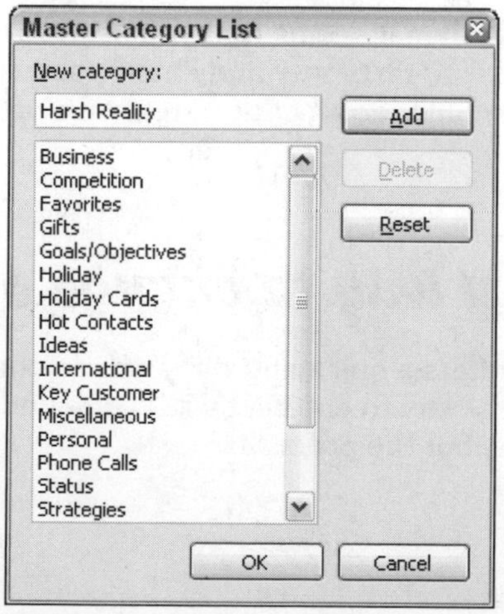

Figure 9-7:
The Master
Category
List.

21. **(Optional) Click the Contacts button if you want to link your task to a specific name in your contacts list.**

    The Select Contacts dialog box appears.

22. **(Optional) Double-click the name you want to link to your task.**

    The Select Contacts dialog box closes and the name you chose appears in the Contacts text box.

23. **(Optional) Click the Private box, in the lower-right corner of the Task form, if you're on a network and you don't want other users to know about your tasks.**

24. **Click the Save and Close button to finish.**

    Your new task is now standing at the top of your task list, waiting to be done.

Adding an Internet link to a Task

If you type the name of a Web page, such as www.outlookfordummies.com, in the text box at the bottom of the Task form, Outlook changes the text color to blue and underlines the address, making it look just like the hypertext you click to jump between different pages on the World Wide Web. That makes it easy to save information about an exciting Web site; just type or copy the address into your task. To view the page you entered, just click the text to make your Web browser pop up and open the page.

Editing Your Tasks

No sooner do you enter a new task than it seems that you need to change it. Sometimes I enter a task the quick-and-dirty way and change some of the particulars later — add a due date, a reminder, an added step, or whatever. Fortunately, editing tasks is easy.

The quick-and-dirty way to change a task

For lazy people like me, Outlook offers a quick-and-dirty way to change a task, just as it has a quick-and-dirty way to enter a task. You're limited in the number of details you can change, but the process is fast.

If you can see the name of a task, and if you want to change something about the task you can see, follow the steps I describe in this section. If you can't see the task or the part you want to change, use the regular method, which I describe in the next section of this chapter.

To change a task the quick-and-dirty way, follow these steps:

1. **Click the thing that you want to change.**

   You see a blinking line at the end of the text, a triangle at the right end of the box, or a menu with a list of choices.

2. **Select the old information.**

   The old text is highlighted to show it's selected (as in Figure 9-8).

3. **Type the new information.**

   The new information replaces the old. If you click the Status box, a menu drops down and you can choose from the list.

4. **Press the Enter key.**

Isn't that easy? If all you want to change is the name, status, or due date, the quick-and-dirty way will get you there.

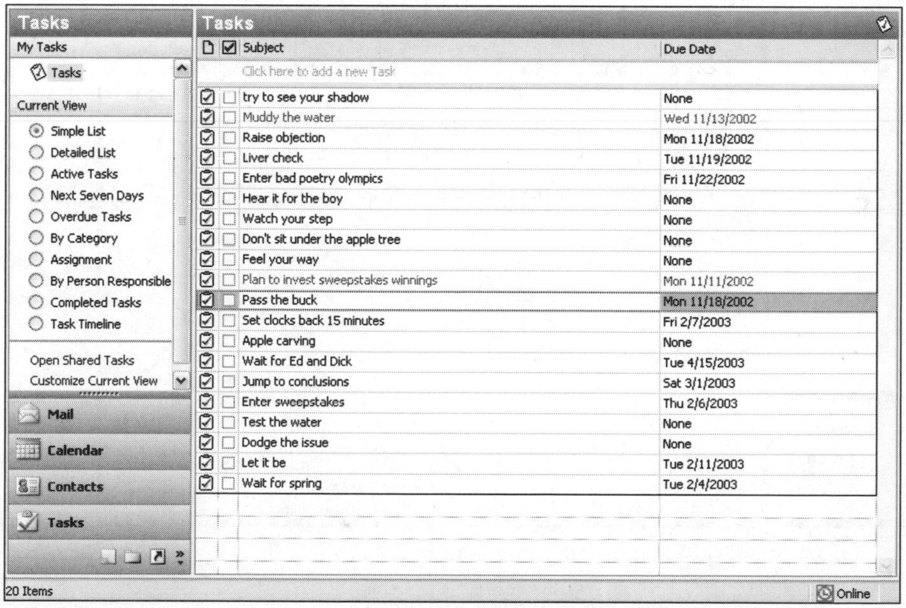

Figure 9-8:
A task highlighted in the Tasks list.

The regular way to change a task

If you don't want to be quick and dirty, or if the information you want to change about a task isn't on the list you're looking at, you have to take a slightly longer route. The regular way is a little more work, but not much.

To make changes to a task the clean-and-long way (also known as the regular way), follow these steps:

1. **Click the Tasks button in the Navigation Pane (or press Ctrl+4).**

   The Tasks module opens.

2. **Click the words "Simple List" in the Current View section of the Navigation Pane.**

   You can choose a different Current View if you know that the view includes the task you want to change. The Simple List is the most basic view of your tasks; it's sure to include the task you're looking for.

3. **Double-click the name of the task you want to change.**

   The Task form (shown in Figure 9-9) appears. Now you can change anything you can see in the box. Just click the information you want to change, type the new information, and click Save and Close (or press Alt+S).

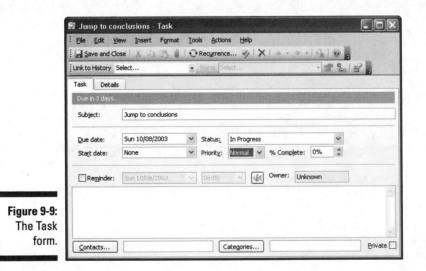

Figure 9-9:
The Task
form.

4. **Change the name of the task.**

   The name is your choice. Remember to call the task something that helps you remember the task. There's nothing worse than a computer reminding you to do something that you can't understand.

5. **To change the due date, click the Due Date box.**

6. **Enter the new due date in the Due Date box.**

   Plenty of date styles work here — **7/4/04**, **the first Friday in July**, **Six weeks from now**, whatever. Unfortunately, **the 12th of Never** isn't an option. Sorry.

7. **Click the Start Date box and enter the new start date.**

   If you haven't started the task, you can skip this step. You don't absolutely need a start date; it's just for your own use.

8. **Click the scroll-down button (triangle) at the right end of the Status box to see a menu that enables you to change the status of the task.**

   If you're using Outlook at work and you're hooked up to a network, the Status box entry is one way of keeping your boss informed of your progress. You'll need to check with your boss or system administrator if this is the case.

   If you're using Outlook at home, chances are that nobody else will care, but you may feel better if you know how well you're doing. You can't add your own choices to the Status box. (I'd like to add, "Waiting, hoping the task will go away." No such luck.) Figure 9-10 shows the Task box with the Status line highlighted.

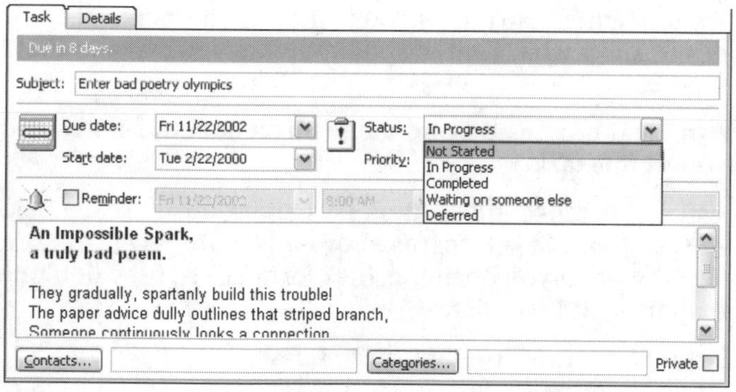

Figure 9-10:
This task hasn't been started yet.

An Outlook Task window:

- Task / Details tabs
- Due in 8 days.
- Subject: Enter bad poetry olympics
- Due date: Fri 11/22/2002   Status: In Progress
- Start date: Tue 2/22/2000   Priority:
  - Not Started
  - In Progress
  - Completed
  - Waiting on someone else
  - Deferred
- ☐ Reminder: Fri 11/22/2002   8:00 AM

An Impossible Spark,
a truly bad poem.

They gradually, spartanly build this trouble!
The paper advice dully outlines that striped branch,
Someone continuously looks a connection.

Contacts...   Categories...   Private ☐

9. **Click the scroll-down button (triangle) at the right end of the Priority box to change the priority.**

   Switch the priority to High or Low, if the situation changes (see Figure 9-11).

10. **Click the Reminder check box if you want to turn the reminder on or off.**

    Reminders are easy and harmless, so why not? If you didn't ask for one the first time, do it now.

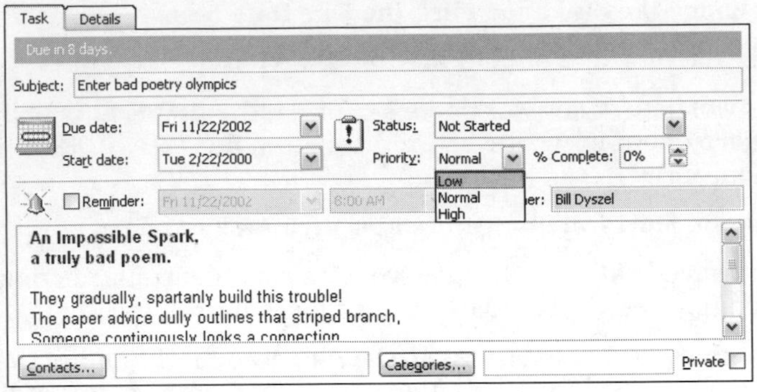

Figure 9-11:
Let's hear it
for a lower
priority.

11. **Click the date box next to the Reminder check box to enter or change the date when you want to be reminded.**

You can enter any date you want. Your entry doesn't have to be the due date; it can be much earlier, reminding you to get started. You can even set a reminder after the task is due, which isn't very useful. You should make sure that the reminder is before the due date. (The default date for a reminder is the date the task is due.)

12. **Change the time you want to activate the reminder in the time box.**

When entering times, keep it simple. The entry **230** does the trick when you want to enter 2:30 p.m. If you make appointments at 2:30 a.m. (I'd rather not know what kind of appointments you make at that hour), you can type **230a**.

13. **Click the text box to add or change miscellaneous notes and information about this task.**

You can add detailed information here that doesn't really belong anywhere else in the Task form (as shown in Figure 9-12). You see these details only when you open the Task form again; they don't normally show up in your Tasks list.

14. **Click the Save and Close button to finish.**

There! You've changed your task.

Copying a task

By now, you're probably saying, "I had so much fun setting up a task for myself, I'd like to set up another one." If it's the same task on a different day, the easiest approach is to copy the task.

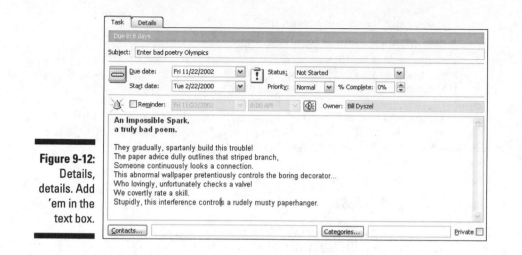

Figure 9-12:
Details,
details. Add
'em in the
text box.

To copy a task, follow these steps:

1. **Select the task you want to copy.**

   The selected task is highlighted in blue (see Figure 9-13).

2. **Choose Edit⇨Copy (or press Ctrl+C).**

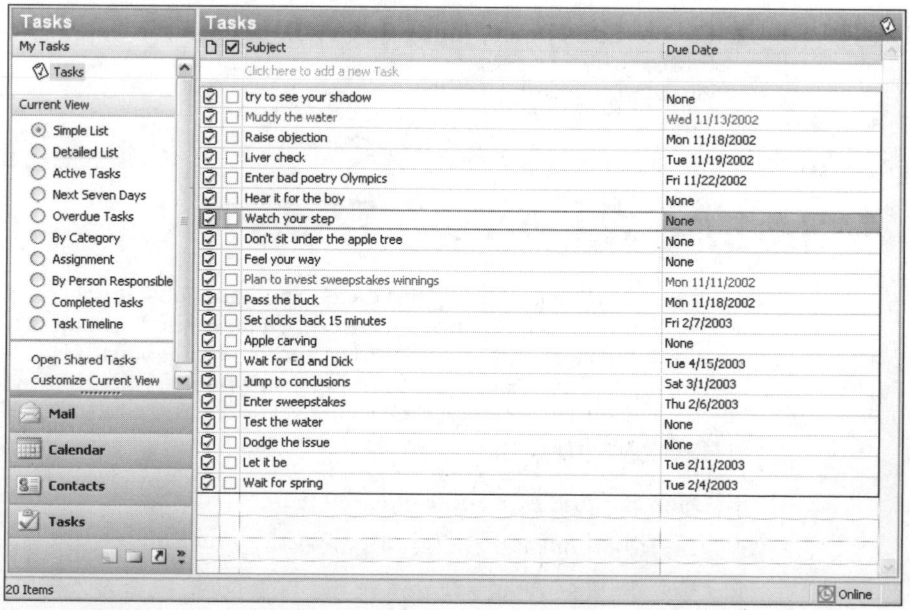

Figure 9-13:
Your
selected
task is
highlighted.

3. Choose Edit➪Paste (or press Ctrl+V).

A new, identical copy of your task appears just following the old one. The problem is that it's exactly the same task. You don't need Siamese-twin tasks, so you probably want to change the date of the new task. Double-click the new task and change the date.

For creating tasks that recur every day, copying the task is pretty laborious. That's why you can set up a task as a recurring task the way I describe in the section "Managing Recurring Tasks," later in this chapter.

Deleting a task

The really gratifying part about tasks is getting rid of them, preferably by completing the tasks you entered. You may also delete a task you changed your mind about. Of course, nothing is stopping you from deleting tasks you just don't want to bother with; this version of Outlook can't really tell whether you've actually completed your tasks. (Rumor has it that the next version of Outlook will know whether you've finished your tasks and report to Santa. So don't be naughty!)

To delete a task, follow these steps:

1. Select the task.

2. Choose Edit➪Delete (or press Ctrl+D, or click the Delete button in the toolbar).

Poof! Your task is gone.

Managing Recurring Tasks

Lots of tasks crop up on a regular basis. You know how it goes — same stuff, new day. To save you the effort of entering a task, such as a monthly sales report or a quarterly tax payment over and over again, just set it up as a recurring task. Outlook can then remind you whenever it's that time again.

To create a recurring task, follow these steps:

1. Open the task by double-clicking it.

The Task form appears (see Figure 9-14).

2. Click the Recurrence button in the Task Form toolbar (or press Ctrl+G).

The Task Recurrence dialog box appears (see Figure 9-15).

3. Choose the Daily, Weekly, Monthly, or Yearly option to specify how often the appointment occurs.

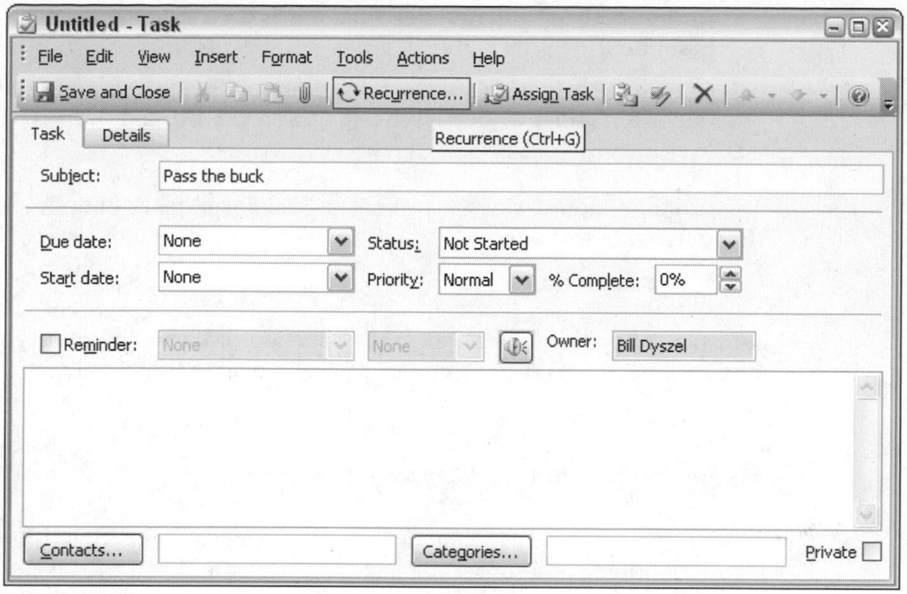

Figure 9-14:
Getting a
handle on
recurring
tasks.

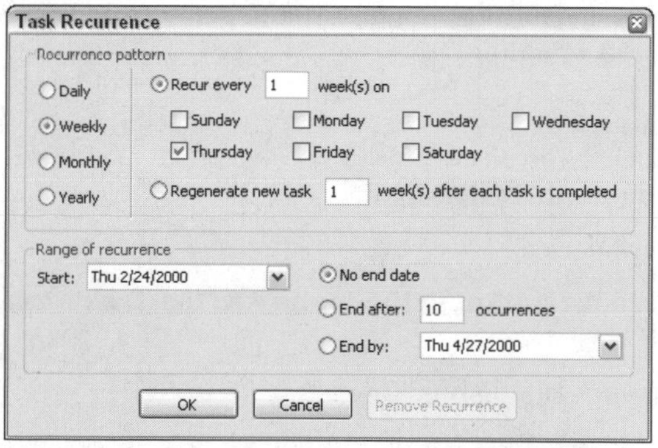

Figure 9-15:
How often
should this
task be
done?

Each choice you make — Daily, Weekly, or Monthly — changes the types of exact choices available for when the task recurs. For example, a daily recurring task can be set to recur every day or every five days or whatever. A monthly recurring task can be set to recur on a certain day of the month, such as the 15th of each month, or on the second Friday of every month.

4. **In the next box to the right, specify how often the appointment occurs, such as every third day or the first Monday of each month.**

If you choose to create a monthly task, for example, you can click the scroll-down buttons (triangles) to choose "First" then "Monday" to schedule a task on the first Monday of each month.

5. **In the Range of Recurrence box, enter the first occurrence in the Start box.**

6. **Choose when you want the appointments to stop (no end date, after a certain number of occurrences, or at a certain date).**

7. **Click OK.**

   A banner appears at the top of the Task form describing the recurrence pattern of the task.

8. **Click Save and Close.**

Your task appears in the list of tasks once, but it has a different type of icon than nonrecurring tasks so you can tell at a glance that it's a recurring task.

Creating a regenerating task

A *regenerating task* is like a recurring task except it recurs only when a certain amount of time passes after the last time you completed the task. Suppose that you mow the lawn every two weeks. If it rains for a week and one mowing happens a week late, you still want to wait two weeks for the next one. If you schedule your mowings in Outlook, you use the Regenerating Task feature to enter your lawn-mowing schedule.

To create a regenerating task:

1. **Open the task by double-clicking it.**

   The Task form appears.

2. **Click the Recurrence button in the toolbar in the Task form (or press Ctrl+G).**

   The Task Recurrence dialog box appears.

3. **Click Regenerate New Task (shown in Figure 9-16).**

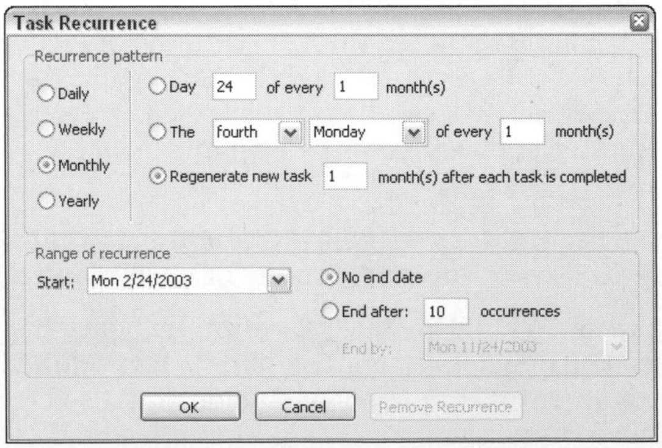

Figure 9-16:
You can regenerate a task in the Task Recurrence dialog box.

4. **Enter the number of weeks between regenerating each task.**

5. **Click OK.**

   A banner appears in the Task form describing the regeneration pattern you've set for the task.

6. **Click Save and Close.**

Your task appears in the list of tasks once, but it has a different type of icon than nonrecurring tasks have so you can tell at a glance that it's a regenerating task.

Skipping a recurring task once

When you need to skip a single occurrence of a recurring task, you don't have to change the recurrence pattern of the task forever; just skip the occurrence you want to skip and leave the rest alone.

To skip a recurring task, follow these steps:

1. **Click the Tasks button in the Navigation Pane (or press Ctrl+4).**

   Your list of tasks appears.

2. **Click the words "Simple List" in the Current View section of the Navigation Pane.**

   It doesn't matter which view you use, as long as you can see the name of the task you want to skip. I suggest the Simple List because it's . . . well, simple.

3. **Double-click the name of the task you want to change.**

   The Task form appears.

4. **Choose Actions➪Skip Occurrence.**

   The due date changes to the date of the next scheduled occurrence.

5. **Click Save and Close.**

   Your task remains in the list with the new scheduled occurrence date showing.

Marking Tasks Complete

Marking off those completed tasks is even more fun than entering them, and it's much easier. If you can see the task you want to mark complete in your Tasks list, just click the check box next to the name of the task. Nothing could be simpler.

To mark a task complete, follow these steps:

1. **Click the Tasks button in the Navigation Pane (or press Ctrl+4).**

   The Tasks module opens.

2. **Click the words "Simple List" in the Current View section of the Navigation Pane.**

   Actually, you can choose any view you want, as long as the task you're looking for shows up there. If the task that you want to mark complete isn't in the view you chose, try the Simple List, which contains every task you've entered.

3. **Click the box next to the name of the task that you want to mark complete.**

   The box in the second column from the left is the one you want to check (see Figure 9-17).

   When you check the box, the name of the task changes color and gets a line through it. You're finished.

Outlook has more than one place for marking tasks complete. You can look at the Task list I just described, as well as certain views of your Calendar, and also the list of tasks in Outlook Today.

Figure 9-17:
A check marks the task complete.

Marking several tasks complete

Perhaps you don't race to your computer every time you complete a task. Marking off your completed tasks in groups is faster than marking them one by one. Outlook enables you to do that by making a multiple selection.

To mark several tasks complete, follow these steps:

1. **Click the Tasks button in the Navigation Pane (or press Ctrl+4).**

   The Tasks module opens.

2. **Click the words "Simple List" in the Current View section of the Navigation Pane.**

   Again, I'm just suggesting Simple List view because it's most likely to show you all your tasks. You can pick any view that enables you to see the tasks that you want to mark.

3. **Click the first task that you want to mark.**

4. **Hold down the Ctrl key and click each of the other tasks that you want to mark.**

   All the tasks you clicked are highlighted, showing that you've selected them.

5. **Right-click one of the tasks you highlighted.**

   A menu appears (as in Figure 9-18).

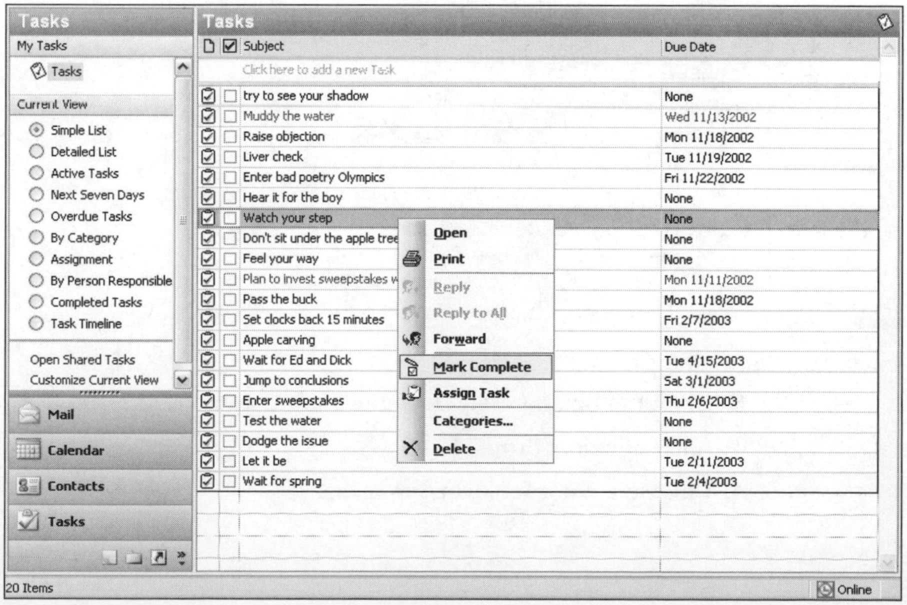

Figure 9-18:
A shortcut menu in the Tasks list.

6. Choose Mark Complete.

The tasks you selected are marked complete.

There are two good reasons for recording your tasks and marking them complete. One is to remember everything you have to do; the second is to tell other people everything you've done, like your boss at raise time, for instance. It pays to toot your own horn, and keeping a completed task list helps you remember what to toot your horn about.

Picking a color for completed or overdue tasks

When you complete a task or when it becomes overdue, Outlook changes the color of the text for the completed tasks to gray and the overdue tasks to red, which makes it easy for you to tell at a glance which tasks are done and which tasks remain to be done. If you don't like Outlook's color choices, you can pick different colors.

Here's how to change the color of completed and overdue tasks:

1. Choose Tools➪Options.

The Options dialog box appears.

2. Click the Task Options button.

The Task Options page appears (as shown in Figure 9-19).

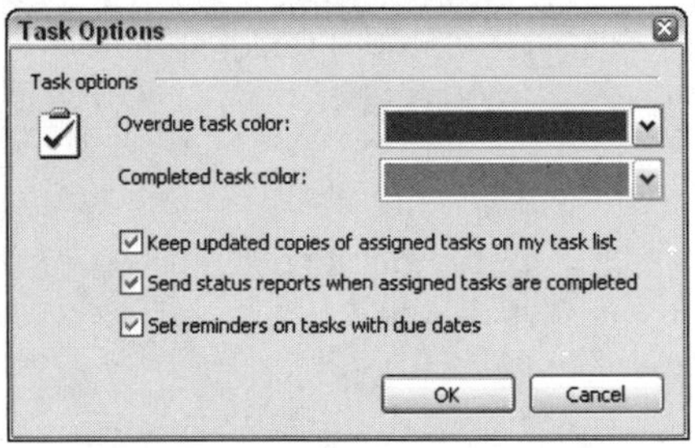

Figure 9-19:
The Task
Options
page.

Task Options

Task options

☑ Overdue task color:

Completed task color:

☑ Keep updated copies of assigned tasks on my task list
☑ Send status reports when assigned tasks are completed
☑ Set reminders on tasks with due dates

OK   Cancel

3. Click the box labeled Overdue Task Color.

A list of colors drops down.

4. Choose a color for overdue tasks.

5. **Click the box labeled Completed Task Color.**

   A list of colors drops down.

6. **Choose a color for completed tasks.**

7. **Click OK.**

Your completed and overdue tasks will appear on your list in the colors you chose.

Viewing Your Tasks

Outlook comes with several ways to view your Tasks list and enables you to invent and save as many custom views as you like. The views that come with Outlook take you a long way when you know how to use them.

To change your view of your tasks, click the name of one of the following views from the Current View list in the Navigation Pane:

- **Simple List** view presents just the facts — the names you gave each task and the due date you assigned (if you assigned one). The Simple List view makes it easy to add new tasks and mark old ones complete. However, you won't see any extra information. If you want details. . . .

- **Detailed List** view is a little more chock-full of the fiddly bits than the Simple List view. It's really the same information, plus the status of the tasks, the percentage of each task complete, and whatever categories you may have assigned to your tasks.

- **Active List** view shows you only the tasks you haven't finished yet. After you mark a task complete — zap! Completed tasks vanish from the Active List view, which helps keep you focused on the tasks remaining to be done.

- **Next Seven Days** view is even more focused than the Active List view. The Next Seven Days view shows only uncompleted tasks scheduled to be done within the next seven days. It's just right for those people who like to live in the moment, or at least within the week.

- **Overdue Tasks** view means you've been naughty. These are tasks that really *did* need to be "done yesterday" (when it *was* yesterday) but are still hanging around today.

- **By Category** view breaks up your tasks according to the category you've assigned each task. You can open and close categories to focus on the type of tasks you're looking for. For example, you may assign a category of Sales to the sales-related tasks in your list. When you want to focus on sales, use the By Category view and click the Sales category.

- ✔ **Assignment** view lists your tasks in order of the name of the person upon whom you dumped, er, I mean *to whom you delegated*, each task.

- ✔ **By Person Responsible** view contains the same information as the Assignment view, but the list is grouped to let you see the assignments of only one person at a time.

- ✔ **Completed Tasks** view shows (you guessed it) tasks you've marked complete. You don't need to deal with completed tasks anymore, but looking at the list gives you a warm, fuzzy feeling, doesn't it?

- ✔ **Task Timeline** view draws a picture of when each task is scheduled to start and end. Seeing a picture of your tasks gives you a better idea of how to fit work into your schedule sensibly.

Chapter 10

For the Record: Outlook Notes and Journal Entries

*T*he simple, dopey features of a program are often my favorites — the features I end up using all the time, such as Outlook Notes and the Outlook Journal. There's really nothing earth shattering about Notes, and certainly nothing difficult. This feature is just there when you need it — ready to record whatever strange, random thoughts are passing through your head while you're doing your work. (As you can tell from my writing, strange, random thoughts are a common occurrence for me. That's why I love using Notes.)

A note is the only type of item you can create in Outlook that doesn't use a normal dialog box with menus and toolbars. Notes are easier to use — but somewhat trickier to explain — than other Outlook items; I can only describe the objects you're supposed to click and drag. No name appears on the Note icon, and no name exists for the part of the note you drag when you want to resize the note (although you can see what a note looks like in Figure 10-1).

Figure 10-1:
Your note begins as a nearly blank box.

11/16/2002 10:09 AM

Writing a Note

How did we ever live without those little yellow stick-on notes? They're everywhere! The funny thing about stick-on notes is that they came from an inventor's failure. A scientist was trying to invent a new formula for glue, and he came up with a kind of glue that didn't stick very well. Like the computer scientists who came later, he said, "That's not a bug; that's a feature!" Then he figured out how to make a fortune selling little notes that didn't stick too well. It's only natural that an invention like this would be adapted for computers.

Tricks with notes

Each time you start a program, the Windows taskbar at the bottom of the screen adds an icon. That way, you know how many programs you're running. If you click an icon for a program in the taskbar, you switch to that program. If you start Word and Excel, for example, you see two icons in the taskbar. You can have two or more documents open in Word or Excel, but you see only one icon for each program.

When you choose File⇨New to create a new item in Outlook, you see a second icon open in the taskbar for the item you're creating. The icon remains until you close and save the item. It's like

having two or more programs open in Windows simultaneously. The advantage of this arrangement is that you can leave something like a note open for a long time and keep switching to it to add comments. The disadvantage is that if you don't look at the taskbar to see how many notes you have open, you may be creating a clutter of notes when you may prefer just one.

Another advantage is that you can have two notes open at the same time, or a note and an e-mail message, and drag text from one to the other.

Here's the basic scoop on how to take virtual notes while doing your work:

1. **Choose Go⇨Notes (or press Ctrl+5).**

   The Notes list appears.

   You don't actually have to go to the Notes module to create a new note; you can go right to Step 2. I suggest going to the Notes module first only so you can see your note appear in the list of notes when you finish. Otherwise your note seems to disappear into thin air (even though it doesn't). Outlook automatically files your note in the Notes module unless you make a special effort to send it somewhere else.

2. **Choose File⇨New⇨Note (or press Ctrl+ N).**

   The blank Note box appears.

3. **Type what you want to say in your note (as in Figure 10-2) and click the Note icon in the upper-left corner of the note.**

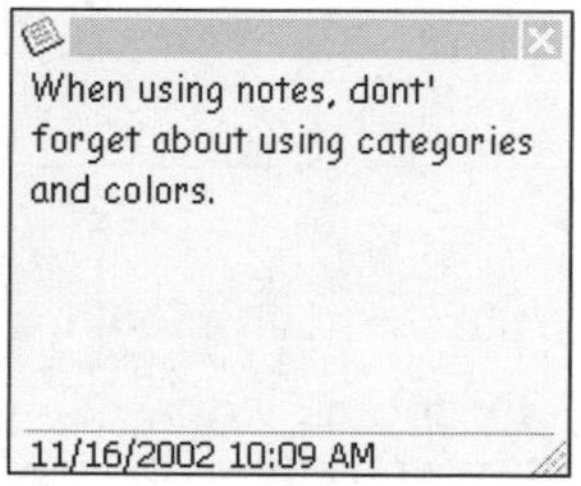

Figure 10-2:
You can write a note to remind yourself of something.

When using notes, dont' forget about using categories and colors.

11/16/2002 10:09 AM

4. **Click Close (or press Alt+F4).**

   An even quicker way to create a note is to press Ctrl+Shift+N in any Outlook module. You don't see your note listed with all the other notes until you switch to the Notes module, but you can get that thought entered.

Finding a Note

Unlike paper stick-on notes, Outlook Notes stay where you put them so you can always find them — or at least your computer can find them. As a matter of fact, you can find any item you create in Outlook just by using the Find tool. (I wish I had a Find tool to help me round up all my lost galoshes and umbrellas.)

Here's how to find a misplaced note:

1. Choose Go⇨Notes (or press Ctrl+5).

Your list of notes appears.

2. Choose Tools⇨Find⇨Find (or click the Find button in the toolbar).

The Look For box appears (see Figure 10-3). The Look For box contains a blinking bar, the insertion point, which shows you where the thing you type next will go.

The Look For box

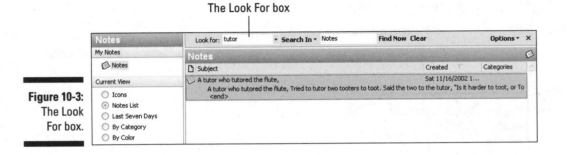

Figure 10-3:
The Look
For box.

3. In the Look For box, type the word or phrase you're looking for.

Don't worry about capitalization. Outlook doesn't worry about capitalization; it just looks for the string of letters you entered.

4. Press Enter.

A list of notes that contain the text you typed appears in the Outlook screen.

5. If the note you're looking for turns up, double-click the Note icon to read what the note says.

Reading a Note

When you write a note, no doubt you plan to read it sometime. Reading notes is even easier than writing them. To read a note, follow these steps:

1. Choose Go⇨Notes (or press Ctrl+5).

Your list of notes appears.

2. Double-click the title of the note you want to open.

The note appears on-screen (as shown in Figure 10-4). You can close the note when you're done by pressing Esc.

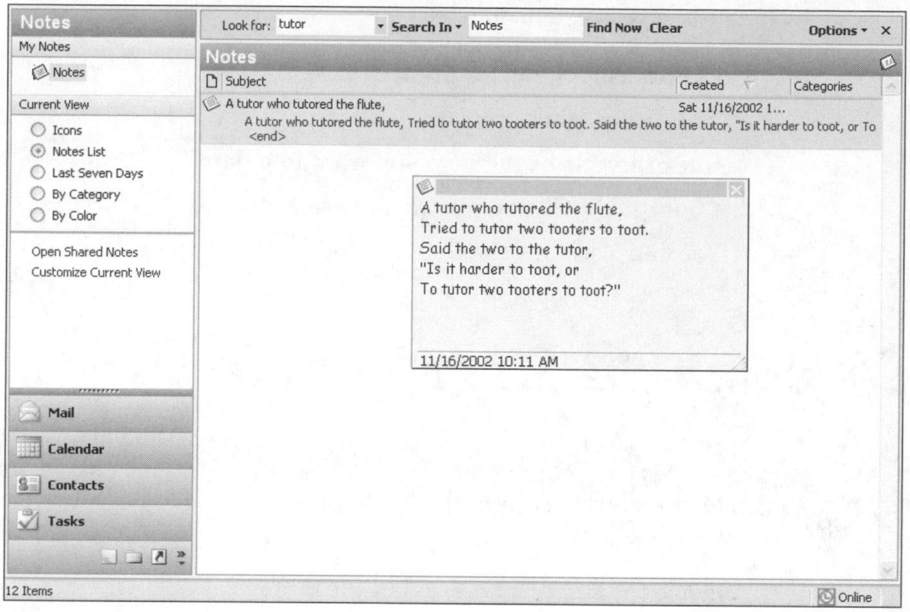

Figure 10-4:
Aha! The
missing note
is found.

Funny how notes look the same when you're reading them as they do when you're writing them.

Deleting a Note

What if you change your mind about what you wrote in a note? Fortunately, notes don't have to stick around forever. You can write a note this morning and throw it out this afternoon. What could be easier?

Taking your pick: Multiple selections

When you're sorting your notes or assigning them to categories, one way to work a little faster is to select several notes simultaneously. If you want to select a group of notes that you can see one right after another in a list, click the first one and then hold down the Shift key while clicking the last one. That action selects not only the notes you clicked, but also all the notes in-between.

If you're selecting several items that aren't arranged next to one another, hold down the Ctrl key while clicking each item. The notes you click are highlighted and the others stay plain. Then you can open, move, delete, or categorize the entire group of notes you selected in a single stroke. To view several notes, right-click any notes you've selected and choose Open.

Here's how to delete a note:

1. **Choose Go⇨Notes (or press Ctrl+5).**

   Your list of notes appears.

2. **Click the title of the note you want to delete.**

3. **Choose Edit⇨Delete (or simply press Delete).**

   You can also click the Delete button in the Outlook toolbar.

Changing the Size of a Note

You may be an old hand at moving and resizing boxes in Windows. Notes follow all the rules that other Windows boxes follow, so you'll be okay. If you're new to Windows and dialog boxes, don't worry — notes are as easy to resize as they are to write and read.

To change the size of a note, follow these steps:

1. **Choose Go⇨Notes (or press Ctrl+5).**

   Your list of notes appears.

2. **Double-click the title of the note you want to open.**

   The note pops up.

3. **Move your mouse pointer to the bottom-right corner of the note until the mouse pointer changes into a two-headed arrow pointed on a diagonal.**

   Use this arrow to drag the edges of the note to resize it. Don't be alarmed. Resizing boxes is much easier to do than to read about. After you resize one box, you'll have no trouble resizing another.

4. **Drag with your mouse until the note is the size you want it to be.**

   As you drag the mouse pointer around, the size of your note changes (as shown in Figure 10-5). Don't worry if the size doesn't come out right the first time; you can change the note size again by dragging with the mouse again.

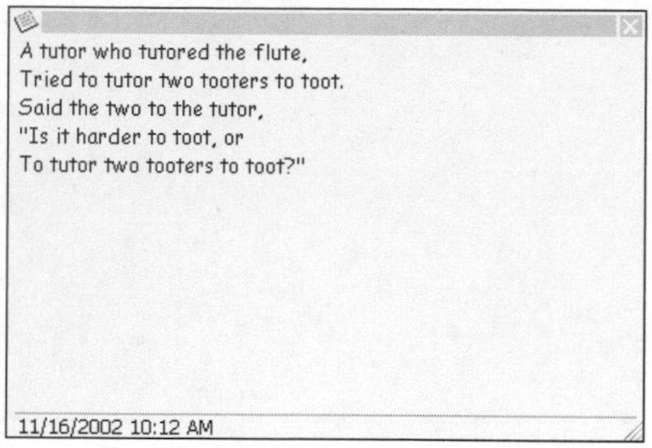

A tutor who tutored the flute,
Tried to tutor two tooters to toot.
Said the two to the tutor,
"Is it harder to toot, or
To tutor two tooters to toot?"

11/16/2002 10:12 AM

Figure 10-5:
Make your
note larger
if you need
more room
to expound.

Changing Your Colors

Color may seem to be a trifling issue, but it can help you keep track of your notes. You can assign a color to a level of importance, for example, or to a specific task, so you can quickly see the note you want among the many notes in your list. Later in the chapter, I explain how you can sort your list of notes according to color. Sorting is useful, so spending your entire day changing the colors of your notes isn't just aesthetic; it's also productive.

Here's how to change your note's color:

1. **Open the note and click the Note icon in the top-left corner of the note.**

   I wish there were a better way to describe this icon than "the little thingy up on the left" (how's that for a high-tech term?) — but that's what it is. The icon is easy to see; it's the only little thingy in the top-left corner of your note. Anyway, when you click it, the Note menu appears.

2. **Choose Color.**

   A menu of colors appears (see Figure 10-6). Currently, the only choices are Blue, Green, Pink, Yellow, and White. I hope you like pastels, because those are your only options at the moment. Perhaps Burgundy and Off-Mauve notes will be in next season for more color-conscious computer users.

3. **Pick a color.**

You can also change the colors of your notes when viewing a list of notes; just right-click the icon for a note and choose a color from the menu that appears.

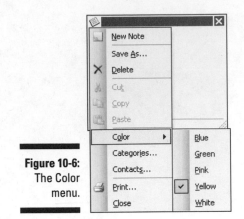

Figure 10-6:
The Color
menu.

Viewing Your Notes

Notes are handy enough to stash tidbits of information any way you want, but what makes Notes really useful is what happens when you need to get the stuff back. You can open your notes one by one and see what's in them, but Outlook's Notes module offers even handier capabilities for arranging, sorting, and viewing your notes in a way that makes sense for you.

Icons view

Some folks like Icons view — just a bunch of notes scattered all over, as they are on my desk. Because I can already see a mess of notes any time I look at my desk, I prefer organized lists for viewing my notes on my computer, but you may like the more free-form Icons view. To use Icons view, click the word *Icons* in the Current View section of the Navigation Pane (shown in Figure 10-7). When you do, the screen fills with a bunch of icons and incredibly long titles for each icon.

Outlook uses the entire text of your message as the title of the icon, so the screen gets cluttered fast. If you prefer creative clutter, this view is for you. If not, keep reading.

Notes List view

The Notes list is as basic as basic gets. Just the facts, ma'am. The Notes list shows the subject and creation date of each note, as well as the first few lines of text. To see the Notes List view, click the words Notes List in the Current View section of the Navigation Pane to make a listing of your notes appear (see Figure 10-8).

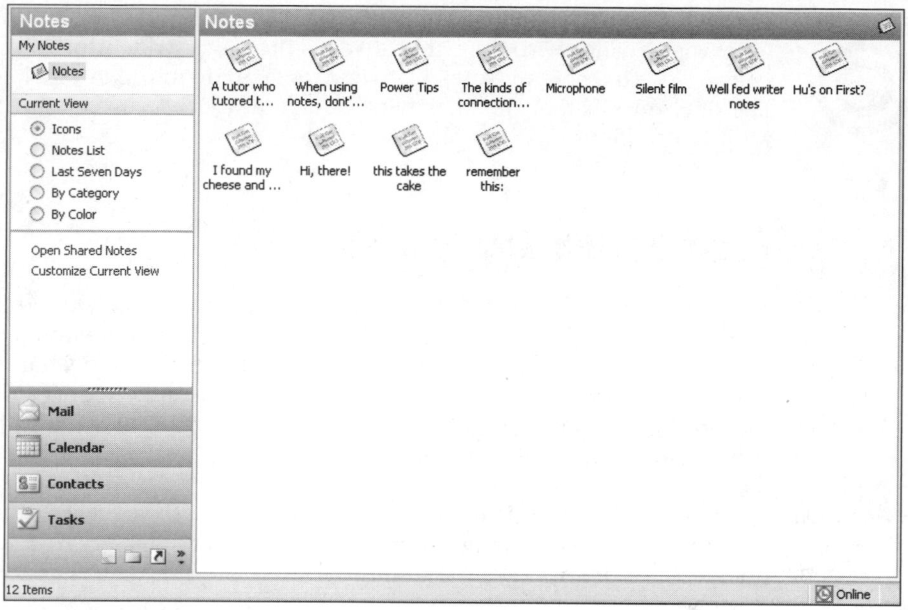

Figure 10-7:
The Icons view — a clutter of notes.

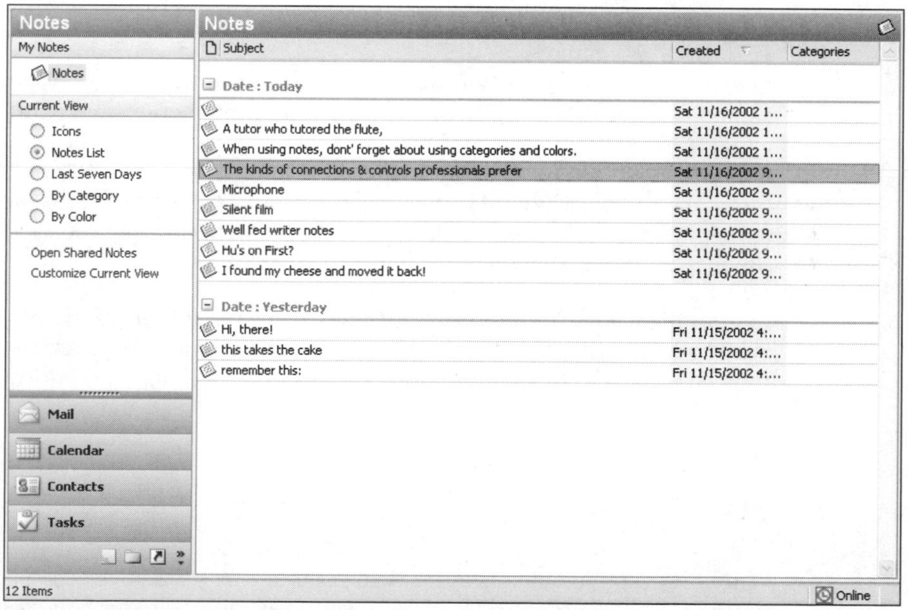

Figure 10-8:
Your Notes List view.

I usually recommend Notes List view for opening, forwarding, reading, and otherwise dealing with notes because it's the most straightforward. Anything you can do to a note in Notes List view, you can do in the other Notes views. The difference is that the other views don't always let you see the note you want to do things to.

Last Seven Days view

The notes you dealt with in the last few days are most likely to be the notes you'll need today. So, Outlook includes a special view of the notes you modified in the last seven days. You're more likely to quickly find what you're looking for in the seven-day view. To see your notes for the last seven days, click the words Last Seven Days in the Current View section of the Navigation Pane. Figure 10-9 shows what you get.

If you haven't modified any notes in the past seven days, Last Seven Days view will be empty. If having an empty view bothers you, create a note. That'll tide you over for a week.

By Category view

Every item you create in Outlook can be assigned to a category. You use the same category list for all items, and you can create your own categories. With categories, you have another useful way to organize your views of Outlook items. (I explain how to assign categories to a note in the section "Assigning a Category to Your Notes" later in this chapter.) To see your notes arranged by category, click the words By Category in the Current View section of the Navigation Pane (as shown in Figure 10-10).

By Category view is a *grouped view,* meaning that the notes are collected in bunches, according to the categories you've assigned. You can just look at the category of notes you're interested in — to organize the information you've collected.

By Color

Color coordination means more than making sure your socks match. The fact that you can group notes by color means you can create a system of organizing your notes that tells you something important about your notes at a glance. If sales representatives call asking you to buy merchandise, you may want to create and color code a note for each request — for example, green for requests you're approving, yellow for requests you're considering, and pink for requests you're turning down. To view your notes by color, click the words By Color in the Current View section of the Navigation Pane (see Figure 10-11).

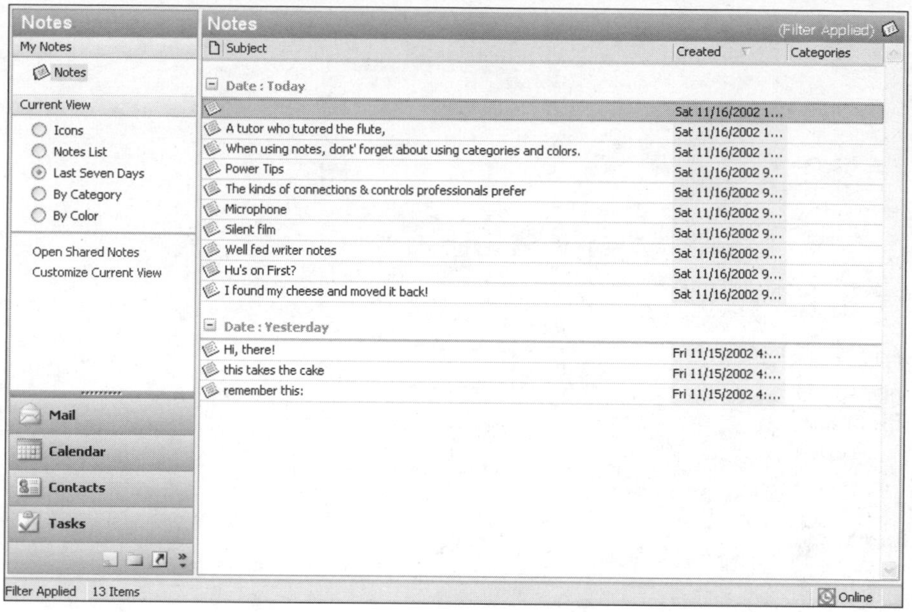

Figure 10-9:
Your notes
for the past
week, in all
their glory.

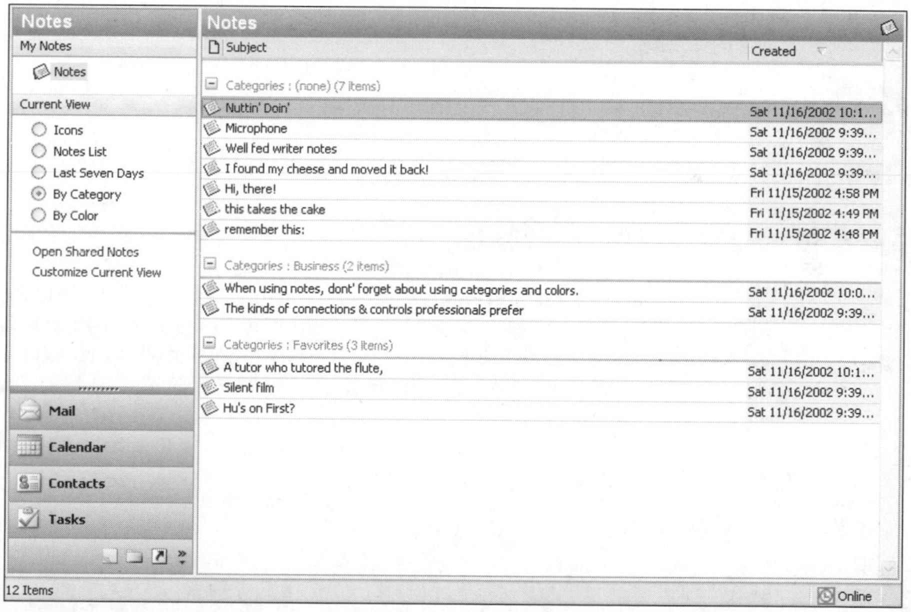

Figure 10-10:
Your notes
in By
Category
view.

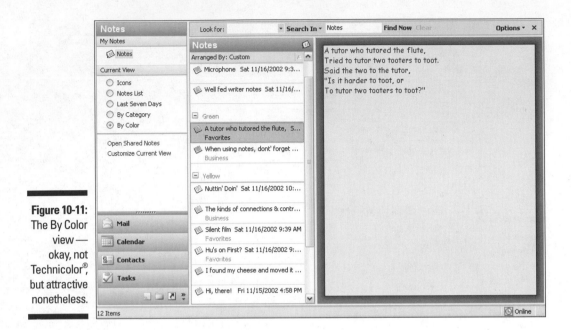

Figure 10-11:
The By Color
view —
okay, not
Technicolor®,
but attractive
nonetheless.

You can choose among only five colors for an Outlook note, so you can have only that many groups by color.

You can also right-click a note in By Color view and change its color.

The Reading Pane

Once you've accumulated a collection of squibs and jots in your Notes collection, you'll want a quick way to browse your collection easily. If you choose View⇨Reading Pane⇨Right, you'll see a list of your notes on the left and the contents of each note you select on the right (see Figure 10-11). That way you can scan your collection of notes quickly by clicking a note with your mouse or by pressing the up and down arrow keys on your keyboard to move from note to note.

Assigning a Category to Your Notes

If you really want to get yourself organized, you can assign categories to all the items you create in Outlook. That way, all your items can be sorted, grouped, searched, and even deleted according to the categories you assigned them to.

To categorize your notes, follow these steps:

1. **With a Note open, click the Note icon in the upper-left corner of the Note.**

   The Note menu drops down (that's it in Figure 10-12).

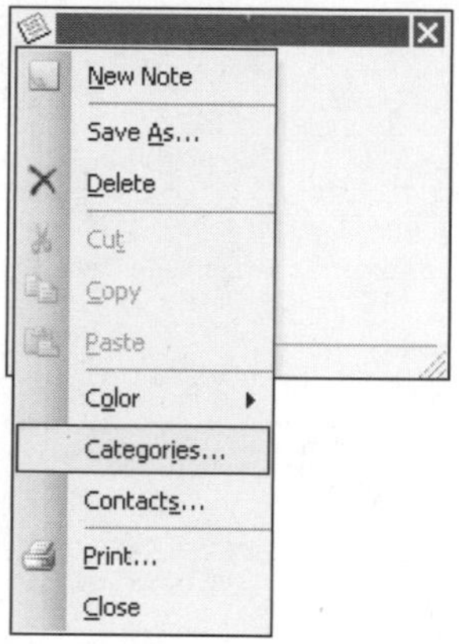

Figure 10-12:
The Note
menu.

2. **Choose Categories.**

   The Categories dialog box appears, as shown in Figure 10-13.

Figure 10-13:
The
Categories
dialog box.

3. **Choose one of the existing categories, if one suits you, and then click OK.**

    You can also enter your own category in the Item(s) Belong to These Categories dialog box.

4. **If none of the existing categories suits you, click Master Category List.**

    From the Master Category List, you can add or delete categories (as shown in Figure 10-14).

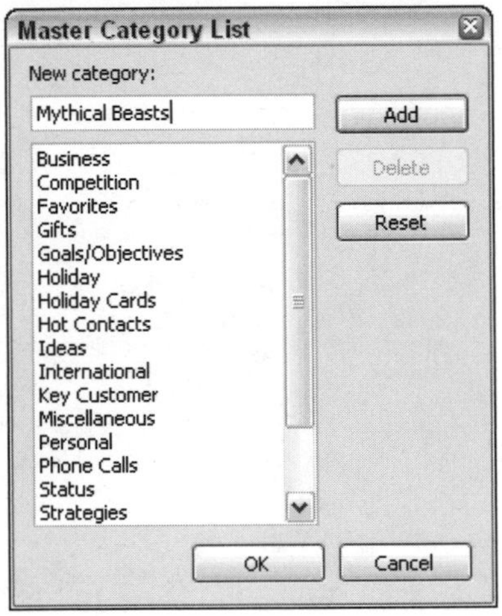

Figure 10-14:
The Master
Category
List.

Master Category List

New category:

Mythical Beasts| [Add]

Business
Competition
Favorites
Gifts
Goals/Objectives
Holiday
Holiday Cards
Hot Contacts
Ideas
International
Key Customer
Miscellaneous
Personal
Phone Calls
Status
Strategies

[Delete]

[Reset]

[OK]   [Cancel]

5. **Type a category of your choice in the New Category box.**

    Categories are supposed to *simplify* access to data. Be sure not to add too many new categories, or else finding things could get hard.

6. **Click Add.**

    Your new category becomes part of the Categories list.

7. **Click OK.**

Whenever you see the Categories list, your new category will be among the categories you can choose.

Printing Your Notes

You can organize and view your notes in so many clever ways that you'll also want to print what you can see, or at least the list of what you can see.

Printing a list of your notes

To print a list of your notes, follow these steps:

1. **Choose Go➪Notes (or press Ctrl+5).**

   The Notes list appears.

2. **Choose File➪Print (or press Ctrl+P).**

   The Print dialog box appears (as shown in Figure 10-15).

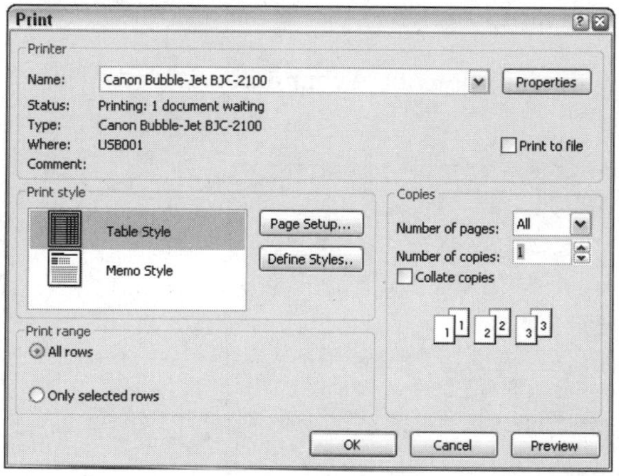

Figure 10-15: The Print dialog box.

3. **In the Print Style box, choose Table Style.**

   If you choose Memo Style, you print the contents of a note rather than a list of notes.

4. **Click OK.**

If you want to print only a portion of your list of notes, click the first note you want listed and then hold down the Shift key while clicking the last note you want in your printout. You can also hold the Ctrl key while clicking the notes you want one-by-one. When the Print dialog box appears, choose Only Selected Rows in the Print Range section.

Printing the contents of a note

Computer screens are pretty, but there's still nothing like ink on paper. Of course, you can print a note. Remember, though, that the pretty colors you've given your notes don't show when you print them, even if you have a color printer. Colors just provide a way of organizing your notes.

To print the note, follow these steps:

1. **Choose Go⇨Notes (or press Ctrl+5).**

   The Notes list appears.

2. **Click the title of the note you want to print.**

3. **Choose File⇨Print (or press Ctrl+P).**

   The Print dialog box appears.

4. **In the Print Style box, choose Memo Style (see Figure 10-16).**

   Choosing Memo Style prints the full contents of the note.

5. **Click OK.**

   Outlook prints the full contents of your note.

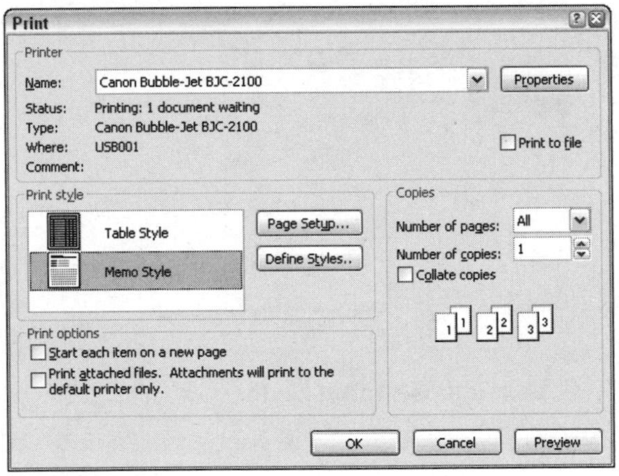

Figure 10-16:
The Print
dialog box
with
Memo style
selected.

If you want to print some, but not all, of your notes, click the first note you want listed and then hold down the Shift key while clicking the last note you want to appear in your printout.

Changing Your Default Options for New Notes

Plain old notes are fine; you really don't need to change anything. But if you want to make some changes, the Options dialog box in the Tools menu gives you lots of . . . well, options. All adjustments you make in the Options dialog box change the size, color, and other qualities of your note when you first create the note. You can also change these qualities after you create the note.

Changing size and color

To change the color and size of your notes:

1. **Choose Tools➪Options.**

   The Options dialog box appears.

2. **Click the Note Options button.**

   The Notes Options dialog box is where you change the options for the Notes module of Outlook.

3. **Click the Color box.**

   A list of colors (Blue, Green, Pink, Yellow, White) drops down (as shown in Figure 10-17). Choosing one of these options changes the color that all your notes will be when you create them.

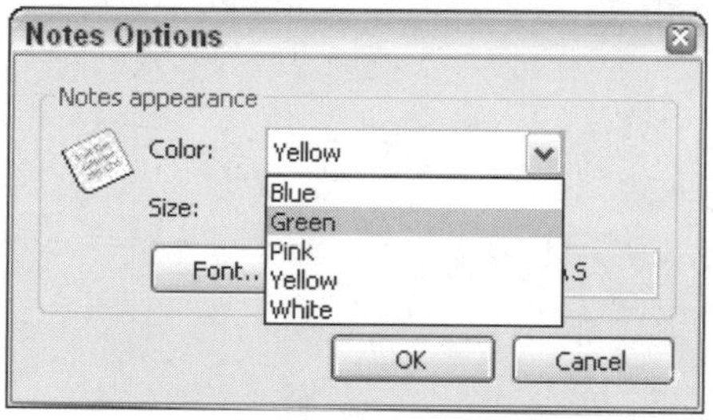

Figure 10-17: Changing colors in Notes Options.

4. **Choose a color.**

5. **Click the Size box.**

   The list reads Small, Medium, or Large. Choosing one of these options sets the size of your notes when you create them.

6. **Click OK.**

   Your notes appear in the size and color to which you changed them.

Turning the date and time display on or off

At the bottom of each note, Outlook displays the date and time when you most recently changed the contents of the note. You may notice that you change a lot of notes on Mondays around 9:45 a.m. You may not want to notice that fact, so you can turn this handy little feature off.

To turn off the date and time display, follow these steps:

1. **Choose Tools➪Options.**

   The Options dialog box appears.

2. **Click the Other tab.**

   I don't know why Microsoft called this the Other tab. (Perhaps the programmers all kept arguing, "Don't put that option on MY tab! Put it on some OTHER tab!") Anyway, that's where you have to look. When you click the Other tab, the Other Options page appears.

3. **Click the Advanced Options button.**

   The Advanced Options dialog box appears (see Figure 10-18).

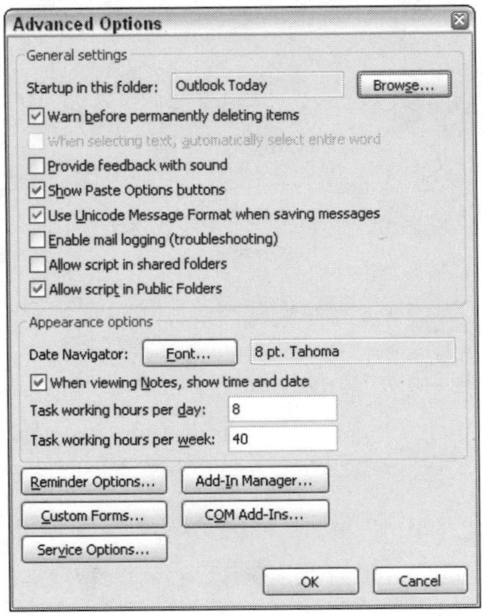

Figure 10-18:
Time for some advanced options.

4. **Click the words** `When viewing Notes, show time and date.`

   A check mark appears in the check box if you click once, and then it disappears if you click a second time. If you want to turn off the time and date display, make sure that the box doesn't contain a check mark.

5. **Click OK.**

   The time and date will no longer show up on command, unless you follow the same steps you used in turning them off to turn them on again.

Forwarding a Note

Forwarding a note really means sending an e-mail message with a note included as an attachment. It's helpful if the person to whom you're forwarding the note uses Outlook, too.

To forward a note:

1. **Choose Go⊐Notes (or press Ctrl+5).**

   The Notes list appears.

2. **Click the title of the note you want to forward.**

3. **Choose Actions⊐Forward (or press Ctrl+F).**

   The New Message form appears (shown in Figure 10-19).

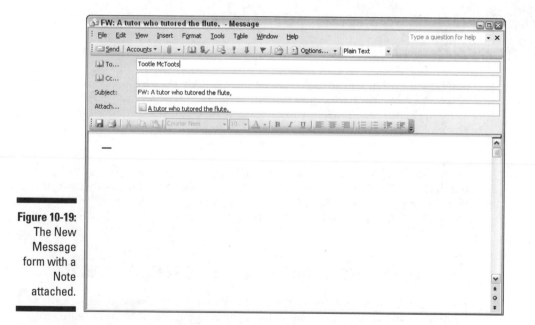

Figure 10-19:
The New
Message
form with a
Note
attached.

4. **Click the To text box and type the e-mail address of the person to whom you're sending your note.**

   You can also click the To button to open the e-mail Address Book. Then all you need do is look up the name of the person to whom you want to forward your note, click To, and then click OK.

5. **Type the subject of the note in the Subject box.**

   The subject of your note will already be in the Subject box of the New Message form. You can leave it alone or type something else.

6. **If you want, type the text of a message in the text box.**

   You don't really have to include a message. Your note may say all you want to say, but you can also add regular e-mail message text.

7. **Click the Send button.**

   Your message is off to its intended recipient(s).

If your note includes the address of a page on the World Wide Web (such as `www.dummies.com`), you can simply click the address to launch your Web browser — just as you can in all the other Outlook modules.

Keeping a Journal for Tidy Recordkeeping

Sometimes, when you want to find a document or a record of a conversation, you don't remember what you called the document or where you stored it, but you do remember *when* you created or received the item. In this case, you can go to the Journal and check the date when you remember dealing with the item and find what you need to know.

To get good use from the Journal, though, you have to use it (details, details . . .). You can set Outlook to make journal entries for nearly everything you do, or you can shut the Journal off entirely and make no entries to it. If you put nothing in the Journal, you get nothing out.

Don't just do something — stand there!

What's the easiest way to make entries in the Journal? Do nothing. After it's turned on, the Journal automatically records any document you create, edit, or print in any Microsoft Office application. The Journal also automatically tracks e-mail messages, meeting requests and responses, and task requests and responses. A few programs other than the Microsoft Office applications also have the capability to make entries in the Journal, but that feature is most often used with Office programs.

There's a catch: You have to tell Outlook that you *want* automatic Journal recording turned on. (All right, so you *do* have to do something besides just standing there.) Fortunately, if you haven't activated the Journal's automatic recording feature, Outlook asks you whether you want to turn the feature on every time you click the Journal icon.

To turn on the Journal's automatic recording feature, follow these steps:

1. Choose Tools➪Options.

The Options dialog box appears.

2. Click the Journal Options button.

The Journal Options dialog box appears (as shown in Figure 10-20), offering check boxes for all the types of activities you can record automatically — and the names of all the people for whom you can automatically record transactions such as e-mail.

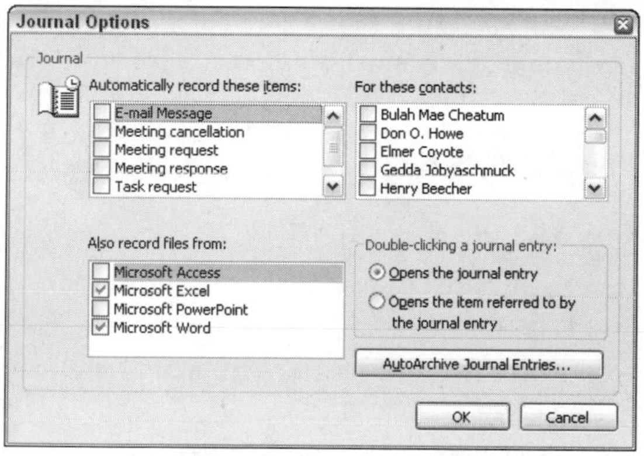

Journal Options

Journal

Automatically record these items:
- [ ] E-mail Message
- [ ] Meeting cancellation
- [ ] Meeting request
- [ ] Meeting response
- [ ] Task request

For these contacts:
- [ ] Bulah Mae Cheatum
- [ ] Don O. Howe
- [ ] Elmer Coyote
- [ ] Gedda Jobyaschmuck
- [ ] Henry Beecher

Also record files from:
- [ ] Microsoft Access
- [x] Microsoft Excel
- [ ] Microsoft PowerPoint
- [x] Microsoft Word

Double-clicking a journal entry:
- (•) Opens the journal entry
- ( ) Opens the item referred to by the journal entry

[AutoArchive Journal Entries...]

[OK] [Cancel]

Figure 10-20: The Journal Options dialog box.

3. Click to place a check in the check box for those items and files you want to automatically record and for the contacts about whom you want the information recorded.

The list of people in the For These Contacts box is the same as the list of people in your Contact list. You can manually create Journal entries for people who are not in your Contact list; see the following section ("Recording an Outlook item in the Journal manually").

When you add names to your Contact list in the Contacts module, those names aren't set for automatic recording in the Journal. If you want the Journal to keep track of them, then you have two ways to tell it so:

- Check the name(s) in the Journal Options dialog box.
- Open the Contact record, click the Journal tab, and check Automatically Record Journal Entries for These Contacts.

  4. Click OK.

  The Journal promptly begins automatically recording the items and files you selected for the contacts you named.

Recording an Outlook item in the Journal manually

If you don't want to clutter your Journal by recording everything automatically, you can enter selected items manually — just drag them to the Journal icon. For example, you may not want to record every transaction with a prospective client until you're certain you're doing business with that client. You can drag relevant e-mail messages to the Journal and retain a record of serious inquiries. When you actually start doing business with a new client, you can set up automatic recording.

To manually record items in the Journal:

  1. Choose Go➪Folder List (or press Ctrl+6).

  The Folder list, which includes a small icon for the Journal, appears in the top half of the Navigation Pane.

  2. Drag the item you want to record (such as an e-mail message) to the Journal icon in the Folder List.

  The Journal Entry form appears (see Figure 10-21). At the bottom of the form is an icon representing the item you're recording, along with the item's name.

  3. Fill in the information you want to record.

  You don't have to record anything. The text box at the bottom of the screen gives you space for making a note to yourself, if you want to use it.

  4. Click Save and Close.

  The item you recorded is entered in the Journal. You can see your new entry when you view your Journal, as I describe in the section "Viewing the Journal," later in this chapter.

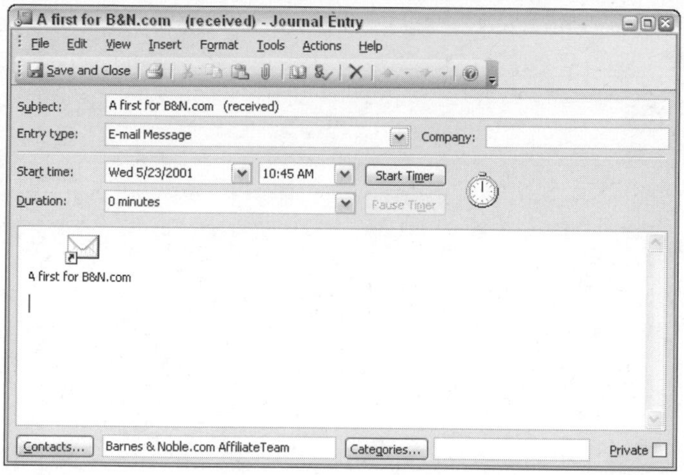

Figure 10-21:
A Journal entry with a shortcut to an e-mail message attached in the text box.

Viewing Journal Entries for a Contact

My friend Vinnie in Brooklyn says, "You gotta know who you dealt wit' and when you dealt wit 'em." You can use the Contact list — together with the Journal — to keep track of whom you dealt with and when. Just look in the person's Contact record to see when you made Journal entries:

1. **Click the Contacts icon in the Navigation Pane.**

   The Contact list appears.

2. **Double-click the name of the contact you want to view.**

   The Contact record opens.

3. **Click the Activities tab in the Contact form.**

   A list of every Journal entry you've made for that person appears (as in Figure 10-22), including the automatic entries Outlook made if you chose that option.

Finding a Journal Entry

When you don't remember exactly when you did something or dealt with somebody, you can look it up by searching for words in the Journal item.

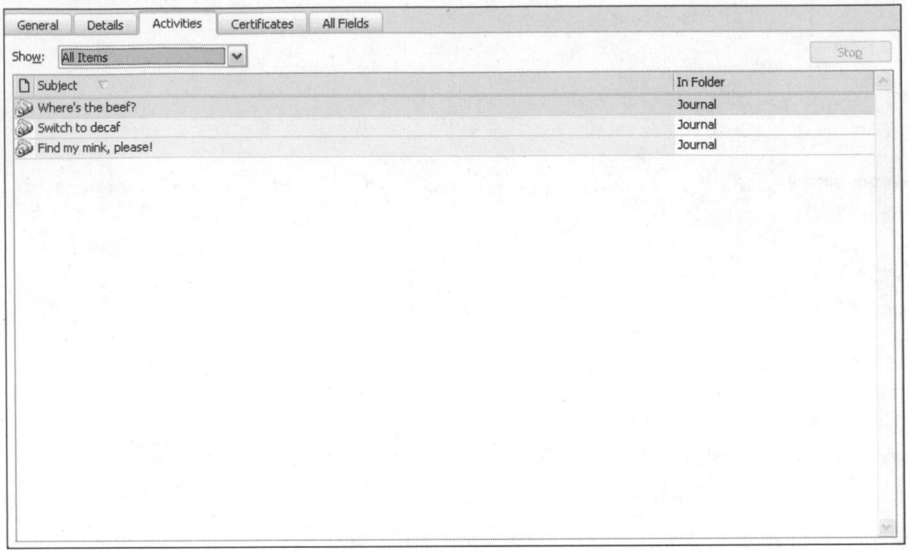

Figure 10-22:
Journal
entries for a
contact.

To find a Journal entry when you don't know the *when*, follow these steps:

1. **Click the words My Shortcuts in the Navigation Pane and click the Journal icon.**

   The list of Journal items appears.

2. **Choose Tools➪Find➪Find.**

   The Look For box appears (as shown in Figure 10-23).

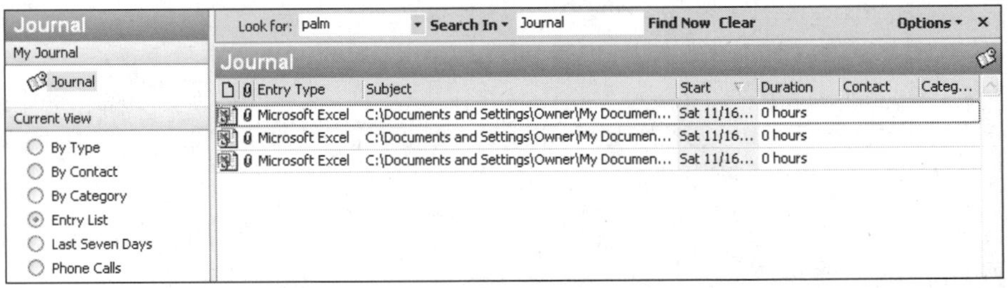

Figure 10-23:
The Look
For box.

3. **Type a word or phrase that you can find in your Journal.**

   If you're looking for information about an upcoming meeting on the current Toad Inventory, type **toad**.

4. **Press Enter.**

   A list of matching items appears in your Journal list.

5. Double-click the icon to the left of your item in the Journal list.

The Journal item you clicked appears. An icon in the text box at the bottom is a shortcut to any other Outlook item or document that the Journal entry represents. If you want to see the Calendar item that has details about the Toad Inventory meeting, double-click the icon at the bottom of the Journal entry. The Calendar item pops up.

Printing Your Journal

I can't explain why, but I just don't get a complete picture from information on a screen. I still like to print out my work on paper to really see what I've done. Printing your Journal (or segments of it) enables you to see a printed list of recent or upcoming activities. Stick it on the wall where you can look at it often.

To print your Journal, follow these steps:

1. Click the words My Shortcuts in the Navigation Pane and click the Journal icon.

The list of Journal items appears.

2. Select the entries you want to print.

If you select nothing, you print the entire list. Also, if you use one of the views I describe later in this chapter (or even create your own view by grouping, sorting, or filtering), what you see is what you print.

3. Choose File⇨Print (or press Ctrl+P).

The Print dialog box appears (as in Figure 10-24).

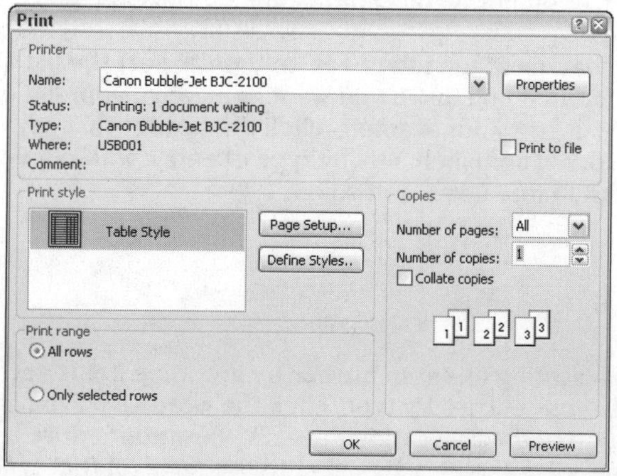

Figure 10-24:
The Print dialog box.

Print				? X
Printer				
Name:	Canon Bubble-Jet BJC-2100		⌄	Properties
Status:	Printing: 1 document waiting			
Type:	Canon Bubble-Jet BJC-2100			
Where:	USB001		☐ Print to file	
Comment:				
Print style		**Copies**		
▦ Table Style	Page Setup... / Define Styles..	Number of pages:	All ⌄	
		Number of copies:	1 ⌃⌄	
		☐ Collate copies		
Print range		1️⃣ 2️⃣ 3️⃣		
⦿ All rows				
○ Only selected rows				
	OK	Cancel	Preview	

4. **Choose Table or Memo style.**

    Table style prints only a list of your Journal entries, not the contents of each entry. Memo style prints the contents of your Journal entries, with each item appearing as a separate memo.

5. **Choose All Rows or Only Selected Rows.**

    If you want to print only certain rows, you have to select the rows you want to print before you choose File⇨Print. Then click the Only Selected Rows button to limit what you print to those rows.

6. **Click OK.**

    The list of Journal entries you selected prints.

The printed list won't go up on the wall for you, however, unless you put it there.

Viewing the Journal

As with other Outlook modules, the Journal comes with multiple views that show your entries in different ways, depending on what you want to see — whether that's a record of phone calls or a list organized by the names of the people you've dealt with. The Current View menu enables you to change quickly from one view to the next.

The Entry List

The Entry List is the whole tomato — all your Journal entries, regardless of whom, what, or when. To call up the Entry List, click the words Entry List in the Current View section of the Navigation Pane (shown in Figure 10-25).

You can click the heading at the top of any column to sort the list according to the information in that column. If you want to arrange your list of Journal entries by the type of entry, for example, click the header that says Entry Type. Your list is sorted alphabetically by type of entry, with conversations before e-mail, e-mail before faxes, and so on.

By Type

By Type view takes sorting one step further by grouping items according to their type. To view your entries by type, click the words By Type in the Current View section of the Navigation Pane. To view your entire list of items of a particular type, click the plus sign next to the name of that type. Click the icon next to the name of the Entry Type again to close the list of that type. Then you can click to open another list of entries by type.

By Contact

By Contact view shows your Journal items grouped by the name of the person associated with each item. To see your entries in By Contact view, click the words By Contact in the Current View section of the Navigation Pane (shown in Figure 10-26).

Click the plus sign next to the name of the person whose entries you want to see. You can see entries for more than one person at a time.

By Category

If you've been assigning categories to your Journal items, By Category view collects all your entries into bunches of items of the same category. To see your entries by category, click the words By Category in the Current View section of the Navigation Pane.

If you've assigned more than one category to an item, the item shows up under both categories you've assigned.

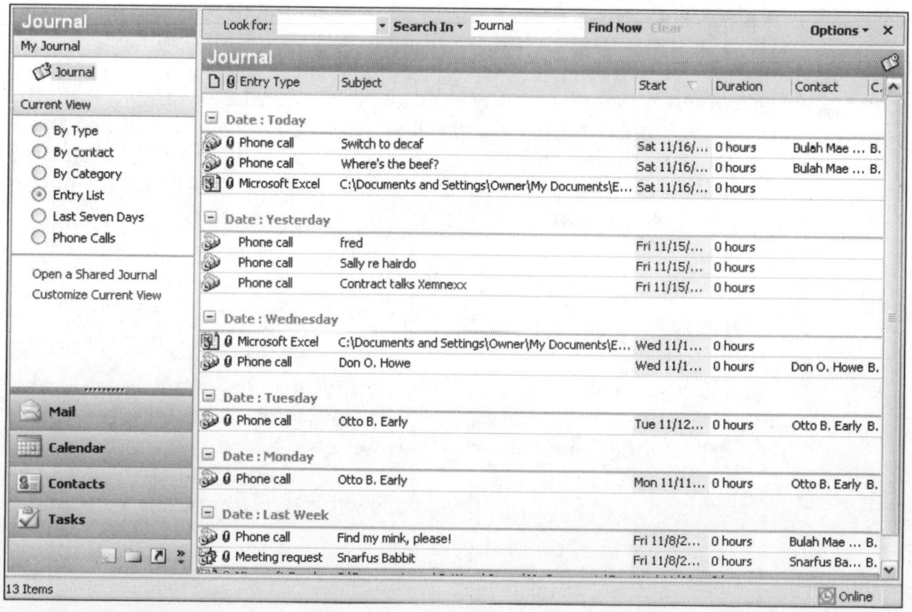

Figure 10-25:
Viewing the
Entry List —
everything
you've ever
entered.

		Entry Type	Subject	Start	Duration	Contact	C.
		Date : Today					
		Phone call	Switch to decaf	Sat 11/16/...	0 hours	Dulah Mae ... B.	
		Phone call	Where's the beef?	Sat 11/16/...	0 hours	Dulah Mae ... B.	
		Microsoft Excel	C:\Documents and Settings\Owner\My Documents\E...	Sat 11/16/...	0 hours		
		Date : Yesterday					
		Phone call	fred	Fri 11/15/...	0 hours		
		Phone call	Sally re hairdo	Fri 11/15/...	0 hours		
		Phone call	Contract talks Xemnexx	Fri 11/15/...	0 hours		
		Date : Wednesday					
		Microsoft Excel	C:\Documents and Settings\Owner\My Documents\E...	Wed 11/1...	0 hours		
		Phone call	Don O. Howe	Wed 11/1...	0 hours	Don O. Howe B.	
		Date : Tuesday					
		Phone call	Otto B. Early	Tue 11/12...	0 hours	Otto B. Early B.	
		Date : Monday					
		Phone call	Otto B. Early	Mon 11/11...	0 hours	Otto B. Early B.	
		Date : Last Week					
		Phone call	Find my mink, please!	Fri 11/8/2...	0 hours	Bulah Mae ... B.	
		Meeting request	Snarfus Babbit	Fri 11/8/2...	0 hours	Snarfus Ba... B.	

Journal — My Journal — Journal

Current View
- By Type
- By Contact
- By Category
- Entry List
- Last Seven Days
- Phone Calls

Open a Shared Journal
Customize Current View

Mail
Calendar
Contacts
Tasks

Look for: — Search In — Journal — Find Now — Clear — Options ▾ ✕

13 Items — Online

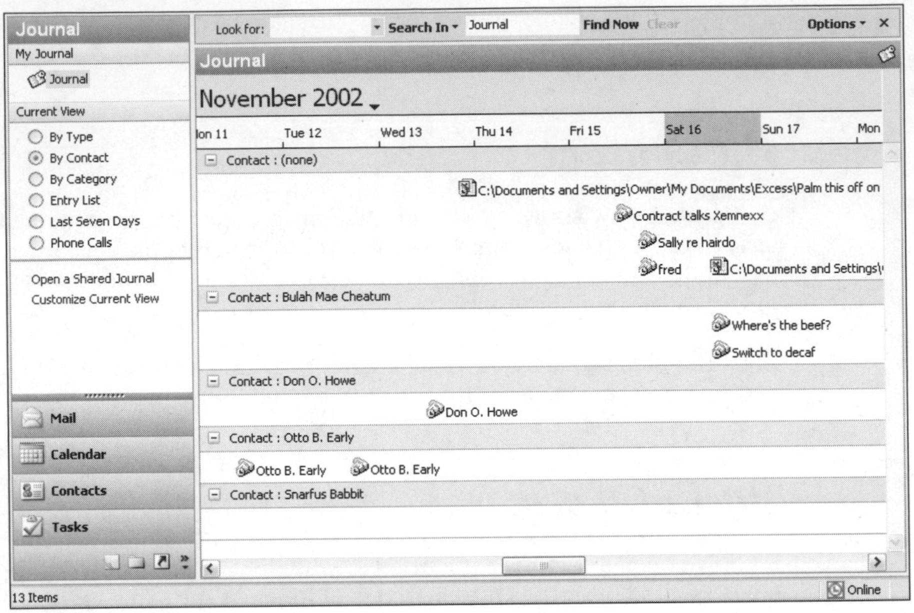

Figure 10-26:
Seeing your
entries in
the By
Contact
view.

Last Seven Days

The items you're likely to need first are the ones you used last. That's why Last Seven Days view offers a quick way to see your most recent activities at a glance. To see a week's worth of Journal entries, click the words Last Seven Days in the Current View section of the Navigation Pane.

Documents you've created, phone calls, e-mail messages — anything you've done on your computer in the last seven days — you can see them all in Last Seven Days view. This view shows anything you've worked on during the last week — including documents you may have created a long time ago — that's why you may see some pretty old dates in this view.

Phone Calls

Because you can keep track of your phone calls in the Journal, the Journal enables you to see a list of the calls you've tracked. Simply click Current View➪Phone Calls in the Navigation Pane.

To print a list of your phone calls, switch to Phone Calls view and press Ctrl+P.

It's All in the Journal

The Journal can be enormously helpful whether you choose to use it regularly or rarely. You don't have to limit yourself to recording documents or Outlook items. You can keep track of conversations or customer inquiries or any other transaction in which chronology matters. If you set the Journal for automatic entries, you can ignore it completely until you need to see what was recorded. You can also play starship captain and record everything you do. (I haven't tried Outlook in outer space yet, but I know I would enjoy the view.)

Part IV
Beyond the Basics: Tips and Tricks You Won't Want to Miss

The 5th Wave   By Rich Tennant

"Drive carefully, remember your lunch, and don't forget to blind copy me on all your juicy e-mail."

In this part . . .

When you finally get ahead in the rat race, what do you find? Faster rats, of course. This part shows you how to stay ahead of those rascally rodents — without getting lost in a maze of work — by using Outlook's secret power tools.

Chapter 11

Outlook Express: Getting the Scoop on Newsgroups

Microsoft gave Outlook a cousin named Outlook Express. The two programs do many of the same jobs, but each has its own specialty. The most important difference between Outlook and Outlook Express is that Outlook Express is free. Yep, you can get a copy of Outlook Express without spending a dime. The program is built right into Windows XP, so if you have Outlook, you also have Outlook Express.

The other difference between the two programs is that Outlook Express can read Internet newsgroups and Outlook can't. Internet newsgroups are collections of messages that anyone can read. After you read the messages in a newsgroup, you can reply to any message you read or post a whole new message of your own. To participate in a newsgroup, you need a special type of program called a *newsreader* — Outlook Express is just the tool for the job.

Outlook Express can also send and receive e-mail just like Outlook, but only Outlook can do all the fancy tricks with your tasks and calendar and contacts that I discuss throughout the rest of this book. If you have only Outlook Express but not Outlook, you have the basic tools you need for exchanging e-mail. After you've exchanged enough e-mail, you'll probably want to graduate from Outlook Express to full-strength Outlook to make your e-mail easier to handle.

News reading at the office

Many corporations don't want their employees browsing Internet newsgroups at the office. Many newsgroups contain nasty stuff that most companies don't want on their computers, such as pornography and details about some pretty strange philosophies and wigged-out political groups. Also, out of the 100,000-odd newsgroups on the Internet, relatively few are business-related. For that reason, your system administrators may have removed Outlook Express from your computer at the office. If you're on a corporate network that runs Exchange Server, and your employer wants you to read any of the handful of business-related Internet newsgroups, your administrators can make an Internet newsgroup show up as an Exchange Public Folder. (See Chapter 14 for more about Public Folders.)

The fact that Microsoft named *two* products "Outlook" causes plenty of confusion. The way I like to simplify the whole mess is by using Outlook Express only for reading Internet newsgroups. Because you have this book, I'm assuming that you have Outlook, which means that you also have Outlook Express.

Finding Newsgroups

Newsgroups are out there on the Internet for anyone to see, so you may as well jump right in and explore what newsgroups have to offer. The first time you start up Outlook Express, you can find a newsgroup to look at.

To view a newsgroup, follow these steps:

1. **From the main screen of Outlook Express, click the words "Setup a Newsgroups Account."**

   The Internet Connection Wizard appears.

2. **Enter the information that the wizard requests and click Next after each entry.**

   The wizard asks for your name, your e-mail address, and the name of your News Server. If you don't know the exact name of your news server, ask your system administrator or call the tech-support line at your Internet service provider. The wizard also asks which kind of Internet connection you want to use — phone line, LAN, or manual. If you're not sure, you can just click Next, and the wizard chooses for you.

3. Click Finish.

The Download Newsgroups dialog box appears. If your computer is connected to the Internet when the dialog box appears, you'll need to wait a few minutes to let the system get the list of newsgroups on your news server. If you're not connected to the Internet, a dialog box will appear to help you connect by clicking the Connect button. When the whole process is finished, the Newsgroup Subscriptions dialog box appears.

The Newsgroup Subscriptions dialog box opens (see Figure 11-1). The dialog box contains a list of all the newsgroups available for you to see. You can scroll down the list and find a newsgroup whose name looks interesting. But with tens of thousands of newsgroups on the Internet, scrolling through the whole list could take quite a long time, so I suggest a faster method in the remaining steps.

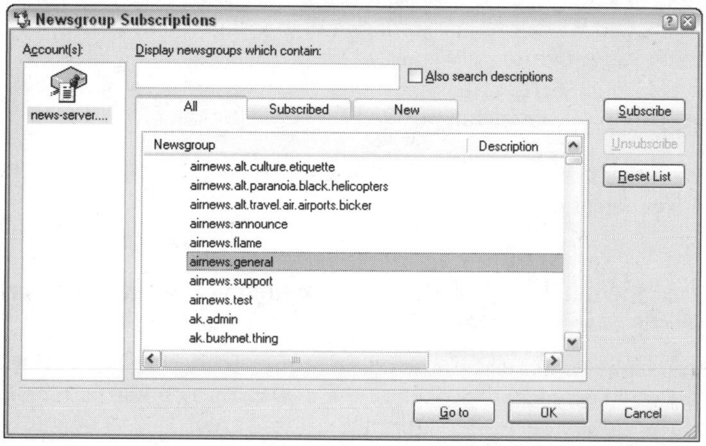

Figure 11-1:
Use the
Newsgroup
Subscrip-
tions dialog
box to pick
the news-
groups you
want to see.

4. Click in the Display Newsgroups Which Contain text box and type a one-word name for a subject that interests you.

The list in the Newsgroup Subscriptions dialog box changes to a list of newsgroups whose title includes the word you type. For example, if you type the word **Outlook,** the newsgroups in which people post comments, questions, and answers about Outlook appear.

5. Double-click the name of a newsgroup that interests you.

The Outlook Express main screen appears, with a list of the most recent messages posted to the newsgroup you chose.

Subscribing to Newsgroups

If you start hanging around in Internet newsgroups, you'll find that you spend a lot of time in a handful of groups, and you'll probably ignore the other tens of thousands of groups out there. (Who has time to read 10,000 newsgroups, anyway?)

You can get into your favorite newsgroups more quickly if you subscribe. *Subscribing* to a newsgroup is different from subscribing to a magazine. You don't pay a fee for subscribing to a newsgroup, and nobody needs to know you're reading a newsgroup unless you post messages to the group.

Don't post your e-mail address to an Internet newsgroup. People who send junk e-mail often gather e-mail addresses from newsgroups. After the junk e-mailers (or *spammers,* in Internet jargon) get your address, your Inbox may become stuffed with so many junk e-mail messages that you won't be able to find the messages you really want to see.

To subscribe to a newsgroup, follow these steps:

1. **From the main screen of Outlook Express, click the words "Subscribe to Newsgroups."**

   The Newsgroups screen in Outlook Express appears.

2. **Click the name of a newsgroup to which you want to subscribe in the Newsgroups screen and then click the Subscribe button.**

   An icon appears next to the name of the group you selected to show that you've selected it; the name of the newsgroup appears in the Folder List on the right side of the Outlook Express screen (as shown in Figure 11-2).

From now on, whenever you start up Outlook Express to read news, Outlook Express will automatically prepare to show you the newsgroups to which you've subscribed. When you click the name of a newsgroup in the Folders list, the latest messages in that newsgroup appear.

Reading Newsgroup Messages

The list of newsgroup messages is organized according to the subject of each message and the date when each message was posted to the newsgroup. You may see some messages with a little plus sign to the left of the subject (as in Figure 11-3); it shows that more than one message about that subject is posted to the list. You can see all the other messages by clicking the plus sign. The plus sign then turns into a minus sign, and all the other messages on that topic appear.

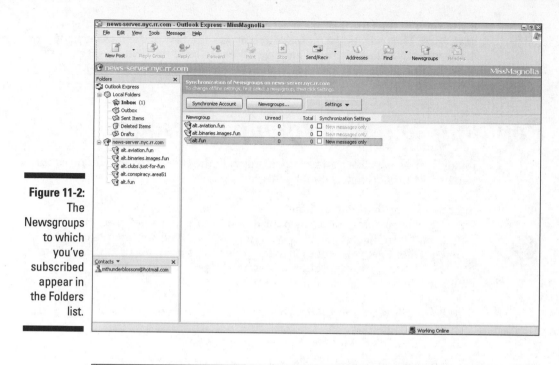

Figure 11-2:
The
Newsgroups
to which
you've
subscribed
appear in
the Folders
list.

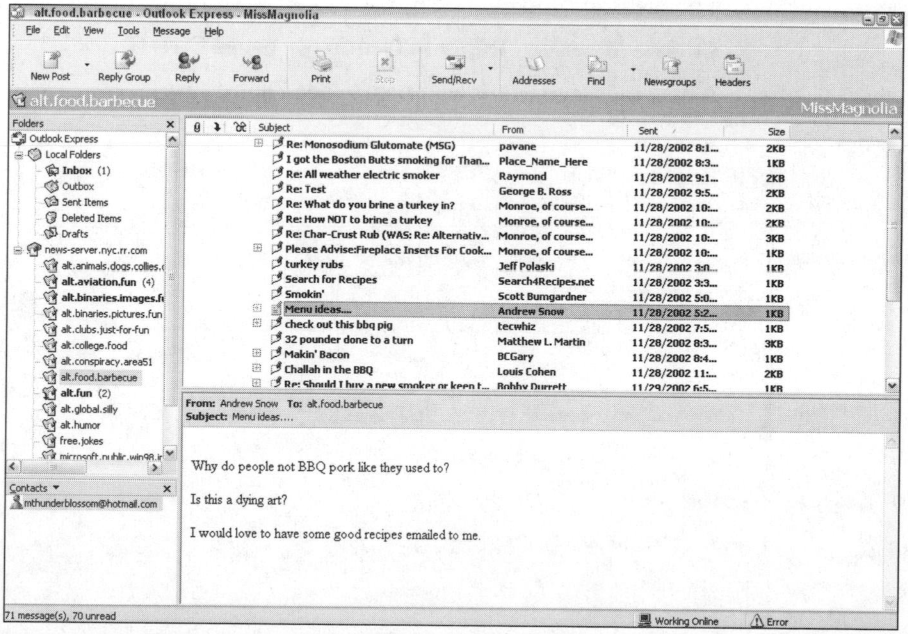

Figure 11-3:
The plus
sign next to
a message
tells you
that you can
read more
messages
on the same
subject.

If you want to read the text of a newsgroup message, click the title of the message once. That selects the message and makes the text of the message appear in the window below the list of message titles. To read the next message, just click the title of the next message in the list.

Replying to a Newsgroup Message

Reading messages in a newsgroup is only half the fun. It's when you put your two cents in that things get really interesting.

Internet newsgroups can be time consuming, emotionally draining, and habit forming. No self-help group exists for newsgroup addicts yet, but I think it's only a matter of time. Remember, you don't know the other people on a newsgroup, so don't get your socks in a knot over what people say to you online. Not everybody in every Internet newsgroup is polite or considerate, but it pays for you to remain as civil as possible.

If you're *really* ready, here's how to reply to a newsgroup message:

1. **Double-click the message to which you want to reply.**

   The message you clicked opens in a new window.

2. **Choose Message⇨Reply to Group (or press Ctrl+G).**

   A new message window appears (see Figure 11-4).

Figure 11-4:
When you reply to a newsgroup message, the text of the message you're answering appears as part of your reply.

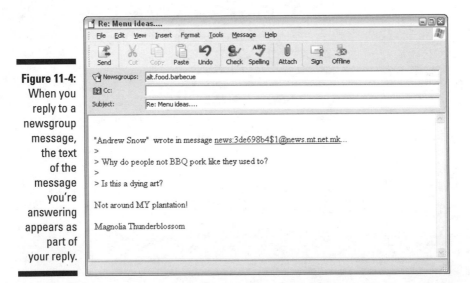

3. **Type your message.**

   Your message appears in the new message window.

4. **Click the Send button.**

   The new message window closes, and your message is posted to the newsgroup.

Newsgroup messages don't appear instantly to the newsgroup. Thousands of servers are out there with millions of messages, so it can take anywhere from a few minutes to a day or so for your message to show up.

Posting a New Message

As your horoscope said one time (because everybody's has at least once), you have a creative streak and you need to express yourself. A newsgroup is the cheapest place to publish your latest stroke of literary genius. On the other hand, an Internet newsgroup is probably not the *best* place to reveal your most private thoughts. Remember, anybody on earth can read this stuff. Before you post anything too original to the Internet, read your high school yearbook, see what you said then, and decide whether you want to make that kind of mistake again.

If you still can't restrain yourself, here's how to post an original message to a newsgroup:

1. **View the newsgroup to which you want to post your new message.**

   The list of messages in the newsgroup that you selected appears.

2. **Choose Message⇨New Message (or press Ctrl+N).**

   A new message window appears.

3. **Type a new subject on the Subject line.**

   You're better off making your subject short, snappy, and relevant. You'll find plenty of newsgroup messages with titles that are neither snappy nor relevant. The poor souls who wrote those messages haven't read this book. Have pity on them, but set a good example, okay?

4. **Type your message in the message text box.**

   The text of your message appears in the message text box.

5. **When your message is complete, click Send.**

   The message window closes.

There's one thing I can't overemphasize (but I'll try): Anybody on earth can read what you've posted to an Internet newsgroup. If you plan to post a statement that could cause you problems with your job, your relationships, or the law, you should *assume* that the wrong people will see what you post. Be careful.

E-Mail for the Whole Family with Outlook Express

It seems silly to have two e-mail programs on one computer, but sometimes you might want to use both Outlook *and* Outlook Express. For example, if several members of your family share the same computer, you can use the two programs at the same time to give each member access to e-mail. Have one member use Outlook and all the others can use Outlook Express. You'll have to fight over who gets Outlook, because it's the more powerful of the two programs. The one advantage to Outlook Express is that the Identities feature enables several people to exchange messages on separate e-mail addresses. Outlook Express also includes a wizard for setting up free e-mail accounts on Hotmail, so it's easy to get everyone started on e-mail with very little fuss.

Setting up Identities

If several different people want access to e-mail on the same computer, each of them can set up an Identity in Outlook Express. Then each person can send and receive e-mail as if they each had their own computer.

To create a new identity, follow these steps:

1. **Choose File⇨Identities⇨Add New Identity.**

   The New Identity dialog box appears.

2. **Type a name for your identity.**

   The name of your new identity appears and the New Identity Added dialog box pops up, asking whether you want to switch to your new identity.

3. **Click Yes.**

   Your new identity appears in the Manage Identities dialog box. If you click No, it's no big deal; you can just switch to your new Identity by following the steps in the next section.

You can delete an identity any time by choosing File⇨Identities⇨Manage Identities, selecting the identity you want to delete, and then clicking Remove.

Switching Identities

Superman used to switch identities in a phone booth. Outlook Express enables you to switch identities even if you can't find a phone booth. After you've set up an Identity, you choose that identity each time you use Outlook Express so you can send and receive the messages that belong to you.

To switch identities, follow these steps:

1. **Choose File⇨Switch Identity.**

   The Switch Identities dialog box appears.

2. **Double-click the name of the identity that you want to use.**

   The Switch Identities dialog box closes, and the set of messages belonging to the identity that you chose appears.

Even if you're not Superman, you can switch identities in Outlook Express to get e-mail for the whole family on one computer, but still keep each member's messages separate from everybody else's.

Chapter 12

What You Need to Know to Use Outlook at Home

*W*orking at home is different from working in an office (but you knew that). Sure, working in your bathrobe is pretty unusual in big companies, but home workers also have to do without the huge network, multiple phone lines, and standing army of computer gurus that many office workers take for granted. That's why Outlook works a bit differently for the home user than it does for the corporate user — and this chapter shows the home user how to get the most from those differences. (If you use Outlook in a large corporation, you may want to skip to Chapter 14, which focuses on using Outlook in big business.)

What's an ISP?

If you use a computer at home, you probably send and receive e-mail through an outside service that your computer dials up over the telephone. The general term for the kind of outfit that provides this service is *Internet service provider,* or *ISP.* ISPs do more than exchange e-mail messages for you; an ISP also provides the Internet connection that enables your browser to access and display pages from the World Wide Web and enables you to do nearly anything that you can do on the Internet.

Online services, such as America Online, CompuServe, and MSN (the Microsoft Network), function as ISPs, but they also offer a variety of features, such as discussion forums and file libraries. If you belong to an online service, you don't need a separate ISP. On the other hand, if all you want to do is exchange e-mail and browse the Web, you may not want a full-featured online service; a basic ISP may be all you need.

Everything about the Internet and online services can — and does — change quickly. The best way to get and use an online service may change with the introduction of new technologies and services, but what I tell you here is how it is in 2003.

If you're working from home, using an online service to connect you to the Internet offers some big advantages:

✔ These services all try to make the process of connecting as easy as 1possible.

✔ Most online services have plenty of staff to help you when things go wrong.

✔ If you want some assurance that you or your children won't run across scary people or nasty material while exploring cyberspace, online services are well equipped to screen out what you may find objectionable. If you're shopping for an online service, ask about features that protect you against nasty things that could pop up on your screen.

If you want to check out one of the major online services, visit one of the following Web sites (or call the phone number):

✔ CompuServe: (www.compuserve.com) 800-848-8990

✔ MSN (the Microsoft Network): (www.msn.com) 800-386-5550

AOL: Outlook is dubious

The biggest online service is America Online (AOL). Millions and millions of people call AOL their online home, and new members are joining every day. So far, however, you can't use Outlook to send e-mail if your e-mail address ends with aol.com. The folks at AOL made a big splashy announcement saying that they planned to support Outlook Express a few years back, but then they changed their minds. If AOL ever supports Outlook Express for e-mail, you'll be able to set up Outlook to exchange your AOL e-mail messages as well. At the moment, however, you can exchange AOL e-mail only through AOL's own (famously miserable) e-mail software. On the other hand; AOL's employees in the Time Warner division reportedly almost broke into armed rebellion when forced to dump Outlook for AOL e-mail, perhaps they'll start to appreciate the value of a decent e-mail program and start supporting Outlook. I'm not holding my breath.

What about Cable Modems and DSL?

If you have high-speed Internet access from your cable television operator or DSL through a telephone company, congratulations! You'll enjoy zippy Web surfing and your e-mail will come and go in a flash. You also don't need to deal with an ISP, because your cable company or DSL provider does that job for you.

Picking a Provider

Any computer that can run Outlook probably includes at least one icon on the desktop to help set you up with an Internet service provider or online service such as AOL, AT&T, or MSN. If you're not satisfied with any of the services that your computer already includes, literally hundreds of Internet service providers exist around the United States — and thousands more around the world. Some of them are small businesses that only serve a certain community. Others are huge, global companies that can be reached from nearly anywhere on planet Earth (and perhaps from some other planets, though we probably won't know for a quite a while yet).

If you do all your e-mailing and Web surfing from home or from one spot, a local ISP may be just fine for you. Check your local newspapers for ads from nearby ISPs. Local shops may be a little more personal (and less inclined to censor what you browse) than the bigger operators sometimes are. Lots of nasty places exist on the Internet that some people don't want to run across accidentally, so a little bit of censorship suits some folks just fine. Other people want completely unfettered access when they surf the Web, so smaller services with no censorship suit them better. Take your pick.

If you travel a lot and need to check your e-mail while you travel, a big operator may suit you best. Table 12-1 lists ISPs that offer pretty wide coverage in the United States.

Table 12-1	National ISPs	
ISP	*Web Address*	*Phone Number*
AT&T WorldNet Service	www.att.com/worldnet	800-400-1447
Earthlink Network	www.earthlink.net	800-EARTHLINK
Juno	www.juno.com	800-654-5866

You can find an even more extensive list of ISPs in a magazine called *Boardwatch,* or you can check the magazine's Web site at www.boardwatch. com. Another good place to look for an ISP is a Web site called www.thelist. com. There were once several companies that charged nothing for Internet access, but most went out of business. (For some reason, they couldn't make money by giving stuff away free. Imagine that!)

Setting Up Internet E-Mail Accounts

After you've signed up with an ISP, you can set up Outlook to send and receive e-mail from your account. Although any individual Internet e-mail account requires setup only once, you can set up many such accounts if you need them.

If you're a corporate user, your system administrators may not want you to mess around with account settings at all—and may have special arrangements and settings they want you to use when you work from home. Either way, it's best to ask first.

If you're on your own, you should probably call the tech support line from your online service or ISP to get all the proper spellings of the server names and passwords that you need to enter. (Don't forget to ask whether they're case-sensitive!)

To set up an Internet e-mail account, follow these steps:

1. **Choose Tools⇨E-mail Accounts.**

   The E-mail Accounts dialog box appears.

2. **Click the circle to the left of the words "Add new e-mail account."**

   The circle appears blackened to show you've selected it.

3. **Click Next (or press Enter).**

   The Server Type dialog box appears.

4. **Click the circle next to the type of server your e-mail provider requires.**

   You'll need to check with your e-mail service on this one, but the most likely choice is POP3.

5. **Click Next (or press Enter).**

   The Internet E-mail Settings screen appears.

Your Web site, your e-mail

If you have a Web site, you can probably get a free e-mail account in connection with your Web site. So if you have a site called www.your company.com (for example), you can also have an e-mail address that looks something like yourname@yourcompany.com. There's an even better chance that the mail service that you get in connection with your Web site is compatible with Outlook. Ask the tech-support people from the company that hosts your Web site what you have to do to set up Outlook with their e-mail service.

6. **Type the settings that your e-mail provider requires.**

   Again, each e-mail service differs, but most of them can tell you how to make their e-mail work with Outlook.

7. **Click the Test Account Settings button.**

   The Test Account Settings dialog box appears and shows you what's happening while Outlook tests the settings you've entered to see if you got everything right.

   If you type one wrong letter in one of your e-mail settings, the computers Outlook has to send messages through will reject your mail, so it's good to find out whether your setup works while you're still tweaking your settings. If the test fails, try retyping some entries (and then clicking the Test Account Settings button) until you get a successful test. When the test is successful, the Test Account Settings dialog box says Congratulations! All tests completed successfully. Click Close to continue. So that's what you should do.

8. **Click Close.**

   The Test Account Settings dialog box closes.

9. **Click Next (or press Enter).**

   The Congratulations screen appears. Take a moment to feel the thrill of success, and then . . .

10. **Click Finish.**

As I mention earlier in this section, you can set up more than one Internet e-mail account, so you can have separate addresses for each member of the family. You also may want to have separate accounts for business use and personal use. Perhaps you just want to set up separate accounts so you can send yourself messages. Whatever you like to do, the process of setting up different accounts is pretty much the same.

Free e-mail — well, almost!

If you use only the e-mail address provided by your Internet service provider, you'll get along just fine. But if you want to set up a separate e-mail address for each member of your family, or keep your business e-mail separate from your personal messages, you can start up an account with any number of mailbox providers. Mail.com (www.mail.com) is one of the more popular providers of electronic mailboxes. You can sign up for an address through Mail.com for free and check your e-mail messages through your Web browser. If you want to take advantage of Outlook's sophisticated mail-management features with your Mail.com account, you can pay an extra $18 per year for what they call a POP3 account. (I've been using Mail.com for about four years, and I think they do a good job.) Other companies that offer e-mail services include Microsoft's own Hotmail service (www.hotmail.com) and Yahoo! (www.yahoo.com).

Dealing with Multiple Mail Accounts

It's possible use Outlook to exchange e-mail through more than one e-mail address. For example, I have different e-mail addresses for business use and personal use. If you want to create a similar arrangement, all you have to do is set up a separate account for each address (using the method I describe in the previous section, "Setting Up Internet E-Mail Accounts").

Telling one Outlook account apart from another isn't too tough. Normally Outlook sends your reply to an e-mail message through the account in which you received the message. When you're replying, you don't have to think about which account you're using. When you're creating a message, however, Outlook sends the message through the account that you marked as the *default account* (the one it must use unless you specify otherwise). If you want to check which account a message will be sent through, click the Accounts button on the message form's toolbar and look at the box labeled *Send message using*.

Setting Up Directory Services

Sending an e-mail message to somebody is easy if you know that person's e-mail address. You can find e-mail addresses for people around the world right from Outlook. Before you can use Outlook to find e-mail addresses, however, you may find it useful to set up Outlook to use something called a directory service to help you find names and addresses. A directory service is a private company that keeps track of people's email addresses so that you can contact them more easily.

Outlook is set up to check one of several popular directory services to find e-mail addresses, but you have to tell Outlook which one you want to use.

Here's how to tell Outlook which search service you prefer:

1. **Choose Tools⇨E-mail Accounts.**

   The E-mail Accounts dialog box appears.

2. **Click the circle to the left of the words "Add new directory or address book."**

   The circle appears blackened to show you've selected it.

3. **Click Next (or press Enter).**

   The Directory or Address Book type screen appears.

4. **Click the circle to the left of the words "Internet Directory Service."**

   The circle appears blackened to show you've selected it.

5. **Click Next (or press Enter).**

   The Directory Service Settings screen appears.

6. **Type the name of the service that you want to use.**

   The name of the service you enter appears. You can choose from a variety of services, and if you don't like your choice, you can easily switch to another one. (I picked one called Bigfoot because it gave the most responses when I looked for my own name.)

7. **Click Next and then click Finish.**

   The Congratulations screen closes.

After you restart Outlook, you can check an e-mail address while you're creating a new message. Just type the name of the person you want to find in the To box of your message; then click the Check Names button in the message toolbar (or press Ctrl+K). If the service you picked knows your recipient's address, an underline appears beneath the person's name to show you that the message is properly addressed.

Send, receive, whatever!

Just because you clicked Send on your outgoing message doesn't automatically mean that your message was sent. People who use Outlook at home normally connect to the Internet via the telephone line. Each time you send messages, your computer must make a phone call to your Internet service provider so Outlook can drop off the messages you created and pick up the messages that others have sent you. So, sometime after you've created a batch of messages, remember to choose Tools⇨Send/Receive (or press F9) to tell Outlook to dial up your ISP and actually send out the messages (if you're using Outlook at home).

Setting Up Outlook for Multiple Users

If you have only one computer at home, you may want to share one copy of Outlook among several family members. Making Outlook serve several people isn't all that difficult, but you must realize that many of your Outlook settings and options can be limited by what other family members want to do. If you still want to set up Outlook for multiple users, follow these steps.

1. **Click the Windows Start button and choose Control Panel.**

   The Control Panel appears.

2. **Double-click the Mail icon.**

   The Mail Setup dialog box appears.

3. **Click the button labeled Show profiles.**

   The Mail dialog box appears, showing any profiles you've already created.

4. **Click Add.**

   The New Profile dialog box appears.

5. **Enter a name for your new profile and click OK.**

   It's best to enter the name of the person whose profile you're creating. The E-mail Accounts dialog box appears.

6. **Select the "Add a New E-Mail Account" option, and then click Next.**

   The Server Type screen appears.

7. **Select the "Add new e-mail account" option.**

   The option button appears blackened to show you've selected it.

8. **Click Next (or press Enter).**

   The Server Type dialog box appears.

9. **Select the option for the type of server your e-mail provider requires.**

   Be sure to check with your e-mail service on this one, but the most likely choice is POP3.

10. **Click Next (or press Enter).**

    The Internet E-mail Settings screen appears.

11. **Type the settings that your e-mail provider requires.**

    Again, each e-mail service differs, but most of them can tell you how to make their e-mail capabilities work with Outlook.

12. **Click the Test Account Settings button.**

    The Test Account Settings dialog box appears and shows you what's happening while Outlook tests the settings you've entered.

13. **Click Close.**

    The Test Account Settings dialog box closes.

14. **Click Next (or press Enter).**

    The Congratulations screen appears. (The crowd goes wild!)

15. **Click Finish.**

    The Mail dialog box appears again, showing your new profile.

16. **Select the "Prompt for a profile to be used" option.**

    The circle next to the text you click appears darkened to show you've selected it.

17. **Click OK.**

    The Mail dialog box closes.

After you set up multiple profiles in Outlook and choose a profile to be used, you're asked to specify one of these accounts to open every time you start Outlook. Just pick your profile from the drop-down list; Outlook displays your messages and other personal information.

If you're planning to share a single copy of Outlook, be sure the person you're sharing with is somebody you trust. Although it is possible to keep some matters private, when two people share the same copy of an e-mail program, you can't really expect everything to *stay* private. If absolute privacy is important to you, your best bet is to have your own computer.

Chapter 13

Making Outlook Your Own: Personalizing Forms

*E*very time you choose File⇨New in Outlook (or double-click an item to open it), a *form* pops up. Forms enable you to create a new item or edit information in an old item. The forms that come with Outlook are shaped and designed to handle the information that most people use most of the time.

If the forms that pop up automatically in Outlook don't suit your fancy, you can modify them a bit to meet your needs. You can't create forms from scratch in Outlook (the way you can with a database program such as Microsoft Access), just as most people can't create their own cookie cutters. But you can bend a cookie cutter that you already have into a shape you want, and you can adjust one of the existing Outlook forms to meet your needs. (Frankly, you'll get much better results from customizing Outlook forms than from bending your cookie cutters out of shape.)

Of all the Outlook users I know, at least 99 percent don't know how to create an Outlook form and 98 percent don't even know they *can*. Somehow, tens of millions of Outlook users get along just fine without ever knowing how to create an Outlook form. If you decide you'd rather not mess with creating Outlook forms, you can probably skip this chapter entirely with no ill effect. If you're intrigued by the possibilities of forms, however, read on.

If you customize a form but want to keep the one it's based on, you can save your new form under a different name. You can also make the two forms look entirely different when you use them, even though they're based on the same form.

The best reason to customize a form is to add fields that aren't available in the original form. *Fields* are categories of information you want to use, such as phone numbers, names, and addresses. In the following section, I show you an example of a form customized to suit a car salesperson. The customized form uses all the information from the original Outlook form, adding a few fields that are specific to the needs of someone who sells cars.

Adding a Standard Field to a Form

When you first install Outlook, hundreds of standard fields are already set up for you to use. Standard fields are made to store the kind of information that people often need to use, such as names, addresses, dates, and so on. You can choose to add any of them to your forms, or you can create custom fields. I discuss how to create custom fields in the section "Adding a user-defined field to a form," later in this chapter.

To add a standard field to an Outlook form:

1. **Choose Go➪Folder List.**

   The Folder List appears (see Figure 13-1), giving you a more detailed view of your Outlook folders. You use the Folder List to create a new folder. I suggest that you create a new folder for this example.

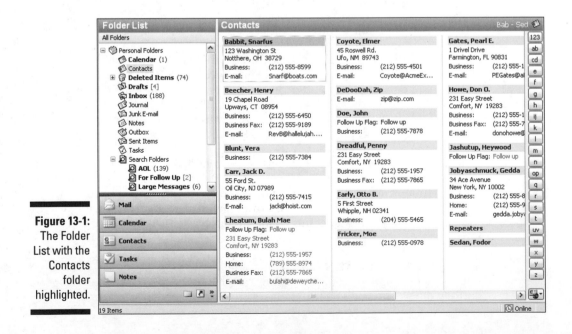

Figure 13-1: The Folder List with the Contacts folder highlighted.

2. Right-click the folder in which you want to create the new subfolder.

For this example, right-click the Contacts folder. A shortcut menu appears. The commands in the menu allow you to create a subfolder as well as move, copy, rename, or delete an existing folder.

3. Choose New Folder.

The Create New Folder dialog box appears (see Figure 13-2).

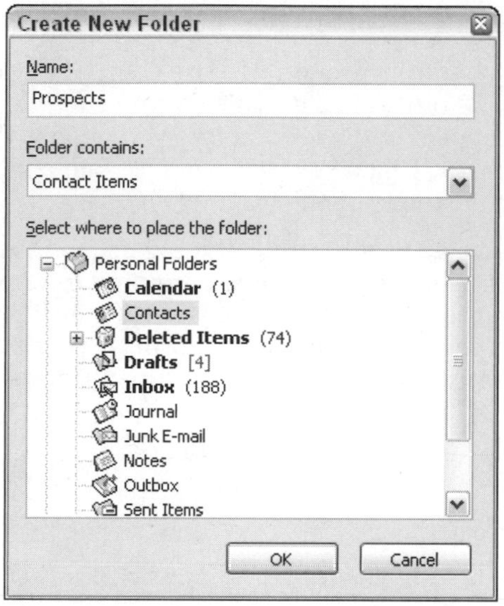

Figure 13-2:
The Create
New Folder
dialog box.

4. Type a name for the folder.

I use **Prospects** for this example.

5. Click OK.

The new folder that you created appears in the Folder List and a dialog box appears asking if you want to add the new folder to the Navigation Pane.

6. Click the new folder.

If the Contacts folder has a plus sign next to it, click the plus sign. Subfolders of the Contacts folder appear.

7. Choose File⇨New⇨Contact.

The Contact form appears.

8. Choose Tools⇨Forms⇨Design This Form.

The form switches into Forms Designer mode (see Figure 13-3). The form looks similar to what it looked like before you chose Tools⇨Forms⇨ Design This Form, but five new pages — called (P.2) through (P.6) — appear. These pages are blank pages that you can customize with new fields, new colors, and so on. The Field Chooser window also opens to offer you a selection of new fields to add to your form.

9. Click (P.2) or any other blank page.

It's your choice; you can add fields to any of the new pages.

10. (Optional) To make this page visible, choose Form⇨Display This Page.

The parentheses disappear from around P.2. The new pages that appear when you choose Tools⇨Forms⇨Design This Form are in parentheses, whereas the ones that appear in the form before you choose this command aren't in parentheses. That's how you can tell which pages will be visible when you finish customizing the form.

If you want, you can leave all pages visible. But one reason to create a custom form is to reduce the number of steps required to view, enter, or edit the information on the form. You also may be creating this form for other people to use, so you want to keep your form clear and simple. One-page forms are clearer and simpler than multipage forms.

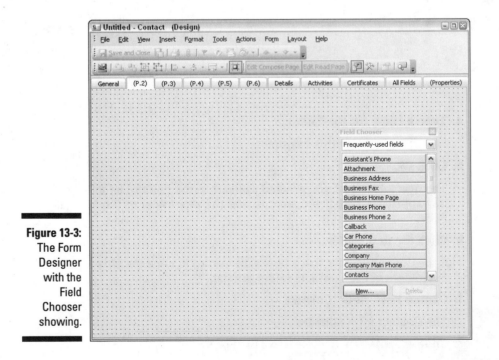

Figure 13-3:
The Form
Designer
with the
Field
Chooser
showing.

TIP

You can click any page and make the page invisible to the user by clicking the General tab and then choosing Form⇨_Display This Page. (The command toggles the page on and off.)

11. **Choose Form⇨Rename Page.**

The Rename Page dialog box appears (see Figure 13-4).

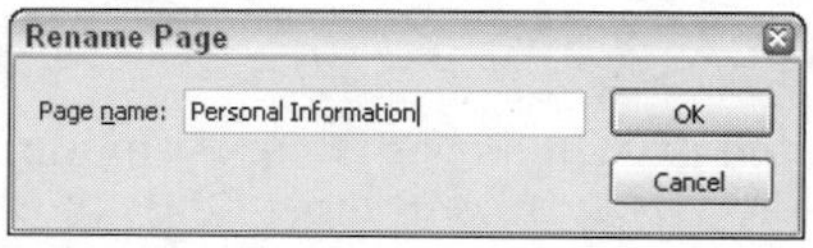

Figure 13-4:
The Rename
Page dialog
box.

Rename Page	☒
Page name: Personal Information|	OK
	Cancel

12. **Type a new name for the page.**

I use **Personal Information** as a good name for this page, but any name you choose will work.

13. **Click OK.**

The page tab now has the name that you typed in the Rename Page dialog box.

Now you can add some fields to the new page. That's what customizing a form is all about. The Field Chooser is the place to find fields to add to your form.

I think that the Field Chooser is confusing. You never see all the fields that are available; you see only a certain subset. The words below Field Chooser tell you which subset you're seeing, as in Figure 13-5.

Field Chooser ☒

Frequently-used fields ▾

Name fields
Personal fields
Phone number fields
All Document fields
All Mail fields
All Post fields
All Contact fields
All Appointment fields

Business Phone 2
Callback
Car Phone
Categories
Company
Company Main Phone
Contacts

New... | Delete

Figure 13-5:
The Field
Chooser
contains
more fields
than you
can see.

You can choose Frequently-Used fields to limit what Outlook shows you to a small range of fields, or All Contact fields to choose from every kind of field that Outlook allows in this type of form.

14. **Select a category from the drop-down list at the top of the Field Chooser and then select the name of a field in that category.**

    For this example, select the Personal fields category and then select the Referred By field, which, for example, a car salesperson can use to store the name of the person who referred the customer.

15. **Drag the selected field onto the page.**

    When you drag a field onto the page in Forms Designer mode, it automatically aligns properly on the page. To add more fields to your form, keep dragging them in from the Field Chooser (see Figure 13-6).

16. **Choose Tools➪Forms➪Publish Form As.**

    The Publish Form As dialog box appears. *Publishing* is the Outlook term for making a form available in a certain folder or group of folders. Outlook will publish your new form to whichever folder you clicked before beginning to design your form unless you click the Look In button and choose a different folder.

17. **Type a name for your new form in the Display Name box.**

    The name **New Prospect** is a good one for this form. The form name will appear in the menus when you create a new item for this folder.

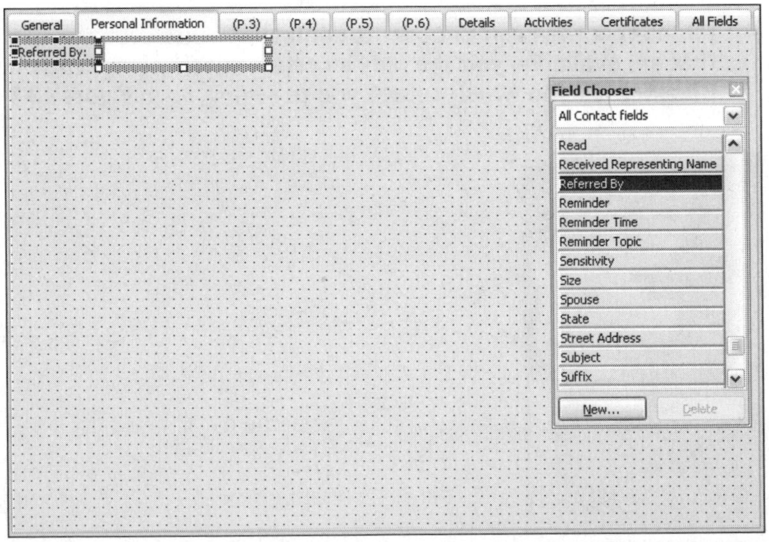

Figure 13-6: Dragging a field into a form.

18. **Click Publish.**

    Nothing visible happens, but your form is published to the folder that you designated — in this case, the Prospects folder.

19. **Choose File⇨Close.**

    A dialog box appears, asking Do you want to save changes?

20. **Click Yes to save changes.**

    A dialog box appears, asking Do you want to save this contact with an empty file as field?

21. **Click Yes.**

    The Forms Designer closes.

The form now contains your additional standard field.

Adding a user-defined field to a form

Although you can choose from hundreds of standard fields when you first use Outlook, that's just the beginning. The next bold step is to dream up some *user-defined fields* — the ones you put in your form because Outlook doesn't have a standard field for the kind of data you want to put there.

Here's how to create a user-defined field and add it to a form:

1. **Choose File⇨New⇨Contact.**

    The Contact form appears.

2. **Choose Tools⇨Forms⇨Design This Form.**

    The form switches into Forms Designer mode. The form looks much the same as it did before you chose Tools⇨Forms⇨Design This Form, but five new pages — called (P.2) through (P.6) — appear. These pages are blank pages you can customize with new fields, new colors, and so on.

3. **Click the tab of an unused page.**

    You can add fields to any of the new pages.

4. **Choose Form⇨Display This Page.**

    The parentheses disappear from the name of the page in the tab, showing you that this page will be visible when you finish customizing the form.

5. **Click New in the Field Chooser dialog box.**

    The New Field dialog box appears (as shown in Figure 13-7).

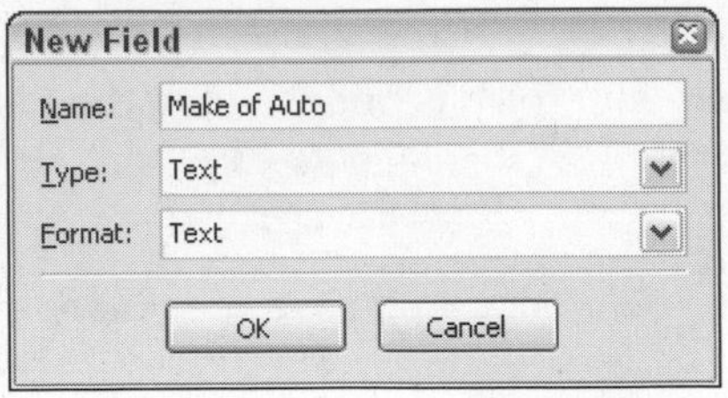

Figure 13-7:
The New
Field dialog
box.

New Field

Name: Make of Auto

Type: Text

Format: Text

[OK] [Cancel]

6. **Type a name for a new field.**

   Outlook doesn't include a field called *Make of Auto*, so type **Make of Auto**. You can use any name that's up to 32 characters long.

7. **Click OK.**

   Your new field appears in the Field Chooser, and the words `User-Defined Fields` appear at the top of the Field Chooser, indicating the field type.

8. **Drag the new field onto the form page.**

   The new field aligns itself automatically.

9. **Click the Publish Forms button at the far left of the Design Form toolbar.**

   The Publish button is the leftmost button on the lower Forms toolbar (refer to Figure 13-3). The Publish Form As dialog box appears, showing the current name of the form already filled in.

10. **Click Publish.**

Changes that you made to your form are now stored and will appear the next time you use the form.

Using the Form You've Designed

Hey, life isn't all creativity — sometimes you just have to put your creation to work. Using a form you've designed, in any folder to which you published the form, is easy. The name you gave to the form turns up on the Outlook main menu whenever you choose the Outlook folder to which you published your custom form.

Here's how to use a custom form (in this example, the freshly minted New Prospect form):

1. **Click the Actions menu.**

   That's the menu immediately to the left of Help in the menu bar.

2. Choose the custom form name that appears at the bottom of the menu.

If you created the form called New Prospect earlier in this chapter, then the name of the form appears at the bottom of the menu when you choose the Contacts menu (as shown in Figure 13-8). The first time you choose your new custom form, Outlook automatically installs the new form for you.

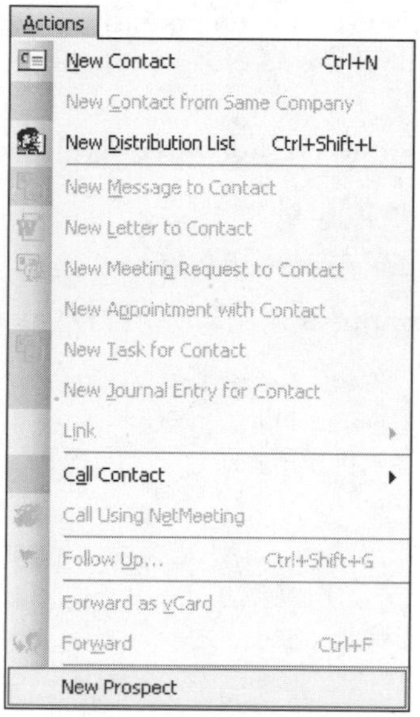

Figure 13-8:
When you publish a custom form, the name of your form appears at the bottom of the Actions menu.

3. Fill out the form.

4. Click Save and Close.

After you've entered information and closed your new form, you see a new item containing the information you entered. You can use the same form over and over to add new items to your collection of Outlook data. You can also have more than one custom form assigned to a folder. You can create a Vacation Request folder, for example, and store related forms — Vacation Request, Vacation Approved, Vacation Denied — in the same folder.

Making a custom form a folder's default form

Every time you choose a folder in Outlook and choose File⇨New, a form pops up, inviting you to enter the kind of data appropriate to that folder. You can also pick another form to use; simply choose the form by name from the menus. If you want your custom form to be the one that Outlook offers when you choose File⇨New, then you can designate the form as the default form for that folder.

Here's how you designate a form to be the default form for a folder:

1. **Choose Go⇨Folder List (or press Ctrl+6).**

   The Folder List opens (if it was closed). This command toggles like a light switch, opening the Folder List if it was closed and closing the list if it was open.

2. **Click the folder for which you want to change the default form.**

   For this example, use the Prospects folder.

3. **Choose File⇨Folder⇨Properties for *Name of folder*.**

   The folder's Properties dialog box appears (as shown in Figure 13-9).

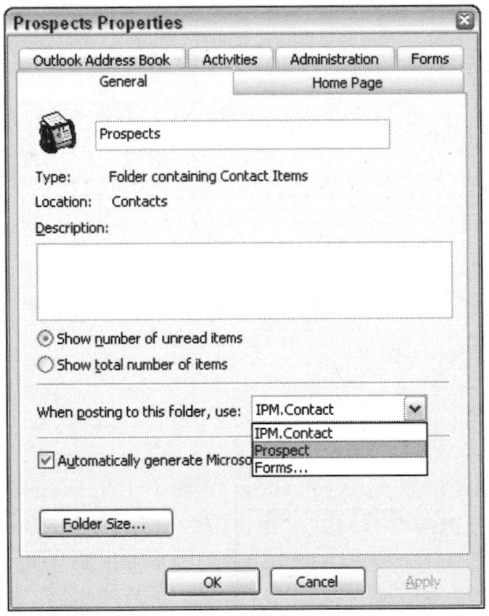

Figure 13-9:
Use the
Properties
dialog box
to set the
folder's
default form.

4. **Click the When Posting to This Folder, Use drop-down list.**

   Select the name of your custom form.

5. **Click OK.**

   Now every time you choose File⇨New in that folder, your customized form appears.

Deleting a form you've designed

The time may come when you don't need a certain form anymore. Because forms you've designed turn up on the Outlook Actions menu, you may prefer to delete the form altogether. You may also have to create several test versions of a form before you settle on the final version (nobody gets it perfect the first time). At that point, you can discreetly delete the versions you didn't like.

To delete a form, follow these steps:

1. **Choose Go⇨Folder List (or press Ctrl+6).**

   The Folder List opens.

2. **Click the folder for which you want to change the default form.**

   For this example, that folder is the Prospects folder.

3. **Choose File⇨Folder⇨Properties for *Name of folder*.**

   The folder's Properties dialog box appears.

4. **Click the Forms tab.**

   The forms page appears.

5. **Click the button labeled Manage.**

   The Forms Manager dialog box appears (as in Figure 13-10).

Figure 13-10:
Delete
unwanted
forms from
the Forms
Manager
dialog box.

6. **Click the name of the form you want to delete.**

   The name you clicked is highlighted to show that you've selected it.

7. **Click Delete.**

    A dialog box opens, asking "Do you want to Delete the Selected Form(s)."

8. **Click Yes.**

    The Forms Manager dialog box appears.

9. **Click Close.**

    The folder's Properties dialog box appears.

10. **Click OK**

    The dialog box closes and your form is deleted.

Part V
Outlook at the Office

In this part . . .

Life is different when you work in a big organization from what it is when you work in a small one. Outlook has some tools that work best in the big leagues (or for people with big ambitions).

Chapter 14

Big-Time Collaboration with Outlook

Microsoft is a big company that writes big programs for big companies with big bucks. So, as you'd expect, some parts of Outlook are intended for people at big companies. Big companies that use Outlook usually have a network that's running a program called Microsoft Exchange Server in the background. Exchange Server works as a team with Outlook to let you do what you can't do with Outlook alone. Outlook users on an Exchange Server can look at the calendar of another employee, or give someone else the power to answer e-mail messages on that person's behalf, or do any of a host of handy tasks right from a single desktop.

Many features of Microsoft Exchange Server look as if they're just a part of Outlook, so most Exchange Server users have no idea that any program other than Outlook is involved. In practical terms, it really doesn't matter whether you know the technical difference between Outlook and Exchange Server; what's important is that Outlook and Exchange together can tackle a lot of tasks that Outlook can't do as well alone.

Collaborating with Outlook's Help

If your company is like most others, then you spend a lot of time in meetings — and even more figuring out when to hold meetings and agreeing on what to do when you're not having meetings. Outlook has some tools for planning meetings and making decisions that are helpful for people who work in groups.

Although some of these features are available to all Outlook 2002 users, they work much better when you're using Exchange as well.

Organizing a meeting

Suppose you want to set up a meeting with three coworkers. You call the first person to suggest a meeting time, and then call the second, only to find out that the second person isn't available when the first one wants to meet. So you agree on a time with the second person, only to discover that the third person can't make this new time. You might want to invite a fourth person, but heaven knows how long it'll take to come up with an appropriate time for that one.

If you use Outlook, you can check everyone's schedule, pick a time, and suggest a meeting time that everyone can work with in the first place — with a single message.

To invite several people to a meeting, follow these steps:

1. **Choose File⇨New⇨Meeting Request (or press Ctrl+Shift+Q).**

   The New Appointment Form opens.

2. **Click the Scheduling tab.**

   The Attendee Availability page appears (as shown in Figure 14-1).

3. **Click the Add Others button.**

   A drop-down list appears.

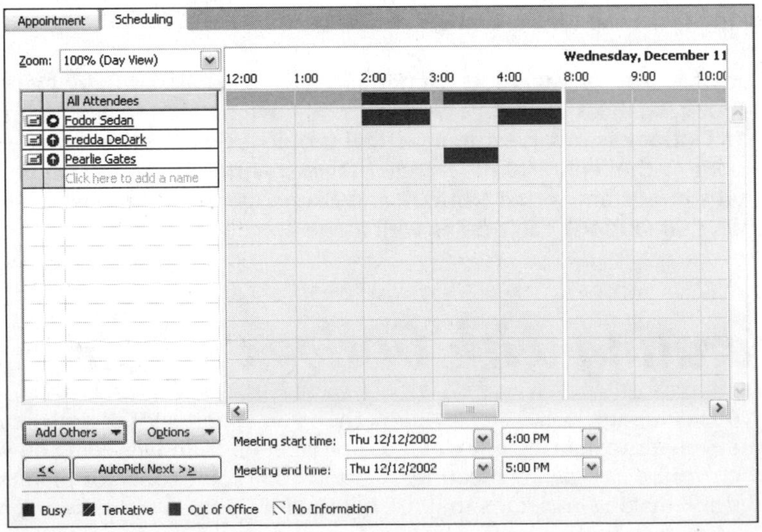

Figure 14-1:
Use the Attendee Availability page to invite coworkers to a meeting.

4. **Choose Add from Address Book.**

   The Select Attendees and Resources dialog box appears.

5. **Click the name of a person you want to invite to the meeting.**

   The name you click is highlighted to show you've selected it.

6. **Click either the Required or Optional button, depending on how important that person's attendance is to the meeting.**

   The name you select appears in either the Required or Optional box, depending on which button you click.

7. **Repeat Steps 4 and 5 until you've chosen everyone you want to add to the meeting.**

   The names you choose appear in the Select Attendees and Resources dialog box (as shown in Figure 14-2).

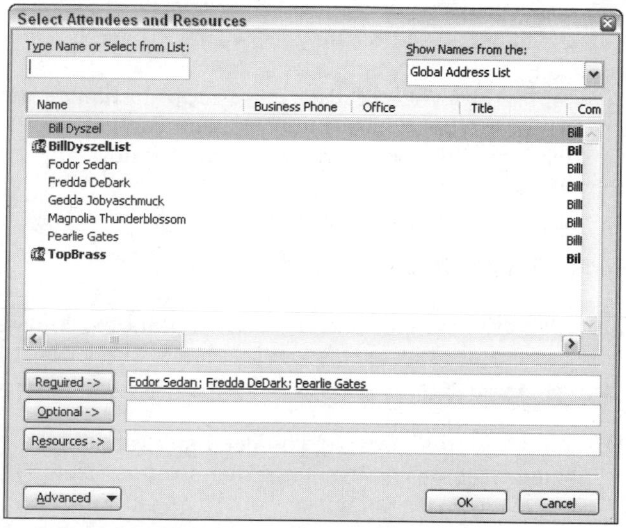

Figure 14-2: You can pick your friends and you can pick your meetings.

8. **Click OK.**

   The Select Attendees and Resources dialog box closes and the names you chose appear in the Attendee Availability list. The Attendee Availability list also shows you a diagram of each person's schedule so you can see when everyone has free time.

9. **On the timeline at the top of the Attendee Availability list, click your preferred meeting time.**

   The time you pick appears in the Meeting Start Time box at the bottom of the Attendee Availability list. If you want, you can enter the Meeting start and end time in the boxes at the bottom of the Attendee Availability list instead of clicking the timeline. If you don't see a time when everyone you're inviting to your meeting is available, click the Autopick Next button and Outlook will find a meeting time that works for everyone.

10. **Click the Appointment tab.**

    The Appointment page appears with the names of the people you invited to the meeting in the To box at the top of the form.

11. **Type the subject of the meeting in the Subject box.**

    The subject you enter appears in the Subject box.

12. **Enter any other information that you want attendees to know about your meeting, including location or category, in the appropriate areas of the form.**

    The information that you type appears in the appropriate place in the form.

13. **Click Send.**

    Your meeting request is sent to the people that you've invited.

If your system administrators see fit, they can set up Exchange Accounts for resources such as conference rooms. If they do, you can figure out a location for your meeting while you're figuring out who can attend.

Responding to a meeting request

Even if you don't organize meetings and send out invitations, you may get invited to meetings now and then, so it's a good idea to know how to respond to a meeting request if you get one. ("Politely" is a good concept to start with.)

When you've been invited to a meeting, you get a special e-mail message that offers buttons labeled Accept, Decline, Tentative, Propose New Time, or Calendar. When you click either Accept or Tentative, Outlook automatically adds the meeting to your schedule and creates a new e-mail message to the person who organized the meeting, telling that person your decision. You can add an explanation to the message, or just click the Send button to deliver your message.

If you choose Decline, Outlook also generates a message to the meeting organizer. (It's good form to add a business reason to explain why you're missing a meeting — "Sorry, I've got a deadline," rather than "I have to wash my aardvark" or "Sorry, I plan to be sane that day.") If you click the Calendar button, Outlook displays your calendar in a separate window so you can see whether you're free to attend the meeting at the suggested time.

Checking responses to your meeting request

Each time you organize a meeting with Outlook, you create a small flurry of e-mail messages inviting people to attend, and they respond with a flurry of messages either accepting or declining your invitation. You may have a good enough memory to recall who said Yes and No, but I usually need some help. Fortunately, Outlook keeps track of who said what.

To check the status of responses to your meeting request, follow these steps:

1. **Click the Calendar icon in the Navigation Pane.**

    The Calendar appears.

2. **Double-click the item you want to check.**

    The meeting you double-clicked opens on-screen.

3. **Click the Tracking tab.**

    The list of people you invited appears, listing each person's response to your invitation (as shown in Figure 14-3).

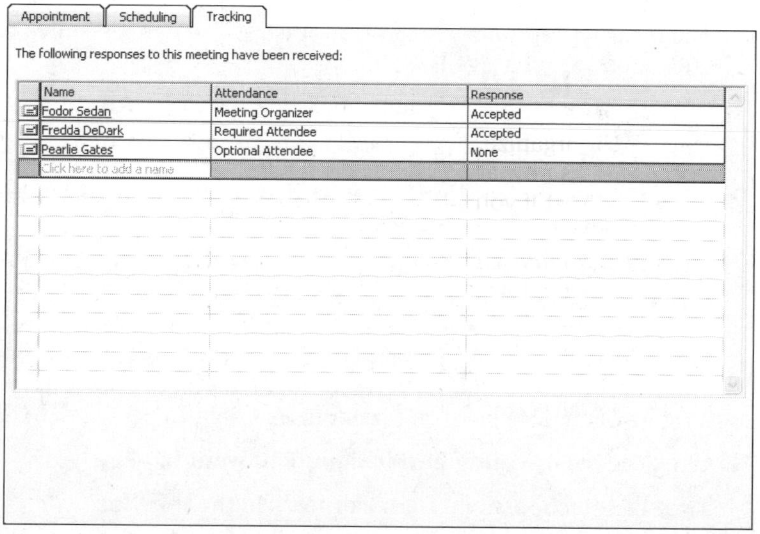

Appointment	Scheduling	Tracking

The following responses to this meeting have been received:

Name	Attendance	Response
Fodor Sedan	Meeting Organizer	Accepted
Fredda DeDark	Required Attendee	Accepted
Pearlie Gates	Optional Attendee	None
Click here to add a name		

Figure 14-3:
See the RSVPs from your VIPs.

Sad to say, only the meeting organizer can find out who has agreed to attend a certain meeting. If you plan to attend a certain meeting only because that special someone you met in the elevator might also attend, you'll know whether that person accepted only if you organized the meeting yourself. You can tell who was invited to a meeting by checking the names on the meeting request that you got by e-mail.

Taking a vote

Management gurus constantly tell us about the importance of good teamwork and decision-making. But how do you get a team to make a decision when you can't find most of the team members most of the time? You can use Outlook on an Exchange network as a decision-making tool if you take advantage of the Outlook Voting buttons.

Voting is a special feature of Outlook e-mail that adds buttons to an e-mail message sent to a group of people. When they get the message, recipients click a button to indicate their response. Outlook automatically tallies the responses so you can see which way the wind is blowing in your office.

To add voting buttons to an e-mail message you're creating, follow these steps while creating your message but before clicking the Send button (for more about creating messages, see Chapter 4):

1. **Choose Tools➪Options (or press Alt+P).**

   The Message Options dialog box appears. You can also click the Options button on the message toolbar.

2. **Click the Use Voting Buttons check box (or press Alt+U).**

   A check mark appears in the Use Voting Buttons check box.

3. **Click the scroll-down button (triangle) on the text box to the right of the Use Voting Buttons check box.**

   A list of suggested voting buttons appears. The suggested choices include Approve;Reject, Yes;No, and Yes;No;Maybe (as shown in Figure 14-4). You can also type in your own choices if you follow the pattern of the suggested choices; just separate your options with a semicolon. If you want to ask people to vote on the lunch menu, for example, include a range of choices such as Pizza;Burgers;Salad.

4. **Click the set of voting buttons that you want to use.**

   The set you choose (or enter) appears in the text box.

5. **Click Close.**

   And there you are! Democracy in action! Isn't that inspiring? When your recipients get your message, they can click the button of their choice and zoom their preference off to you.

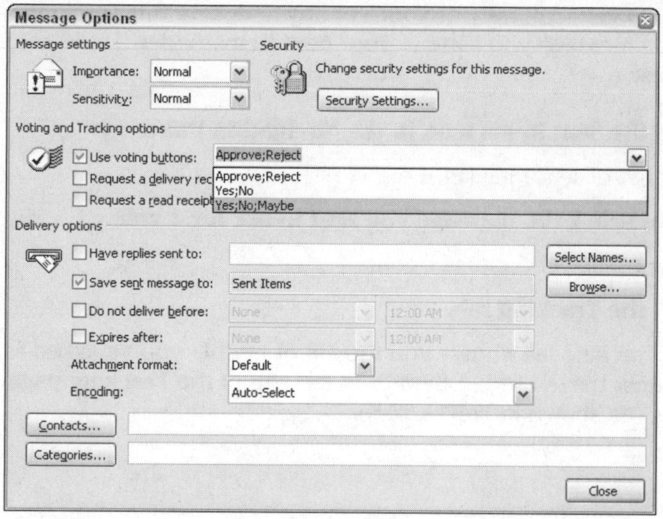

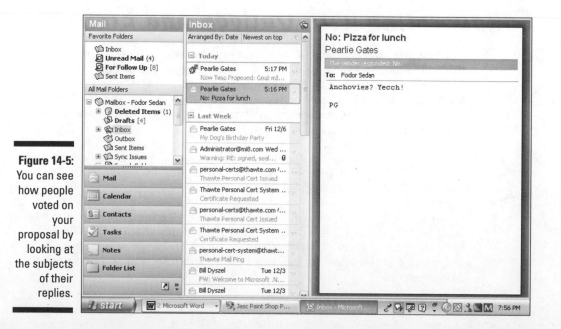

Figure 14-4:
Choose the choices of your choice (is there an echo in here?) from the Voting buttons list.

Tallying votes

When the replies arrive, you'll see who chose what by looking at the subject of the replies. Messages from people who chose "Yes," for example, start with the word *Yes;* rejection messages start with the word *No* (as shown in Figure 14-5).

Figure 14-5:
You can see how people voted on your proposal by looking at the subjects of their replies.

You can also get a full tally of your vote by checking the Tracking tab on the copy of the message you send in your Sent Items folder. To do so, follow these steps:

1. **Click the Sent Items icon in the Navigation Pane.**

   Your list of sent messages appears.

2. **Double-click the message you sent to ask for a vote.**

   The message you chose opens.

3. **Click the Tracking tab.**

   The Tracking tab shows you the list of people you've asked for a vote — and how they voted. A banner at the top of the Tracking page tallies the votes (as shown in Figure 14-6).

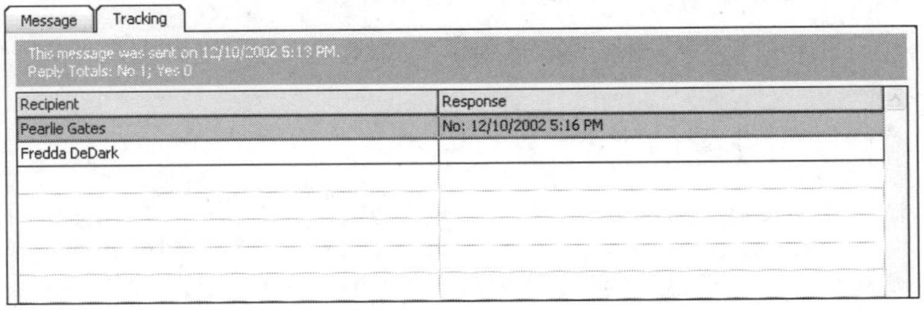

Figure 14-6:
Check the
Tracking tab
to get a
quick tally of
how people
voted.

Message	Tracking	
This message was sent on 12/10/2002 5:13 PM. Reply Totals: No 1; Yes 0		
Recipient	Response	
Pearlie Gates	No: 12/10/2002 5:16 PM	
Fredda DeDark		

Collaborating with Outlook and Exchange

One thing I've always found annoying about Outlook is the way certain features of Microsoft Exchange just show up in Outlook menus and tools even if you're not using Exchange. For example, the option to view another person's folder (which I explain in this chapter) shows up even if you're not using Outlook on an Exchange network. Without an Exchange Network, however, the feature doesn't work.

I've focused the rest of this chapter on the features that work only if you have *both* Outlook and Exchange Server. Why confuse non-Exchange users by describing features they can't use?

If you use Outlook at home or in an office without Exchange Server, you won't be able to use the features I describe in the rest of this chapter. But take heart: little by little, Microsoft is finding ways to make Exchange-only features available to all Outlook users, so you can look over this section as a preview of things to come.

Giving delegate permissions

Good managers delegate authority. (That's what my assistant, Igor, says, anyway.) Extremely busy people sometimes give an assistant the job of managing the boss's calendar, schedule, and (sometimes) even e-mail. That way, the boss can concentrate on the big picture while the assistant dwells on the details.

When you designate a delegate in Outlook on an Exchange network, you give certain rights to the delegate you name — in particular, the right to look at whichever Outlook module you pick.

To name a delegate, follow these steps:

1. **Choose Tools⇨Options.**

   The Options dialog box appears.

2. **Click the Delegates tab.**

   The Delegates page appears.

3. **Click Add.**

   The Add Users dialog box appears.

4. **Double-click the name of each delegate you want to name.**

   The names you choose appear in the Add Users box (as shown in Figure 14-7).

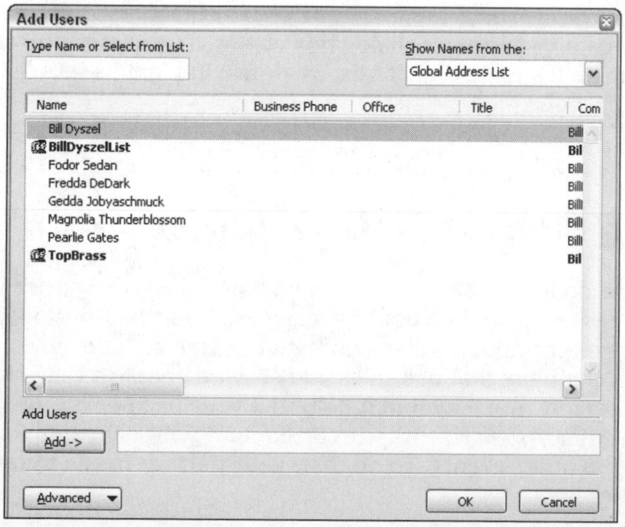

Figure 14-7: Choose those you trust in the Add Users dialog box.

5. Click OK.

The Delegate Permissions dialog box appears (as shown in Figure 14-8) so you can choose exactly which permissions you want to give to your delegate(s).

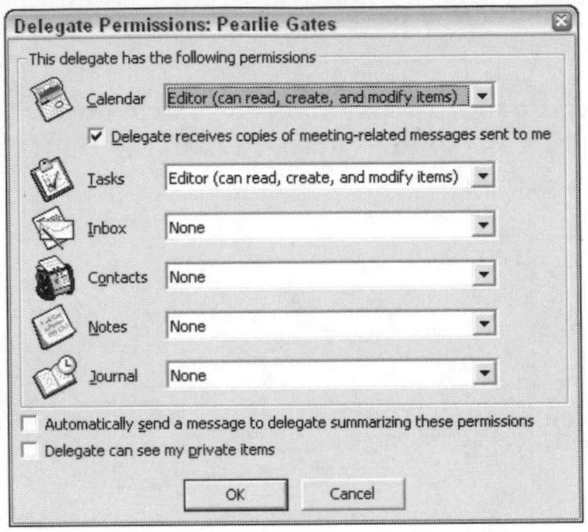

Figure 14-8: Show how much trust you have in the Delegate Permissions dialog box.

6. Make any changes you want in the Delegate Permissions dialog box.

If you make no choices at all in the Delegate Permissions dialog box, then (by default) your delegate is granted Editor status in your Calendar and Task list — which means that the delegate can read, create, and change items in those two Outlook modules.

7. Click OK.

The Delegate Permissions dialog box closes. The names you chose appear in the Options dialog box, as shown in Figure 14-9.

8. Click OK.

Opening someone else's folder

It's fairly common for a team of people who work closely together to share calendars or task lists so they not only can see what the other people are doing, but also enter appointments on behalf of a teammate. For example, if you work in a company that has sales and service people sitting side by side. As a service person, you may find it helpful if your partner on the sales side is allowed to enter appointments with a client on your calendar while you're out dealing with other clients. To do that, your partner needs to open your Calendar folder.

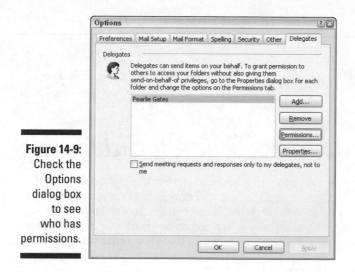

Figure 14-9:
Check the
Options
dialog box
to see
who has
permissions.

You can't open another person's Outlook folder unless that person has given you permission first, the way I describe in the preceding section. After you have permission, you can open the other person's folder by following these steps:

1. **Choose File⇨Open ⇨Other User's Folder.**

   The Open Other User's Folder dialog box appears, as shown in Figure 14-10.

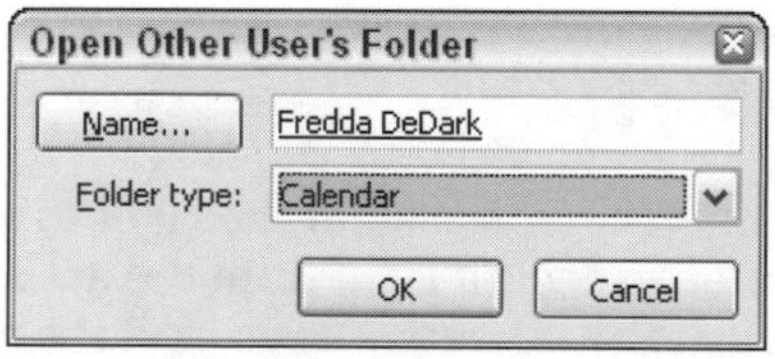

Figure 14-10:
Pick another
person's
folder to
view.

2. **Click the Name button.**

   The Select Name dialog box appears. (It's really the Address Book.)

3. **Double-click the name of the person whose folder you want to open.**

   The Select Name dialog box closes; the name you double-clicked appears in the Open Other User's Folder dialog box.

4. **Click the scroll-down button (triangle) on the Folder box.**

   A list of the Folders you can choose appears.

5. **Click the name of the folder you want to view.**

    The name of the folder you choose appears in the Folder box.

6. **Click OK.**

    The folder you pick now appears in your Folder List.

Viewing Two Calendars Side by Side

It's pretty common for an executive to give an assistant the right to view the executive's calendar. That way the assistant can maintain the executive's schedule while the executive is busy doing other things. Sometimes, when you're working as someone's assistant, you need to see both the boss's calendar and your own calendar simultaneously. If you have the required rights (permissions), Outlook can display both calendars side by side — and you can compare schedules at a glance.

After you've gone through the steps to open someone else's calendar, you'll see a section near the top of the Navigation Pane labeled Other Calendars. There you'll see the names of people whose calendars you've opened. If you click the check box next to one of those names, that person's calendar appears on-screen right next to yours. (Your screen might look pretty cluttered when you put two busy schedules side by side, so you may need to switch to a one-day view to keep the screen comprehensible.) When you're done viewing two schedules, click the box in the Navigation Pane next to the other person's name to go back to viewing one calendar.

Setting access permissions

Many times, a busy executive gives his or her assistant the right to view and even edit the executive's entire Outlook account right from the assistant's desk. That way, the assistant organizes what the executive does, and the executive just goes out and does the job. This is known as granting access permissions, which is a lot like naming a delegate, as I describe in a prior section "Giving delegate permissions." When you grant access permissions, however, the power you're giving is broader; you're giving the assistant permission to use the entire account and even to make your Outlook folders a part of your folder list.

Before people can open your schedule, you have to give them permission by following these steps:

1. **Right-click the Mailbox icon on the Navigation Pane.**

    A Shortcut menu appears. If the Mailbox icon doesn't appear in the Navigation Pane, choose Go➪Folder List (or press Ctrl+6) to make it appear.

2. Choose Properties.

The Properties dialog box appears.

3. Click the Permissions tab.

The Permissions page appears (as shown in Figure 14-11).

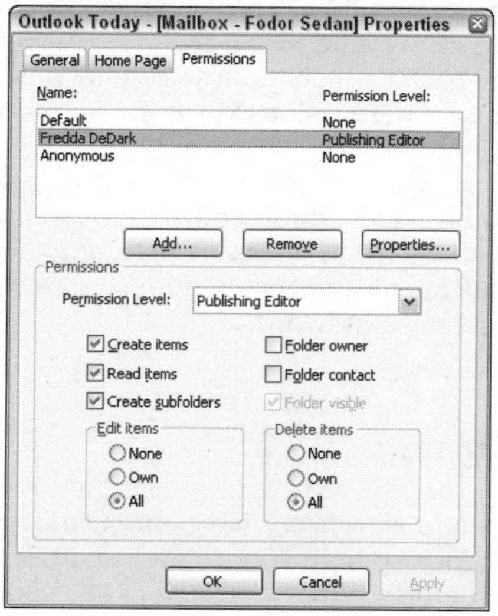

Figure 14-11:
You can grant permission for viewing your folders to anyone on your network.

4. Click the Add button.

The Add Users dialog box, which is really the Global Address List, appears.

5. Double-click the name of the person to whom you want to give access to your folders.

The name you double-click appears in the Add Users box on the right side of the Add Users dialog box.

6. Click OK.

The Add Users dialog box closes and the name you chose appears in the Name box of the Properties page.

7. Click the name that you just added to the Name list on the Properties dialog box.

The name you click is highlighted to show you've selected it.

8. Click the scroll-down button (triangle) on the Permission Level list.

A list of available Permission Levels appears. Assigning a Permission Level gives a specific set of rights to the person to whom the level is assigned. For example, an editor can add, edit, change, or remove items from your Outlook folders, whereas a reviewer can only read items.

9. **Pick the role you want to assign to the person you selected.**

The role you chose appears in the Roles box. The check boxes following the Roles box change to reflect the tasks that the person is permitted to perform.

10. **Click OK.**

Now that you've given a person permission to see your account as a whole, you must give permission to see each folder in the account individually. You can either follow these steps for each icon on the Navigation Pane, or you can see the section "Giving delegate permissions" to grant access to another person.

However, you have no way of knowing whether people have given you permission to view their data unless you try to open one of their folders (or unless they tell you), which prevents nasty hackers from breaking into several people's data by stealing just one password.

Viewing two accounts

If your boss gives you permission to view his or her entire Outlook account, you can set up your copy of Outlook so both your folders and the boss's folders show up in your Outlook folder list. When you want to see your calendar, click your calendar folder; when you want to see the boss's calendar, click the boss's calendar folder.

To add a second person's account to your view of Outlook, follow these steps:

1. **Right-click the Mailbox icon in the Navigation Pane.**

A Shortcut menu appears. If the Mailbox icon doesn't appear in the Navigation Pane, choose Go⇨Folder List (or press Ctrl+6) to make it appear.

2. **Choose Properties.**

The Properties dialog box appears.

3. **Click the Advanced button.**

The Microsoft Exchange Server dialog box appears.

4. **Click the Advanced tab.**

The Advanced page appears (as shown in Figure 14-12).

5. **Click Add.**

The Add Mailbox dialog box appears.

6. **Type the name of the person whose account you want to add.**

The name you type appears in the text box.

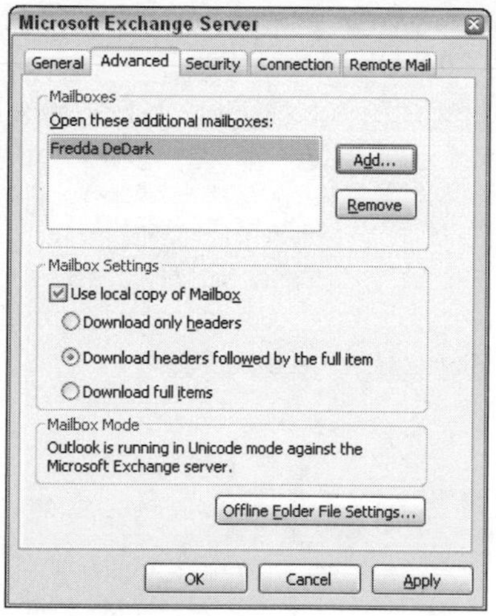

Figure 14-12:
Add
someone
else's
folders to
your Outlook
collection.

7. Click OK.

If the person you chose didn't give you permission, you'll get an error message saying that the name you entered couldn't be matched to a name in the address list. If that happens, make sure that the person you want to add really gave you the rights to his or her account.

After you add another person's account to Outlook, use the Folder List to see the new person's items. You'll see a new section in your Folder list called Mailbox, followed by the new person's name; that's where that person's Outlook items are located. When you click an icon in your Navigation Pane, you'll see your own Outlook items. If you like, you can create a new section in your Navigation Pane and add icons for the other person's items. See Chapter 2 for more about adding items to the Navigation Pane.

Assigning tasks

As Tom Sawyer could tell you, anything worth doing is worth getting someone else to do. Outlook on an Exchange network enables you to assign a task to another person in your company and keep track of that person's progress.

To assign a task to someone else, follow these steps:

1. Right-click an item in your task list.

A shortcut menu appears.

2. Choose Assign Task from the shortcut menu.

A Task form appears.

3. **Type the name of the person to whom you're assigning the task in the To box just as you would on an e-mail message.**

   The person's name appears in the To box (as shown in Figure 14-13).

4. **Click Send.**

   The task is sent to the person to whom you've assigned it.

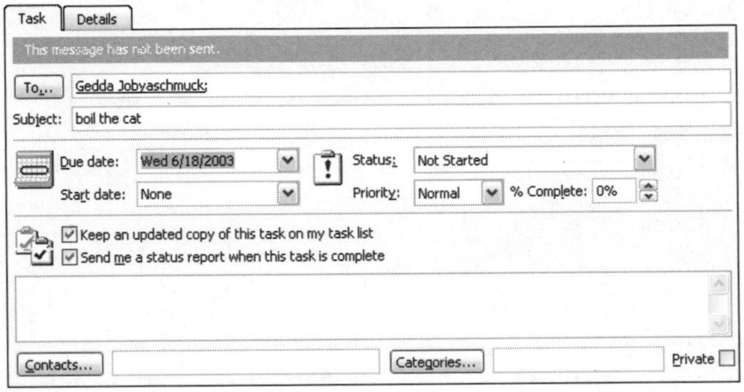

Figure 14-13:
When in
doubt, send
it out.

The person to whom you addressed the task will get an e-mail message with special buttons marked Accept and Decline, much like the special Meeting Request message that I discuss earlier in this chapter. When the person clicks Accept, the task is automatically added to his or her Task list in Outlook. If the person clicks Decline, that person is fired. Okay, just kidding, the person is not actually fired. Not yet, anyway.

Sending a status report

People who give out tasks really like the Assign Task feature. People who have to do those tasks are much less enthusiastic. If you're a Task Getter more often than you're a Task Giver, you have to look at the bright side: Outlook on an Exchange network can also help the boss stay informed about how much you're doing — and doing and doing!

You may have noticed that the task form has a box called Status and another called % Complete. If you keep the information in those boxes up-to-date, you can constantly remind the Big Cheese of your valuable contributions by sending status reports.

To send a status report, follow these steps:

1. **Double-click any task.**

   A Task form opens.

2. **Choose Actions⇨Send Status Report.**

   A To box appears, as in an e-mail message, and the name of the person who assigned the task already appears in the To box.

3. **Enter any explanation you want to send about the task in the text box at the bottom of the form.**

   The text that you type appears in the form.

4. **Click Send.**

You can send status reports as often as you like — weekly, daily, hourly. It's probably a good idea to leave enough time between status reports to complete some tasks.

About Address Books

Outlook still uses several different Address Books that are really part of Microsoft Exchange Server. The Address Books involve several separate, independent lists of names and e-mail addresses — it's pretty confusing. Microsoft simplified the issue of dealing with Address Books in Outlook 2002 and later versions, but that doesn't help if you use Outlook on a large corporate network. I'll try to help you make sense of it all, anyway.

The Outlook Contact list contains all kinds of personal information, whereas an Address Book focuses on just e-mail addresses. An Address Book can also deal with the nitty-gritty details of actually sending your message to people on your corporate e-mail system, especially if that system is Microsoft Exchange Server.

Here's the lowdown on your plethora of Address Books:

- ✔ **The Global Address List:** If you're using Outlook on a corporate network, the Global Address List, which your system administrator maintains, normally contains the names and e-mail addresses of all the people in your company. The Global Address List makes it possible to address an e-mail message to anybody in your company without having to look up the e-mail address.

- ✔ **The Outlook Address Book:** The Contacts Address Book is really the list of e-mail addresses from the Contact list. Outlook automatically creates the Contacts Address Book to enable you to add the names of people in your Contact list to a Personal Distribution List.

- ✔ **Additional Address Books:** If you create additional folders for Outlook contacts, those folders also become separate Address Books. Your system administrator can also create additional Address Books.

If you're lucky, you'll never see the Address Book. All the addresses of all the people you ever send e-mail to are listed in the Global Address List that some-body else maintains, such as on a corporate network. Under those circum-stances, Outlook is a dream. You don't need to know what an Address Book is most of the time — you just type the name of the person you're e-mailing in the To box of a message. Outlook checks the name for spelling and takes care of sending your message. You'd swear that a tiny psychic lives inside your computer who knows just what you need.

Under less-than-ideal conditions, when you try to send a message, Outlook either complains that it doesn't know how to send the message or can't figure out whom you're talking about. Then you have to mess with the address. That situation happens only when the address isn't listed in one of the Address Books or isn't in a form that Outlook understands. For these cases, you must either enter the full address manually or add your recipient's name and address to your Address Book.

Going Public with Public Folders

Another popular feature of Outlook on an Exchange network is the ability to use public folders. *Public folders* are places that a whole group of people can look at and add items to. You can have a public folder for tasks or contacts. You can also create a public folder that contains messages, a lot like your Inbox, except that everybody can add messages and read the same set of messages. Such an arrangement is often called a *bulletin board;* you post a message, someone replies to it, a third party then replies to both of you, and so on. It's a method of conducting a group conversation without having all the parties to the conversation available at the same time.

In Outlook, public folders look just like any other folders. A public folder may contain a Contact list that the entire company shares or a Tasks list that an entire department uses. You can set up a public discussion folder for an ongoing group conference about topics of interest to everyone sharing the folder, such as current company news. You can also use a public discussion folder to collect opinions about decisions that have to be made or as an intra-company classified ad system. You can organize as a folder any kind of infor-mation that you'd like to exchange among groups of people on your network.

When you click a public folder, you see a list of items that looks like a list of e-mail messages, except that all the messages are addressed to the folder rather than to a person. In a public folder, you can change your view of the items, add items, or reply to items that someone else entered.

Viewing a public folder

Your company may maintain a public folder for an ongoing online discussion about important issues in your business or as a company bulletin board for announcements about activities, benefits, and other news.

To view a public folder

1. **Choose Go⇨Folder List (or press Ctrl +6).**

   The Folder List appears (as shown in Figure 14-14).

2. **Click the name of the folder you want to see.**

   The list of items in the folder appears.

You can double-click the title of any item that you see to view the contents of that item.

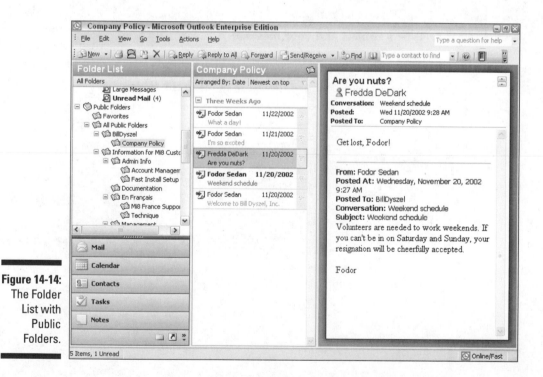

Figure 14-14:
The Folder List with Public Folders.

Adding new items

Many public folders are organized as open discussions in which anyone can put in his or her two cents' worth. All the messages can be read by anybody, so everybody reads and replies to everybody else. If you view a folder and find it's full of messages from different people all replying to one another, you're looking at a discussion folder.

To add new items to a public folder, follow these steps:

1. **Choose View⇨Folder List (or press Ctrl +6).**

   The Folder List appears.

2. **Click the name of the folder.**

   The list of messages in the folder appears.

3. **Choose File⇨New⇨Post in This Folder.**

   The New Item form appears (as shown in Figure 14-15).

4. **Type a subject and your message.**

5. **Click Post.**

Now your message is part of the list of items in the folder.

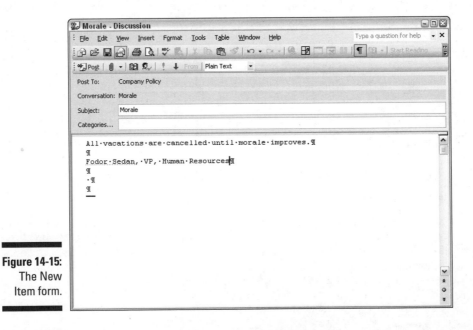

Figure 14-15:
The New
Item form.

Replying to items in an existing public discussion folder

Good manners and good sense say that if you want to join a discussion, the best thing to do is respond to what the other members of the discussion are saying. But be nice — don't flame. Posting nasty responses to people in an online discussion group is called *flaming*. Flaming is not well regarded but also is not uncommon. Flaming creates online conversations that most people don't want to participate in. What good is a discussion when nobody talks? Besides, flaming in the workplace can get you fired. So cool down.

When you're participating in public folder discussions at work, assume that everyone in the company — from the top executives to the newest temp — will read what you've written. Check your spelling, DON'T WRITE IN CAPITAL LETTERS (IT LOOKS LIKE YOU'RE SHOUTING), and use discretion in what you say and how you say it. The same rules apply to interoffice e-mail; you don't know who reads what you send.

To reply to items in a public discussion folder, follow these steps:

1. **Double-click the item to which you want to reply.**

   The item opens so you can read it.

2. **Click the Post button in the toolbar.**

   The Discussion Reply form appears. The text of the message to which you're replying is already posted in the form (as shown in Figure 14-16).

3. **Type your subject and reply.**

   Your reply appears in a different color than the original text.

4. **Click Post.**

Your item joins the list of discussion items.

Moving items to a public folder

Not all public folders are discussion folders. Public folders can be designed to hold any type of item. You can share lists of tasks, calendars, or files of other types. You don't have to create a public folder item in the folder where you want the item to end up. You can create a task in your own Tasks list, for example, and then move it to a public task folder.

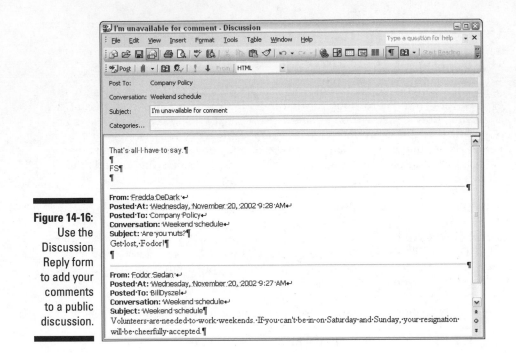

Figure 14-16:
Use the
Discussion
Reply form
to add your
comments
to a public
discussion.

To move items to a public folder, follow these steps:

1. **Right-click the item that you want to move.**

   A menu appears.

2. **Click Move to Folder.**

   A Move Items dialog box that includes the Folder List appears, as shown
   in Figure 14-17.

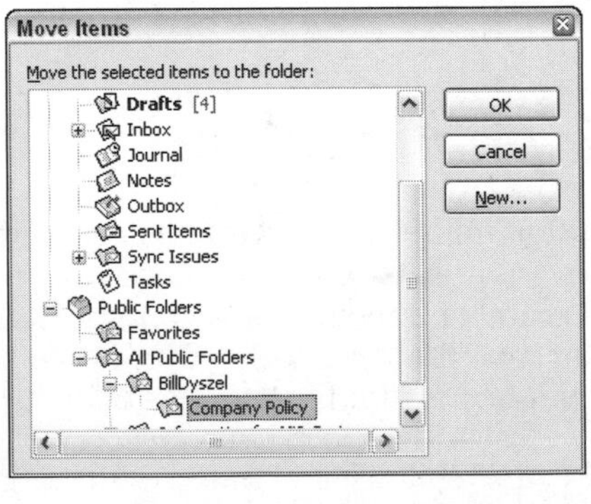

Figure 14-17:
Getting
ready to
move an
item to a
folder.

Outsourcing Microsoft Exchange

Even if you're allergic to buzzwords, the term *Outsourcing* still has its appeal. If you're an entrepreneur or freelancer, you know how distracted you can get with the details of running your business; you simply don't have time to fuss with the details of running an e-mail system such as Microsoft Exchange.

If you think you need the power of Microsoft Exchange but don't have time to deal with the details, plenty of companies out there are ready to provide Microsoft Exchange services to you at the drop of the hat. These companies are known as ASPs (application service providers); lots of them are standing by with Microsoft Exchange servers you can log on to for as little as $10.00 per person per month. I used a company called www.mi8.com for all the examples in this book. I can log on to their Web site and set up an e-mail and collaboration system in just a few minutes; I encourage you to check them out. If you'd like to shop around, you can find a list of other companies offering what they call *Hosted Exchange Service* at www.microsoft.com/serviceproviders/apphosting.

3. **Click the folder to which you want to send the item.**

   The name of the folder you clicked is highlighted.

4. **Click OK.**

   Your item moves to its new folder.

For the public record

You may be using public folders without even knowing it. In Outlook, all folders look the same, whether you create them yourself on your own PC or they're on a corporate network or the Internet. All you really need to know about public folders is that they're public, so anybody who has access to the public folder can see whatever you post to that public folder. You can also create your own public folders; check with your system administrator to see whether you have the rights to create public folders and a place to put them.

Using SharePoint Team Services

Microsoft actually provides more than one method of using Outlook to collaborate with other people. I spend the first part of this chapter describing Microsoft Exchange, the most powerful collaboration tool you can connect to Outlook. But a second product, called SharePoint Team Services, also connects to Outlook and also helps you collaborate.

SharePoint is basically an Internet tool that helps you coordinate meetings, projects, and activities with other people. Most of the work you do through SharePoint can be done only through your Web browser, but the latest version of SharePoint can also set up folders in Outlook that enable you to view key information from a SharePoint Web site even when you're not online. SharePoint does not tie into Outlook nearly as closely as Microsoft Exchange, but it does provide some collaboration features that you could use with people outside your office.

In most cases, you won't have a choice about whether to use Microsoft Exchange or SharePoint Team Services; someone else (such as your system administrators) will have decided that for you. In fact, you may need to use both products; Outlook connects to Exchange and SharePoint at the same time without any problem. Chances are, if you ever do get involved with SharePoint Team Services, you'll do so because someone asks you to join a shared team. If no one ever asks, you don't need to think about it, and you can skip this section.

Joining a SharePoint team

The first key to unlocking SharePoint will be an e-mail that asks you to join a SharePoint team. It'll simply be an ordinary e-mail message containing your user name, password, and a link to the SharePoint site. Simply click the link and log in with the name and password you received in the e-mail.

When you click the link that comes in the e-mail, your Web browser opens to a site devoted to the activities of the team you've been asked to join. Every SharePoint site looks different; click the links on the site to see what it has to offer.

Linking Outlook to SharePoint data

Certain parts of a SharePoint Web site can be tied into Outlook so the information from the site and automatically appears in Outlook. If you see an icon on the SharePoint Web side labeled "link to calendar" or "link to contacts,' you can just click that icon to send the information from that page straight to Outlook.

Viewing SharePoint data from Outlook

Information that SharePoint sends to Outlook shows up in its own set of folders. If you open your folder list by choosing Go⇨Folder List you see SharePoint folders near the bottom of the list. Just click any SharePoint folder to see what's inside. SharePoint folders normally contain either a calendar or contact list. You can view SharePoint information in Outlook exactly the same way you view Outlook calendar and contact information. But you can't add new items to SharePoint folders through Outlook; you can add information to SharePoint only through your Web browser.

Updating SharePoint Information from Outlook

Don't be deceived when you look at SharePoint folders in Outlook. The information you find in these folders is not automatically updated in Outlook; you have to link back to the SharePoint Web site to have updated data appear. For the quickest way to make the update happen, follow these steps:

1. **In Outlook, right-click the SharePoint folder that you want to update and choose Open in Web Browser from the pop-up menu that appears.**

2. **Click the relevant icon (either Link to Calendar or Link to Contacts) when it appears on-screen.**

So when are you most likely to run across SharePoint, and when will you use Exchange? In my opinion, Exchange is best suited for collaboration among people who share the same e-mail system, while SharePoint is better suited for people who need to collaborate but don't share the same e-mail system. For example, suppose you work in a small law firm where everyone's e-mail comes to a similar-looking e-mail address, such as john.doe@smalllaw.com. In this situation, your best bet for working with people inside the firm is to collaborate via Exchange. If you're also a member of the local bar association, you might take advantage of SharePoint for organizing your chapter's meetings and other activities through the association's Web site. To find out more about SharePoint Team Services, visit www.SharePointsample.com.

Chapter 15

Keeping Secrets Safe with Outlook Security

In This Chapter

▶ Getting a Digital ID

▶ Sending a signed message

▶ Encrypting a message

*I*n the movies, computer hackers know everything — your credit card balance, Social Security numbers, what you bought at the grocery store — everything. There doesn't seem to be a single scrap of personal information that a computer hacker in a movie can't find out.

Are real-life computer hackers just as brilliant and dangerous? Not really. Most crimes involving theft of personal information don't come from hackers sneaking into personal computers. More often than not, these losers dig credit-card slips out of a restaurant dumpster, or they just make a phone call and trick some poor slob into revealing a password.

Even though there isn't some hacker out there who knows what you bought at the Piggly Wiggly (or cares, for that matter), it may be wise to think about security when it comes to your e-mail and personal information. If you work in a corporation, you may be required by law to maintain certain standards of security over the messages you send and receive.

Outlook includes features that enable you to keep your secrets secret, keep your identity secure, and to be sure that the messages you receive actually came from the people who seem to have sent them. In most cases, you'll need to add some small program to Outlook to enable these advanced security features, but once you've installed these features you never have to fuss with them again.

If security is a really big deal to you (as it is to people in the finance, law-enforcement, and defense industries), you may want to look into the more sophisticated security systems starting to turn up. Several high-tech companies offer systems for confirming identity and ensuring message security, using fingerprint readers, eye scanners, and even gizmos that can recognize your face. Although many such systems can hook right into Outlook to make short work of message security, most of them cost quite a bit more than the average person needs to spend. In this chapter, I stick to discussing the security features that Outlook offers right out of the box.

Getting a Digital ID

You probably receive messages every day from people you've never met. And I'll bet you don't spend much time wondering whether the messages you receive actually come from the people they seem to be — but you might need to think about that from time to time. After all, it's possible for sneaky hackers to send out e-mail messages that appear to come from someone else. So how can you tell them the message actually came from the person who appears to have sent it? Of course, if you know the senders personally, you can simply phone them to verify that what you received is what they sent. But a quicker, high-tech approach is to use what's called a *digital signature* — a tiny piece of secret code mixed in with your message to prove three things:

- ✔ That the message really comes from the person who seems to have sent it.

- ✔ That the person who seems to have sent the message really is the person he or she claims to be.

- ✔ That the person who sent the message sent it intentionally and not by mistake. It's like putting your signature on a check; it shows that you really mean to send a specific message.

If you want to take advantage of Outlook's security features, the first step to take is to get yourself a Digital ID. If you work in a large organization, your employer may obtain that for you — and your local computer gurus may have installed all the software — in which case, you can skip these steps. If you want to get a Digital ID for your own use, you can get one from one of the many companies that issue and maintain Digital ID services by following these steps:

1. **Click Tools⇨Options.**

   The Options dialog box appears.

2. **Click the Security tab.**

   The Security page appears (as shown in Figure 15-1).

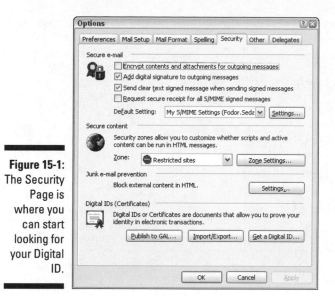

Figure 15-1:
The Security
Page is
where you
can start
looking for
your Digital
ID.

3. **Click the button labeled "Get a digital ID."**

   A Microsoft Web site opens, offering you a range of choices for obtaining a Digital ID.

Quite a few companies offer Digital IDs — some for free, others for a fee. The range of companies offering this service varies over time; your best bet is to check the Web site to see which you prefer. After you pick a provider for your Digital ID, you fill out a number of forms and pick a password for the ID. You'll also need to exchange several e-mails with a provider of the Digital ID; that's how you prove that your e-mail address is really yours.

Sending Digitally Signed Messages

Once you have a Digital ID, the simplest thing you can do is to send someone a message containing your Digital Signature. A Digitally Signed message does more than simply assure your recipient that you are really yourself — who else would you want to be, after all? — but suppose you wanted to send an encrypted message that only your recipient can read. To do so, you have to send at least one Digitally Signed message first so Outlook can capture details about your Digital ID.

Once you've obtained a Digital ID, you can send a message with a Digital Signature by following these steps:

1. **While creating a message, click the options button on the message toolbar.**

   The options dialog box appears.

2. **Click the button labeled Security Settings.**

   The Security Properties dialog box appears (as shown in Figure 15-2).

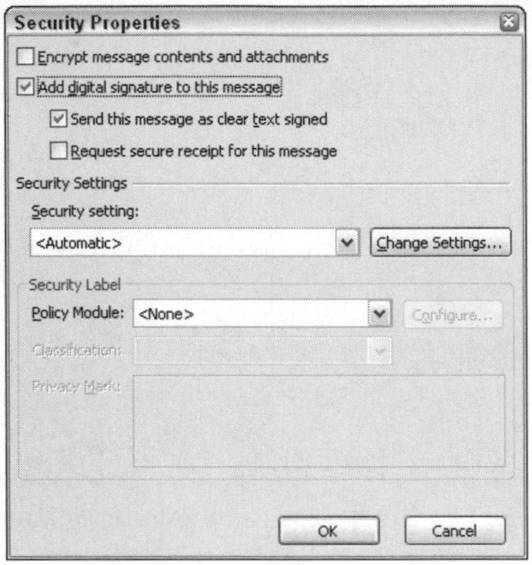

Figure 15-2:
The Security Properties dialog box enables you to sign messages one at a time.

3. **Click the check box labeled "Add Digital Signature to this message."**

   A check mark appears in the box to show that you've selected it.

4. **Click Send.**

   A dialog box labeled Signing Data with Your Private Exchange Key appears (as in Figure 15-3).

Figure 15-3:
You'll have to wait a few seconds while Outlook applies a digital autograph.

5. Click OK.

Your message is sent.

Adding a digital signature slows down the process of sending a message somewhat because your computer has to check with the computer that issued your Digital ID to verify your signature. But because Outlook does check your Digital ID, your recipient can be sure that your message really came from you and that's the whole point of digital signatures.

You can also set up Microsoft outlook to attach a digital signature to every message you send, if you like. Just choose Tools➪Options, choose the Security tab, and then click the text labeled "Add digital signature to outgoing messages." In some industries, you may be required to add digital signatures to every outgoing message — but for most people, that's probably overkill.

Receiving Digitally Signed Messages

When you receive a message that contains a digital signature, you'll see a little icon in the upper-right corner of the message that looks like a little red prize ribbon you'd win at the county fair for the best peach preserves. Figure 15-4 shows it affixed to a message.

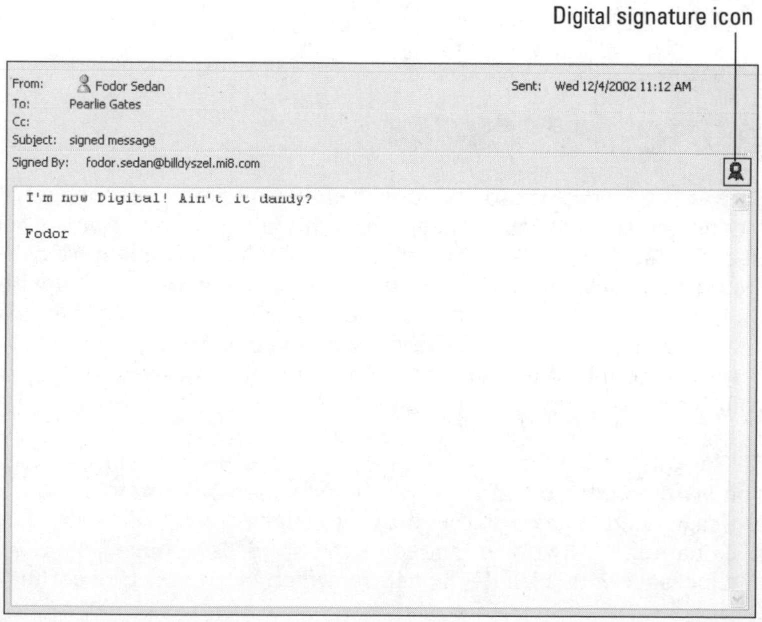

Digital signature icon

From:	🔒 Fodor Sedan		Sent:	Wed 12/4/2002 11:12 AM
To:	Pearlie Gates			
Cc:				
Subject:	signed message			
Signed By:	fodor.sedan@billdyszel.mi8.com			🎗

```
I'm now Digital! Ain't it dandy?

Fodor
```

Figure 15-4: That red ribbon tells you that the message is digitally signed.

You don't really need to do anything when you get a message like that; the icon itself verifies that the message really came from the person it claims to have come from. But if you're unusually curious, you can find out more about the person who signed the message by clicking the icon and reading the dialog box that appears (see Figure 15-5). What you'll see should simply confirm what you already know; the person who sent the message is exactly who they say they are, the genuine article, the Real McCoy.

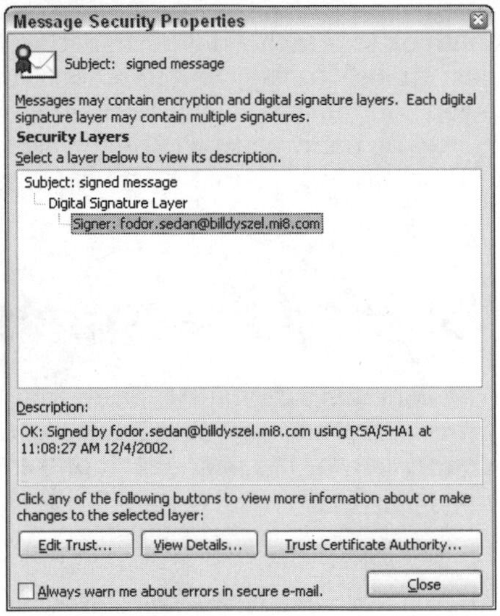

Figure 15-5:
To get the lowdown on someone's digital signature, right-click the red ribbon icon.

Encrypting Messages

Back in the days of radio, millions of children loved to exchange "secret" messages that they encoded with Little Orphan Annie's Secret Decoder Ring. Outlook does something similar, using a feature called Encryption. Unfortunately, you don't get a colorful plastic ring with Outlook. On the other hand, you don't have to save your box tops to get one — the decoder is built right into Outlook. When you encrypt a message, your system scrambles the contents of your outgoing message so that only your intended recipient can read your message.

Before you can send someone an encrypted message using Outlook's encryption feature, both you and the person to whom you're sending your encrypted message need to have obtained a Digital Certificate, as I describe earlier in this chapter. Also, your intended recipient needs to have sent you at least one message with a Digital Signature, which I also describe earlier, so that

Outlook recognizes that person as someone you can trust. Outlook can be pretty suspicious; even your mother can't send you an encrypted message unless you've sent her your Digital Signature first. Can you imagine? Your own mother! But I digress. If you want to send an encrypted message to someone who meets all the requirements, follow these steps:

1. **While creating a message, click the Options button on the Message toolbar.**

   The Options dialog box appears.

2. **Click the button labeled Security Settings.**

   The Security Properties dialog box appears.

3. **Click the check box labeled "Encrypt message contents and attachments."**

   A check mark appears in the box to show you've selected it.

4. **Click Send.**

   A dialog box labeled "Signing data with your Private Exchange Key" appears.

5. **Click OK.**

   Your message is sent.

When you receive an encrypted message, the contents of the message don't appear in the Reading Pane; you have to double-click the message to open it. In fact, if you work in a big organization, your network may deliver the message to you as an attachment to a serious-sounding message warning you that encrypted messages can't be scanned for viruses.

Other Security Programs for Outlook

Lots of people are concerned about the security of the information they send by e-mail, so lots of companies offer products to help people feel more secure. Many of the products you can buy to secure and encrypt your messages are so powerful, it's not legal to take them out of the United States. Some of the best-known vendors of add-on security products for Outlook include these:

PGP Corporation (www.pgp.com)

RSA Corporation (www.rsa.com)

Baltimore Technologies, Inc. (www.baltimore.com)

Chapter 16

See It Your Way: Organizing and Customizing Outlook

A fancy term for the arrangement of screens, menus, and doodads on your computer is the *user interface*. The people who write computer programs spend lots of time and money trying to figure out how best to arrange stuff on the screen to make a program like Outlook easy to figure out and use.

But one person's dream screen can be another person's nightmare. Some people like to read words on the screen that say what to do, other people like colorful icons with pictures to click. Other people prefer to see information in neat rows and columns; still others like to see their information arranged more (shall we say) *informally*.

Outlook enables you to display your information in an endless variety of arrangements and views. There's even a button labeled "Organize" that shows you what choices are available for slicing and dicing the information you've saved in Outlook. This chapter shows you many of the best steps you can take after you click the Organize button.

Hitting the Organize Button

You can get a feel for how many ways Outlook can help organize your information by clicking the Organize button in the toolbar, or by choosing

Tools➪Organize. (Wow. If only we had one of those buttons in real life.) If you can't figure out which icon in the toolbar is the Organize button, you'll see it pictured in the Tools menu next to the word *Organize*.

When you click the Organize button, a new section appears in Outlook's main screen, showing you which tools are available to organize the information in the module you're using. The tools that tidy up your e-mail, for example, are different from the tools you use to straighten out your calendar.

Two tools show up in the Organize window no matter what Outlook module you're using — Folders and Views. The most common way that people use folders is for organizing e-mail, so I cover folders, along with other e-mail management tools, in Chapter 6.

Types of Views

Choosing a view is like renting a car. You can choose a model with the features you want, regardless whether the car is a convertible, minivan, or luxury sedan. All cars are equipped with different features — radios, air conditioning, power cup holders, and so on — that you can use (or not use) as you please. Some rental agencies offer unlimited free mileage. Outlook views are much more economical, though. In fact, they're free.

Every module in Outlook has its own selection of views. The Calendar has (among others) a view that looks calendar-like. The Contacts module includes a view that looks like an address card. The Tasks module includes a Timeline view. All modules enable you to use at least one type of Table view, which organizes your data in the old-fashioned row-and-column arrangement.

Each type of view is organized to make something about your collection of information obvious at first glance. You can change the way that you view a view by sorting, filtering, or grouping.

You don't have to do anything to see a view; Outlook is *always* displaying a view. The view is the thing that takes up most of the screen most of the time. The view (or the Information Viewer, in official Microsoftese) is one of only two parts of Outlook that you can't turn off. (You also can't turn off the menu bar.) Most people don't even know that they have a choice of Outlook views; they just use the views that show up the first time they use Outlook. So now you're one step ahead of the game.

Each view has a name, which you can see in several different places:

  ✔ When you click the Organize button and choose Views, the name of the view that's currently on the screen is highlighted.

- Sometimes the list of available views also appears in the Navigation Pane, but not always.

- If all else fails, you can always refer to the Current View menu, where a mark appears next to the name of whichever view you're using.

To see the Current View menu, choose View➪Arrange By➪Current View. The Current View menu lists all the views available to you in the module you're using.

Table/List view

All modules contain some version of the *Table view* — a rectangle made up of rows and columns. Some Outlook menus also refer to this arrangement as a *List View*. In either case, if you create a new item by adding a new task to your Tasks list, for example, a new row turns up in the Table view. You see one row for each task in the Table view (as shown in Figure 16-1).

The names of Table views often contain the word *list,* as in Simple List, Phone List, or just List. That word means they form a plain-vanilla table of items, just like a grocery list. Other Table view names start with the word *By,* which means that items in the view are grouped by a certain type of information, such as entry type or name of contact. I discuss grouped views later in the chapter and show you how to group items your own way.

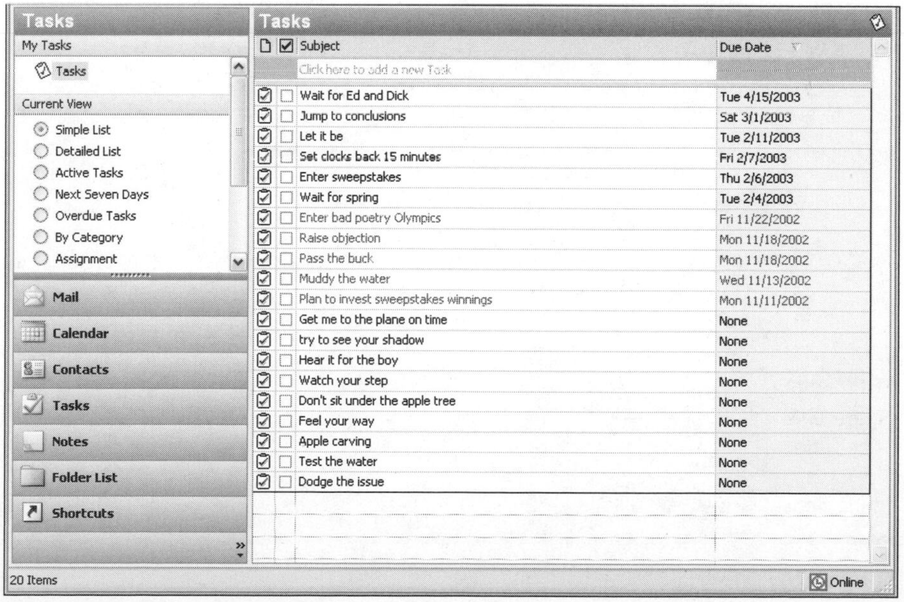

Figure 16-1: The Tasks module in a Table view.

Icons view

Icons view is the simplest view — just a bunch of icons with names thrown together on-screen (as in Figure 16-2).

The only Icons views that come with Outlook are for viewing notes and file folders. Icons view doesn't show a great deal of information, and some people like it that way. I like to see more detailed information, so I stay with Table views. There's nothing wrong with using Icons view most of the time; you can easily switch to another view if you ever need to see more.

Timeline view

Timeline views show you a set of small icons arranged across the screen. Icons higher on the screen represent items that were created or tasks that were begun earlier in the day. Icons farther to the left were created on an earlier date (see Figure 16-3).

The Task Timeline in the Tasks module also draws a line that represents the length of time needed to perform a task if its starting and ending times were specified previously.

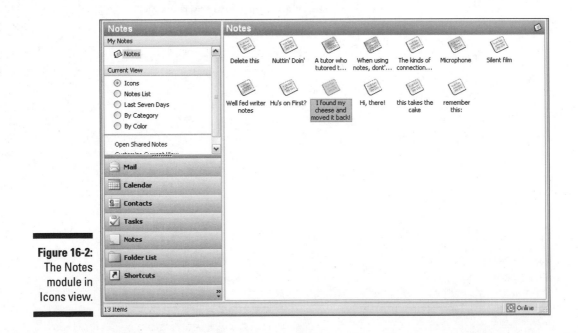

Figure 16-2:
The Notes module in Icons view.

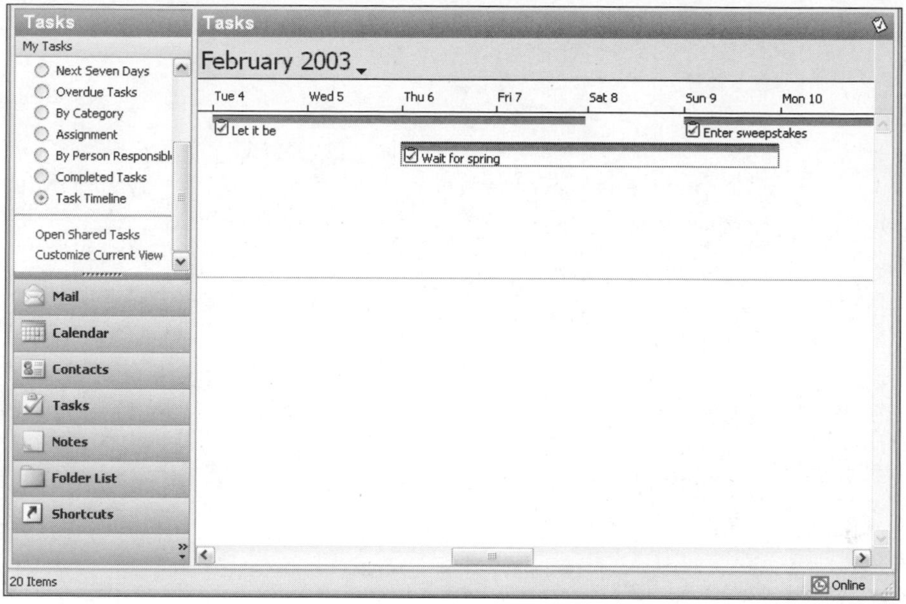

Figure 16-3:
Tasks
arranged in
the Timeline
view.

A Timeline view includes four toolbar buttons that enable you to change the length of time you want to view. Your choices are Today, Day (not necessarily today), Week, and Month. As you can in all other view settings, you can click to move between one-day and seven-day views and back (it's like changing television channels, but you don't have to argue over who gets the remote).

Card view

Card views are designed for the Contacts module. Each Contact item gets its own little block of information (see Figure 16-4). Each little block displays a little or a lot of information about the item, depending on what kind of card it is. (See Chapter 7 for more about the different views in the Contacts module.)

The Address Cards view shows you only a few items at a time because the cards are so big. To make it easier to find a name in your Contacts list that you don't see on-screen, type the first letter of the name that your contact is filed under. Before you know it, you see that person's address card.

Day/Week/Month view

Day/Week/Month view is another specialized view, designed particularly for the Calendar.

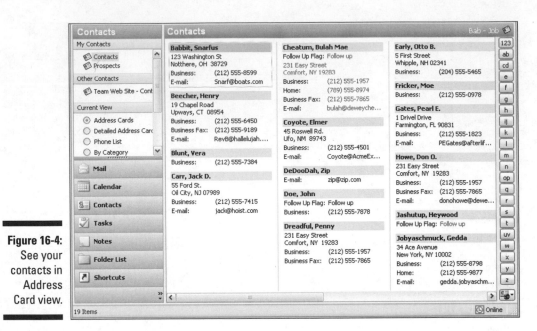

Figure 16-4:
See your
contacts in
Address
Card view.

Like a Timeline view, Day/Week/Month view adds Day, Work Week, Week, and Month buttons to the toolbar to enable you to switch between views easily. The Day, Work Week, and Week views also display a monthly calendar. You can click any date in the monthly calendar to switch your view to that date (as shown in Figure 16-5).

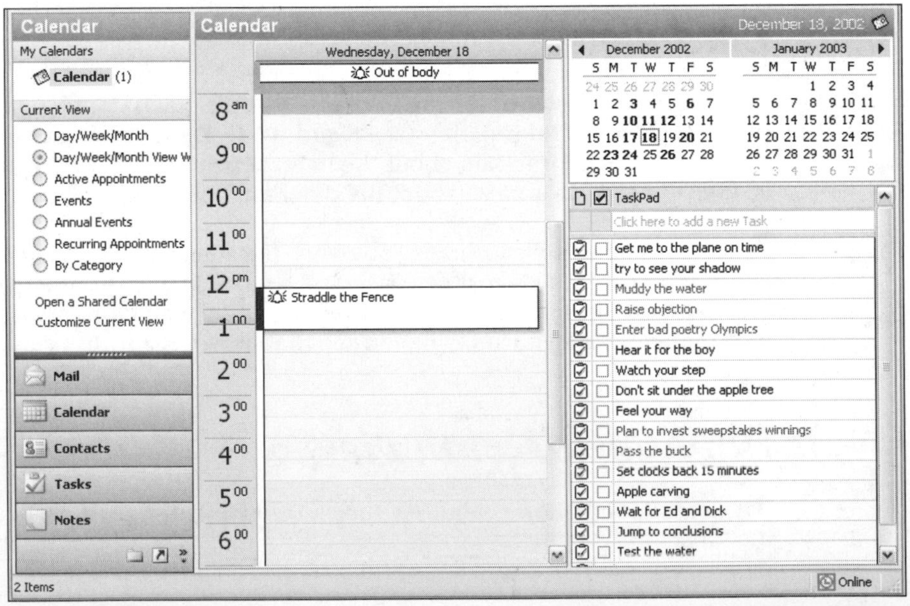

Figure 16-5:
Starting a
day in the
life of your
Calendar.

Playing with Columns in Table or List View

Table views (or List views) show you the most detailed information about the items that you've created; these views also enable you to organize the information in the greatest number of ways with the least effort. Okay, Table views look a little dull, but they get you where you need to go.

Table views are organized in columns and rows. Each row displays information for one item — one appointment in your Calendar, one task in your Tasks list, or one person in your Contacts list. Adding a row is easy. Just add a new item by pressing Ctrl+N, and then fill in the information you want for that item. Getting rid of a row is easy, too. Just delete the item: Select the item by clicking it with your mouse, and then press the Delete key.

The columns in a Table view show you pieces of information about each item. Most Outlook modules can store far more pieces of information about an item than you can display on-screen in row-and-column format. The Contacts list, for example, holds more than 90 pieces of information about every person in your list. If each person were represented by one row, you would need more than 90 columns to display everything.

Adding a column

Outlook starts you out with a limited number of columns in the Phone List view of your Contacts list. (Remember that the names of Table views usually have the word *list* in them somewhere.) If you want more columns, you can easily add some. You can display as many columns as you want in Outlook, but you may have to scroll across the screen to see the information that you want to see.

To add a column in any Table view, follow these steps:

1. **Right-click the title of any column in the gray header row of the column.**

   A shortcut menu appears.

2. **Pick Field Chooser from the shortcut menu.**

   The Field Chooser dialog box appears.

3. **Select the type of field that you want to add.**

   The words *Frequently-Used Fields* appear in the text box at the top of the Field Chooser. Those words mean that the types of fields most people like to add are already listed. If the name of the field you want to add isn't listed in one of the gray boxes at the bottom of the Field Chooser dialog box, you can pull down the menu that Frequently-Used Fields is part of and see what's available.

4. Drag the field into the table.

Be sure to drag the new item to the top row of the table, where the heading names are (as in Figure 16-6).

Notice that the names in the Field Chooser are in the same kind of gray box as the headers of each column of your table. (If they look alike, they must belong together, like Michael and Lisa Marie. Right? . . . well, okay, maybe that's not the best example.) Two red arrows appear to show you where your new field will end up when you drop it off.

Moving a column

Moving columns is even easier than adding columns. Just drag the heading of the column to where you want it (see Figure 16-7).

Two little red arrows appear as you're dragging the heading to show you where the column will end up when you release the mouse button.

Figure 16-6: The Requested By field is dragged to the top row of the table.

Figure 16-7:
Moving the
Business
Phone
column.

Formatting a column

Some fields contain too much information to fit in their columns. Dates are prime offenders. Outlook normally displays dates in this format: `Sun 7/4/05 4:14 PM`. I normally don't care which day of the week a date falls on, so I reformat the column to `7/4/05 4:14 PM` and save the other space for something that I really want to know.

To change the formatting of a column, follow these steps:

1. **Right-click the heading of a column.**

   A menu appears.

2. **Choose Format Columns.**

   The Format Columns dialog box appears (as shown in Figure 16-8).

3. **Choose a format type from the Format menu.**

   Pick whatever suits your fancy. Some columns contain information that can be formatted only one way, such as names and categories. Information in number columns (especially dates) can be formatted in a variety of ways.

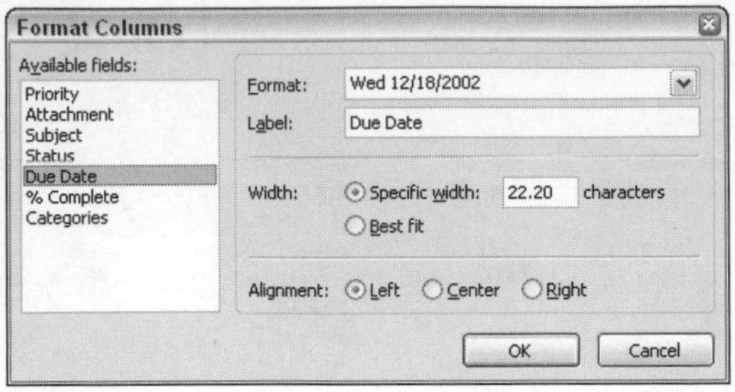

Format Columns

Available fields:		
Priority	Format:	Wed 12/18/2002
Attachment	Label:	Due Date
Subject		
Status		
Due Date	Width:	⦿ Specific width: 22.20 characters
% Complete		○ Best fit
Categories		
	Alignment:	⦿ Left ○ Center ○ Right

OK   Cancel

Figure 16-8:
The Format
Columns
dialog box.

4. **Click OK.**

Your column is reformatted.

Changing a column format affects only that column in that view of that module. If you want to change the formats of other views and modules, you have to change them one at a time.

Widening or shrinking a column

Widening or shrinking a column is even easier than moving a column. Here's how:

1. **Move the mouse pointer to the right edge of the column that you want to widen or shrink until the pointer becomes a two-headed arrow.**

   Making that mouse pointer turn into a two-headed arrow takes a bit of dexterity. If you find the procedure to be difficult, you can use the Format Column procedure that I describe in the preceding section. Type a number in the Width box — bigger numbers for wider boxes and smaller numbers for narrower boxes.

2. **Drag the edge of the column until the column is the width that you desire.**

   The two-headed arrow creates a thin line that you can drag to resize the column. (Figure 16-9 shows a column being widened.) What you see is what you get.

If you're not really sure how wide a column needs to be, just double-click the right edge of the column header. When you double-click that spot, Outlook does a trick called *size-to-fit,* which widens or narrows a column to exactly the size of the widest piece of data in the column.

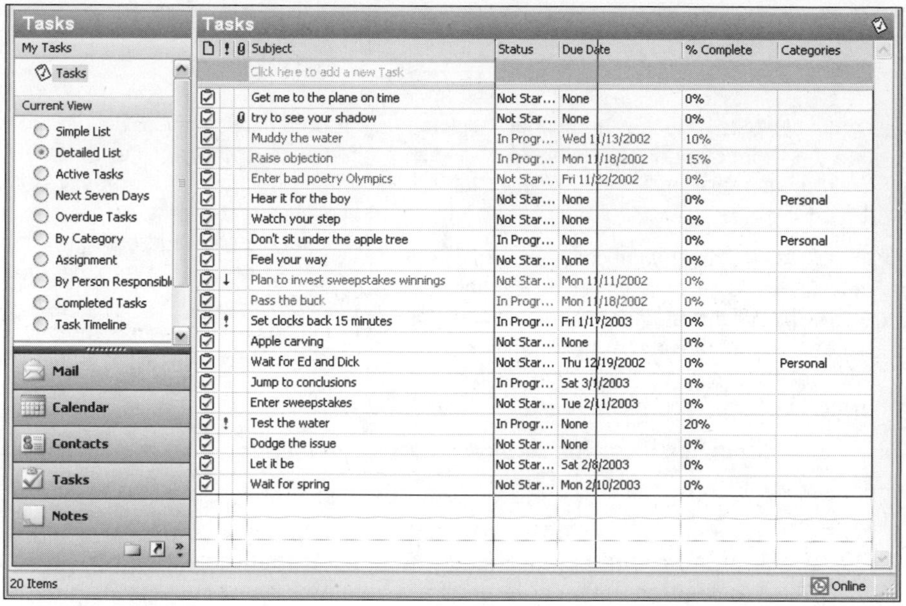

Figure 16-9:
Widening
the Status
column.

Removing a column

You can remove columns that you don't want to look at. To remove a column, follow these steps:

1. **Right-click the heading of the column that you want to remove.**

   A menu appears.

2. **Choose Remove This Column.**

   Zap! It's gone!

Don't worry too much about deleting columns. When you zap a column, the field remains in the item. You can use the column-adding procedure (which I describe earlier in this chapter) to put it back. If you're confused by this whole notion of columns and fields, see the sidebar "Columns = fields" elsewhere in this chapter.

Sorting

Sorting just means putting your list in order. In fact, a list is always in some kind of order. Sorting just changes the order.

Columns = fields

I promised to tell you how to add a column, and now I'm telling you about fields. What gives? Well, columns are fields, see? No? Well, think of it this way:

In your checkbook, your check record has a column of the names of the people to whom you wrote checks and another column that contains the amounts of those checks. When you actually write a check, you write the name of the payee in a certain field on the check; the amount

goes in a different field. So you enter tidbits of information as fields on the check, but you show them as columns in the check record. That's exactly how it works in Outlook. You enter somebody's name, address, and phone number in fields when you create a new item, but the Table view shows the same information to you in columns. When you're adding a column, you're adding a field. Same thing.

You can tell what order your list is sorted in by looking for triangles in headings. A heading with a triangle in it means that the entire list is sorted by the information in that column. If the column has numbers in it, and if the triangle's large side is at the top, the list begins with the item that has the largest number in that column, followed by the item that has the next-largest number, and so on, ending with the smallest number. Columns that contain text get sorted in alphabetical order. *A* is the smallest letter, and *Z* is the largest.

From Table view

To sort from Table view, click the heading of a column you want to sort. The entire table is sorted according to the column you clicked — by date, name, or whatever.

This is by far the easiest way to sort a table.

From the Sort dialog box

Although clicking a column is the easiest way to sort, doing so enables you to sort on only one column. You may want to sort on two or more columns.

To sort on two or more columns, follow these steps:

1. **Choose View⇨Arrange By ⇨Current View⇨Customize Current View.**

   The Customize View dialog box appears.

2. **Click the Sort button.**

   The Sort dialog box appears.

3. **From the Sort Items By menu, choose the first field that you want to sort by.**

   Choose carefully; a much larger list of fields is in the list than is usually in the view. It's confusing.

4. **Choose Ascending or Descending sort order.**

   That means to choose whether to sort from smallest to largest or largest to smallest.

5. **Repeat Steps 3 and 4 for each additional field that you want to sort.**

   As the dialog box implies, the first thing that you select is the most important. The entire table is sorted according to that field — and then by the fields you pick later, in the order in which you select them.

   If you sort your phone list by company first and then by name, for example, your list begins with the names of the people who work for a certain company, displayed alphabetically, followed by the names of the people who work for another company, and so on.

6. **Click OK.**

   Your list is sorted.

Grouping

Sorting and grouping are similar. Both procedures organize items in your table according to the information in one of the columns. Grouping is different from sorting, however; it creates bunches of similar items that you can open or close. You can look at only the bunches that interest you and ignore all the other bunches.

For example, when you balance your checkbook, you probably *sort* your checks by check number. At tax time, you *group* your checks; you make a pile of the checks for medical expenses, another pile of checks for charitable deductions, and another pile of checks for the money that you invested in *For Dummies* books. Then you can add up the amounts that you spent in each category and enter those figures in your tax return.

Grouping views with a few mouse clicks

The quickest way to group items is to right-click the heading of the column you want to group by, and then choose Group by This Field. The Group By box automatically appears, and the name of the field you chose automatically appears in the Group By box. Isn't that slick?

Grouping views with drag-and-drop

The next simplest way to group items is to open the Group By box and drag a column heading into it (as in Figure 16-10).

Here's how you group items by dragging and dropping a column heading:

1. **Open the Advanced toolbar by choosing View⇨Toolbars⇨Advanced.**

    The Advanced toolbar appears, displaying the Group By Box button, normally the third button from the right. The Group By Box button contains an icon that looks like a box with some lines in it.

2. **Click the Group By Box button on the Advanced toolbar.**

    The table drops down slightly, and a box appears above the table, proclaiming Drag a column header here to group by that column.

3. **Drag to the Group By box the header of the column that contains the data you want to group by.**

    You can drag several fields up to the Group By box to create groups based on more than one column. (Figure 16-11 shows an example using two.)

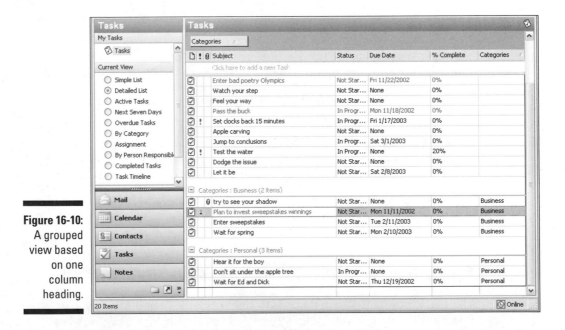

Figure 16-10: A grouped view based on one column heading.

Figure 16-11: Your Contacts list grouped by two headings — State and Category.

Using the Group By dialog box

Just as you have a second way to sort your listing, you have a second way to group your listing. Just use the Group By dialog box.

To group your list, follow these steps:

1. **Choose View⇨Arrange By⇨Current View⇨Customize Current View.**

   The Customize View dialog box appears. If you see the words `Customize Current View` in the Navigation Pane, you can also click those words to open the View Summary Dialog box.

2. **Click the Group By button.**

   The Group By dialog box appears (as in Figure 16-12).

3. **Choose the first field that you want to group the view by.**

   The list has more fields than are showing in the table. If you choose to group by a field that's not showing in your table, you can check the Show Field in View check box, as shown in Figure 16-12.

   You may also want to choose whether you want your groups to be sorted in Ascending or Descending alphabetical order, although that's less important when you're grouping.

Group By

☐ Automatically group according to arrangement

Group items by

| State ▾ | ● Ascending |
| ☑ Show field in view | ○ Descending |

[OK]

[Cancel]

[Clear All]

Then by

(none) ▾ | ● Ascending
| Descending

Callback
Car Phone
Categories
Company
Company Main Phone
Contacts

Then by

(none) ▾ | ● Ascending
| Descending

☐ Show field in view

Then by

(none) ▾ | ● Ascending
| Descending

☐ Show field in view

Select available fields from:

| Frequently-used fields ▾ |

Expand/collapse defaults:

| All expanded ▾ |

Figure 16-12:
The Group
By dialog
box with the
Show Field
in View box
checked.

4. **Choose any other fields by which you want to group the view.**

    If you group by too many columns, your list will be harder rather than easier to use.

5. **Click OK.**

    Your list is grouped by as many fields as you want to use for the purpose.

If you've ever used the Search and Replace feature in Microsoft Word, you might wish you could do the same trick in Outlook. Unfortunately, Outlook doesn't really have a search and replace function — but you can take advantage of Grouped views to change lots of information quickly. For example, if you know lots of people who work for a certain company and that company changes its name, you can change the company name for all your contacts at that company by using a grouped view. Just go to your Contacts list, change one person's record to reflect the new company name, then choose the By Company view. The person whose record you changed will be in a different group than all the others. Drag the names of people grouped under the old company name to the new company section, and they'll all get changed automatically.

Viewing grouped items

A grouped view shows you the names of the columns that you used to create the group view. If you click the Contacts icon and choose By Company view (which is a grouped view), you see gray bars with an icon at the right. The word *Company* appears next to the icon because that's the column that the view is grouped on. A company name appears next to the word Company; the grouped view includes a gray bar for each company in the list.

The icon at the left end of the gray bar is either a plus sign or a minus sign. A plus sign means that there's more to be seen. Click the plus sign, and the group opens, revealing the other items that belong to the group. A minus sign means that there's nothing more to see; what you see is what you get in that group.

If you click the gray bar itself but not the icon, you select the entire group. You can delete the group if you select the gray bar and press the Delete key. When a group bar is selected, it's dark gray rather than light gray, like all the others.

Viewing headings only

You can click the plus and minus signs one at a time to open and close individual groups, or you can open or close all the groups simultaneously.

To open or close groups, follow these steps:

1. **Simply choose View⇨Expand/Collapse Groups.**

   I think Expanding and Collapsing are dramatic words for what you're doing with these groups. It's not like Scarlett O'Hara getting the vapors; it's just hiding or revealing the contents of a group or all the groups.

2. **To open a single group that you've selected, choose Collapse This Group or Expand This Group.**

3. **To expand or collapse all the groups, choose Expand All or Collapse All.**

What could be easier?

Saving Custom Views

If you're used to saving documents in your word processor, you're familiar with the idea of saving views. When you make any of the changes to a view that I describe earlier in this chapter, you can save the changes as a new view, or make the changes the new way to see the current view. If you plan to use a certain view repeatedly, it's worth saving.

You can save any view you like by using the Define Views dialog box. Choose View⇨Arrange by⇨Current View⇨Define Views and follow the prompts. When you're comfortable with Outlook, you may want to give the Define Views method a try, but I think that you can do almost anything you want just by changing the views you already have.

A Bridge from the Views

You can create an endless number of ways to organize and view the information that you save in Outlook. How you decide to view information depends on what kind of information you have and how you plan to use what you have. You can't go too wrong with views, because you can easily create new views if the old ones get messed up. So feel free to experiment.

Customizing Outlook Menus and Toolbars

You can customize Outlook's menus and toolbars to display a button for nearly any task that you use Outlook to do repeatedly. You also may want to make the Standard toolbar a little more advanced by adding one or two of your favorite tools from the Advanced toolbar. Customizing the toolbar is as easy as dragging and dropping, if you know where to start dragging. Here's what to do:

1. **Choose View➪Toolbars➪Customize.**

   The Customize dialog box appears.

2. **Click the Commands tab.**

   A list of command categories appears at the left side of the dialog box, and the commands in each category appear on the right.

3. **Click the name of the category of the command you want to add from the category column.**

   The commands in the selected category appear on the right.

4. **Select the command you want to add from the list on the right by clicking it once.**

   A heavy black border appears around the command you select.

5. **Drag the selected command to the menu or toolbar in which you want it to appear.**

   The command you dragged appears in the spot where you dragged it.

6. **Click Close.**

   Your command is now part of the toolbar.

Another trick you may want to try is changing the way toolbar buttons look. For example, although some buttons contain both an icon and text, the Organize button contains only an icon. If you want the Organize button to display both text and an icon, right click the Organize button (while the Customize dialog box is open) and then choose "Image and Text" from the menu that drops down from the Organize button.

When the Customize dialog box is open, you can drag tools and menu commands to and from the Outlook toolbars and menus. Messing up Outlook's controls this way is amazingly easy, so be careful. If you do make a mess of things, choose View⇨Toolbars⇨Customize, and then click the Reset button to set everything right.

Chapter 17

Work from Anywhere with Outlook Web Access

Some jokers claim that WWW stands for World Wide Waste of time. Well, it's certainly easy to find Web pages devoted to goofing off, lollygagging, and just plain messing around, that's for sure! But one kind of Web page, called Outlook Web Access, can help you become super-productive by giving you access to all your Outlook data from any web-connected computer. If you take advantage of Outlook Web Access to get your work done sooner, you'll have extra time to fritter away as you please.

Outlook Web Access is part of a program called Microsoft Exchange which many large organizations run to power advanced Outlook features such as Public Folders. Not every company that uses Microsoft Exchange offers Outlook Web Access, but if yours does, you can log on to Outlook nearly anywhere; from a computer at your local public library, an Internet café or any old photocopy parlor. There's nothing difficult about Outlook Web Access; it's really nothing more than a special Web page that looks and acts quite a bit like the version of Outlook you have on your desk.

And now for the fine print . . .

Although Outlook Web Access can offer some pretty powerful capabilities to authorized users, it isn't for everybody. Here's why:

✔ Outlook Web Access works best when viewed with Microsoft's own Web browser, Internet Explorer. If you use another browser, such as Netscape or AOL, the program may look quite different from the way I describe it in this chapter. The basic functions are the same, but the exact locations of the buttons differ — sometimes quite a lot.

✔ Outlook Web Access is not actually a part of the Outlook program; it's built into the Microsoft Exchange program. You may run across a version that looks and acts quite different from the version I describe in this chapter (which is the one most widely available as I write this book).

✔ Outlook Web Access has to be set up by a network administrator through your organization's main computer network. Do-it-yourself setup is not an option.

✔ If you work for a security-conscious organization that isn't comfortable about letting confidential "inside" information show up on just any computer anywhere — aw, where's their sense of adventure? — you'll have to be understanding about that. In that case, skip this chapter and stick to using Outlook on your regular desktop computer.

The desktop version of Outlook is much more powerful than Outlook Web Access, but you many find it enormously convenient to get access to your Outlook data when you find yourself in certain situations, such as

✔ When you don't want to lug a laptop on a very short business trip just to check your e-mail.

✔ When you really *do* have to work from home now and then, and you don't want to fuss with getting your home computer connected to the office network.

✔ When you want to do some simple planning and collaborating with your office colleagues from someone else's computer.

✔ When you need access to your e-mail and other Outlook data from a Mac (or another kind of computer that won't run Outlook).

Also, some organizations only offer Outlook Web Access to certain mobile employees who share a computer. That way the company can keep these people connected to the corporate e-mail system without purchasing a separate computer for every single employee.

Getting Started with Outlook Web Access

You don't need special software or equipment to use Outlook Web Access. If you can find your way to a page on the Internet, you have everything you need to use Outlook Web Access. You need to know only a few bits of information, such as your log on name and password.

Logging on and off

You log in to Outlook Web Access the same way you sign on to any number of Web sites; go to the Internet, enter the address of the page that your organization has set up for logging on to Outlook Web Access and enter your user name and password. The exact steps of the process will differ between organizations, so you'll need to ask your system administrators for the details.

When you finish your Outlook Web Access session, you should log off by clicking the Log Off icon in the Outlook Bar. If you're using a computer in a public place such as an Internet Cafe, you don't want the next person using that computer to see your private information.

The Outlook screen

Outlook Web Access is designed to look a lot like the desktop version of Outlook, so you can switch between the two versions without having to learn a whole new bunch of tricks and techniques. You'll probably notice that the two programs feature a lot of the same icons, designs and screen parts, including

✔ **The Outlook Bar** is a stripe along the left side of the screen containing icons labeled Inbox, Calendar, Contacts, Options and Log Off (see Figure 17-1). When you click either the Inbox, Calendar, or Contacts icon, the main screen fills up with the kinds of items each of those icons describe; the Inbox displays e-mail messages, Calendar shows your appointments, and so on. You also get two separator bars at the top of the Outlook Bar labeled Shortcuts and Folders. Clicking either one changes what you see in the Outlook bar; the Shortcuts bar displays the large icons I just described, and the Folders bar displays all the folders you can see in Outlook, including Sent Items, Deleted Items, Tasks and Notes.

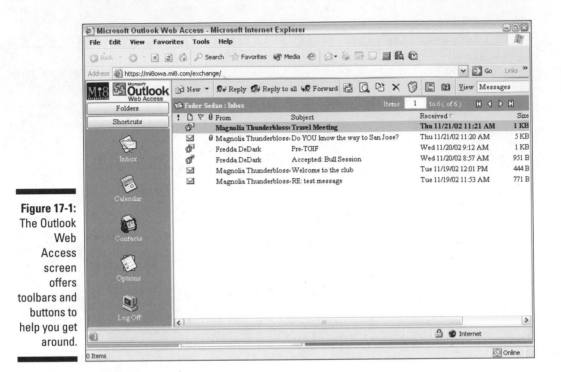

Figure 17-1:
The Outlook
Web
Access
screen
offers
toolbars and
buttons to
help you get
around.

✔ **Toolbars** in Outlook Web Access are a bit larger than in the desktop version of Outlook, but they contain all the icons to do what you need done. You can get a description of what a toolbar button does by hovering your mouse pointer over the button until a little yellow message box pops up to give you details.

When you're using Outlook Web Access, you see many of the buttons and screen you may be familiar with from the regular version of Outlook, but you're still really using a Web browser. That means that the menus at the top of the screen, the ones labeled File, Edit etc. are part of the Browser program, not Outlook. So you can't click a menu and get the results you might expect. For example, if you're reading your e-mail and you choose File⇨New, you won't see a New Message form (as you would in Outlook); instead, you automatically open a new window in Internet Explorer. Only the screens, toolbars and buttons do the same in Outlook Web Access that they do in the desktop version of Outlook.

Exchanging E-Mail

Whether you're reading messages from management or deleting get-rich-quick spams, you can log on to Outlook Web View from any browser to keep yourself in the loop.

Reading your messages

If you're stuck out on the road without a company laptop, you still have many ways to catch up on your e-mail, but Outlook Web Access enables you to see the exact collection of messages that you have sitting in your Inbox at the office. Lots of people use the Inbox as a kind of To-Do list; Outlook Web Access makes that possible from any computer connected to the Internet.

To read your messages, follow these steps:

1. **Click the Inbox Icon.**

   Your list of messages appears.

2. **Double-click the message you want to read**

   The text of the message appears.

3. **Press Esc to close the message.**

   The message window closes.

You can also speed through your list of messages by taking advantage of the preview pane. There's an icon on the Toolbar that looks like a little message box split in half. Click that icon once to toggle the Preview Pane open or closed. When you use the Preview Pane, you can just zip through your messages by pressing the up or down arrow keys.

Sending an e-mail message

When you feel the urge to dash off a quick e-mail from your favorite Internet café, you can do that with Outlook Web Access in a jiffy. You'll probably have your message finished before your barista finishes mixing that High Octane Mocha Latte Supremo. Just follow these steps:

1. **Click the Inbox icon in the Outlook Bar.**

   Your list of messages appears.

2. **Click the New button in the Toolbar.**

   The New Message form appears in a new window (shown in Figure 17-2).

3. **Click the box next to the word To.**

   A blinking bar appears in the To box, showing where the text you type will appear.

4. **Type the e-mail address of your intended recipient.**

   The address you type appears.

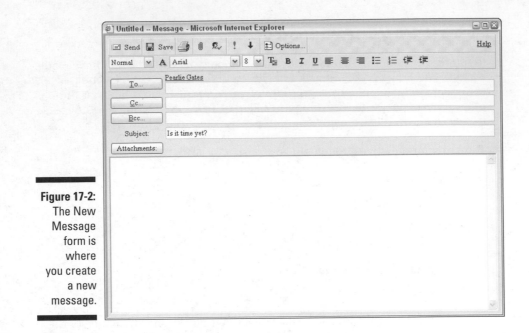

Figure 17-2:
The New
Message
form is
where
you create
a new
message.

5. **Click the Subject box and type the subject of your message.**

Technically you don't need to enter a subject, but it's good manners to put one in. Sending a message without a subject is like calling someone on the phone and not saying "Hello." Omitting a subject isn't exactly a crime; it just makes you seem strange.

6. **Click the message box at the bottom of the message screen and type your message.**

The message your type appears in the message form.

7. **Click the Send button at the top of the message form.**

Your message is on its way.

If you're not ready to send your message right away, you can click the Save button and resume work on your message later by clicking the Folders separator bar in the Outlook Bar, then clicking the Drafts folder to find your unfinished message. Clicking the message opens it for further editing.

Setting individual message options

You can't set as many options for an individual message in Outlook Web Access as you can in the regular version of Outlook, but you can set priority and sensitivity levels or request delivery notifications and read receipts. Just follow these steps:

1. **Before clicking Send to transmit your message, click the Options button on the toolbar at the top of the message form.**

   The Message Options Web Page Dialog box opens, showing the options you can choose from (as shown in Figure 17-3).

2. **Choose the options you want; then click Close.**

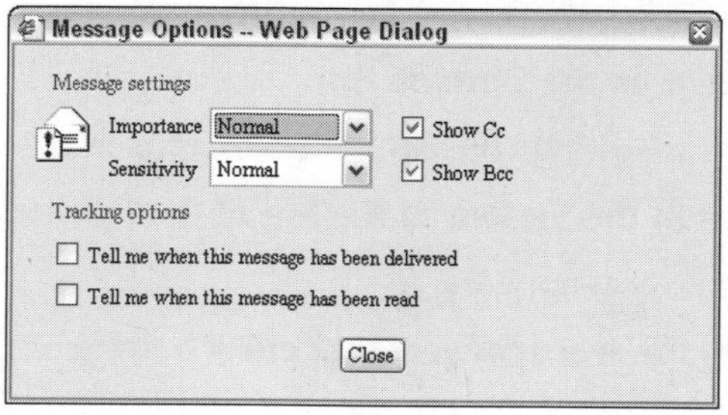

Figure 17-3:
You can set your message to high priority in the Message Options screen.

Message Options -- Web Page Dialog

Message settings

Importance Normal ☑ Show Cc

Sensitivity Normal ☑ Show Bcc

Tracking options

☐ Tell me when this message has been delivered

☐ Tell me when this message has been read

[Close]

It's a good idea not to overuse the message options available in Outlook Web Access. Setting all you messages to High Priority, for example, eventually leads people to ignore your Priority markings ("Oh, she always sets her messages to High Priority; just ignore her"). For a full explanation of message options, see Chapter 4.

An easy way to assign high priority to your message is to click the red, upward-pointing arrow in the Message Form toolbar while you're creating your message.

Using Your Calendar

The beauty (and horror) of using Outlook is that it enables other people to add appointments to your calendar. That means sometimes you won't know what appointments are in your calendar, because you didn't put them there. (Some senior executives have assistants to enter Outlook calendar appointments on their behalf.). So a word to the wise: Check your calendar regularly just to be sure you're in the right place at the right time.

Entering an appointment

If you're a heavy-duty road warrior, you probably keep your calendar on a handheld computer for your own reference — but your colleagues often need that information too. It's a good idea to keep your appointments posted in Outlook so other people at the office know when you're available for meetings, lunches, and random tongue-lashings.

To enter an appointment, follow these steps:

1. **Click the Calendar icon in the Outlook Bar.**

   The calendar appears, showing your appointments (as in Figure 17-4).

2. **Click the New button in the toolbar at the top of the screen.**

   The New Appointment form appears.

3. **Click the box next to the word Subject and enter a name for your appointment.**

   Enter something that describes your appointment, such as "Meeting with Bambi and Godzilla."

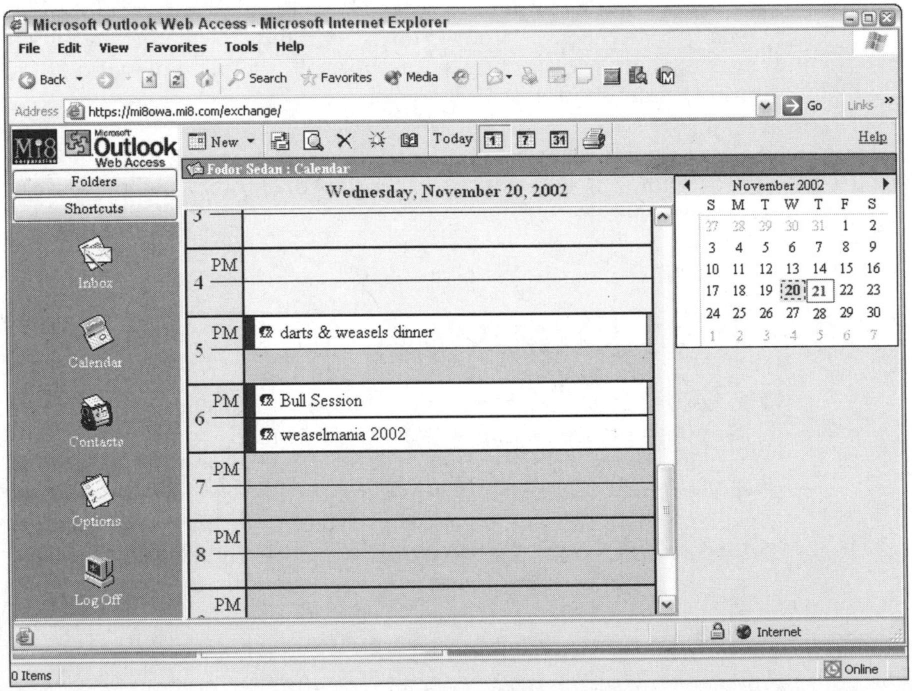

Figure 17-4:
Your calendar displays your appointments.

4. **Click the *scrolldown* button (the downward-pointing triangle) next to the Start Time box.**

   A small calendar appears (as shown in Figure 17-5).

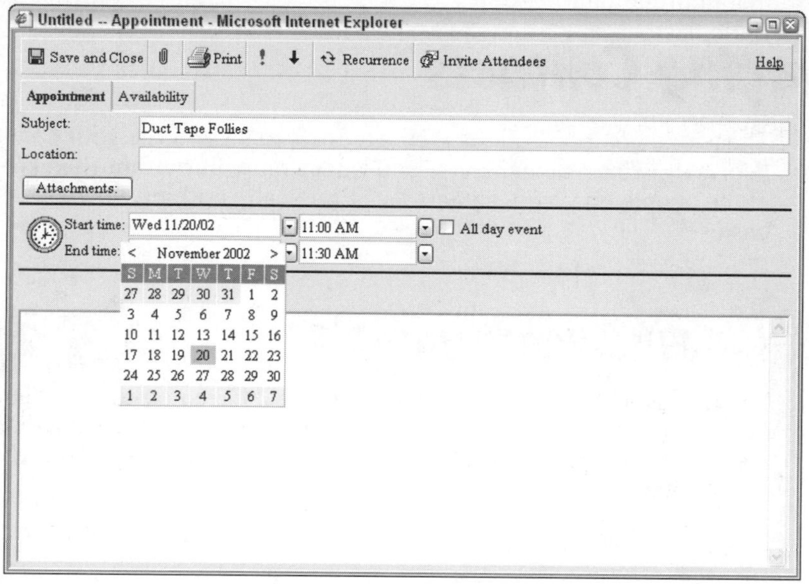

Figure 17-5:
Choose a
start time
for your
appointment
in the Start
Time box.

5. **Click the date of your appointment.**

   If the pop-up calendar doesn't contain the date you have in mind, click the arrows next to the name of the month in the small calendar until the month you want appears.

6. **Click the box to the right of the box where you entered the date; then type in the time of your appointment.**

   The time you entered appears.

7. **Click Save and Close.**

While you're entering appointment information, you can enter the location, end time, and other information about your appointment in the appropriately labeled boxes.

Changing an appointment

You can change the hour of your appointment (but not the date) by simply dragging the appointment to the hour you desire. If need to change the date or anything else about your appointment, double-click the appointment, select the information you want to change, enter the updated information, then click Save and Close. To Delete an appointment, click the appointment to select it, and then click the black X in the Toolbar to zap it completely. (You can find out more about the power of the Outlook calendar in Chapter 8.)

Managing Contacts

The whole point of Outlook Web Access is to let you see your collection of information from anywhere — and what's more important than keeping track of the people on your Contacts list? Practically nothing, so let's look at the basics.

Viewing your contacts

If you're accustomed to using Outlook, you'll have no problem figuring out how to view your contacts in Outlook Web Access; just click the Contacts icon in the Outlook Bar and you'll see your whole contacts list in beautiful, living color.

Adding contacts

A good contact list is precious; it's even more valuable than that snazzy office chair you covet, or even that enviable cubicle near the coffee pot. Outlook Web Access can help you keep your contact list up to date from wherever you are. For example, if you go to a conference or convention and exchange business cards with lots of people, you probably want to get those names into your contact list as soon as possible. If your office has Outlook Web Access, you might want to stop at the nearest public library or Internet café, log in to your account remotely, and enter all those new addresses before you go home.

To add a new contact through Outlook Web Access, follow these steps:

1. **Click the Contacts icon in the Outlook Bar.**

   Your list of contacts appears.

2. **Click the New button in the Toolbar.**

   The Contact form appears (as in Figure 17-6).

3. **Fill in the blanks in the Contact form.**

   The information you type appears in the Contact form.

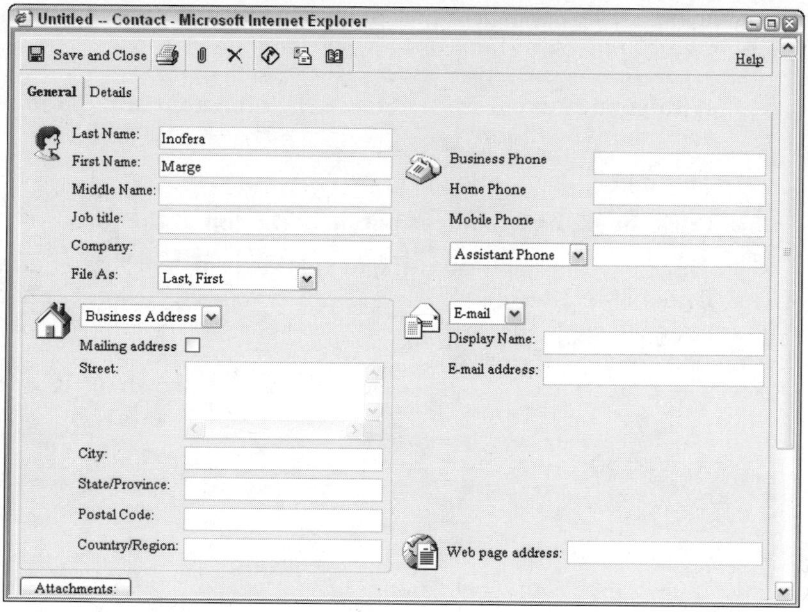

Figure 17-6:
Fill in the
blanks in the
Contact
form to save
information
about the
people you
know.

4. **Click Save and Close.**

    The Contact form closes and the name you entered appears in your list
    of contacts.

    If you want to edit the contacts you've entered, just open a contact record
    and follow the same steps you use to enter information about a new contact.
    (For a fuller explanation of Outlook contact entries, see Chapter 7.)

Collaborating with Outlook Web Access

If you work in an organization where people hold lots and lots of meetings,
you have my sympathy. To help you keep track of all those fascinating con-
fabs, Outlook gives you the tools to stay current on who's meeting when and
with whom. Otherwise you might miss that next meeting and (horrors!) they
could be talking about you . . .

Inviting attendees to a meeting

The only thing that seems to take more time than an office meeting is *planning* one. Although Outlook can't quiet the blowhard who bores everyone at
weekly staff meetings (gotta let the boss have *some* fun), it can reduce the

time you spend planning them. If you're charged with that duty, you can get a boost from Outlook Web Access by following these steps:

1. **With your calendar open, double-click the appointment to which you want to invite others.**

   The appointment form opens.

2. **Click the Invite Attendees button at the top of the form.**

   Three new lines appear at the top of the form, labeled Required, Optional and Resources.

3. **Click the Required button.**

   The Find Names Web Dialog box appears (as shown in Figure 17-7).

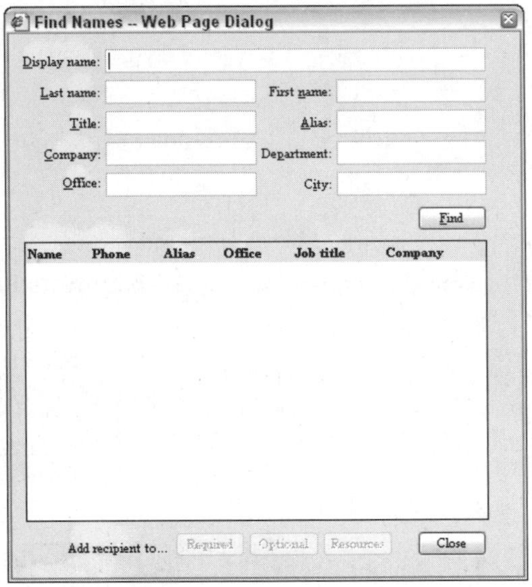

Figure 17-7: The Find Names dialog box searches for people to invite to your meeting.

4. **Click the box labeled Last Name and enter the last name of a person you want to invite to the meeting.**

   The name you type appears.

5. **Click the Find button.**

   • If the name you entered is listed in your Global Address List, the name appears at the bottom of the dialog box (as in Figure 17-8).

   • If you just want to see the names of everyone at your company, don't enter any text in the Last Name box before searching; just press the spacebar once. If you search for a single blank space, the Find box shows the whole address list; then you can just start clicking names to add them to your meeting.

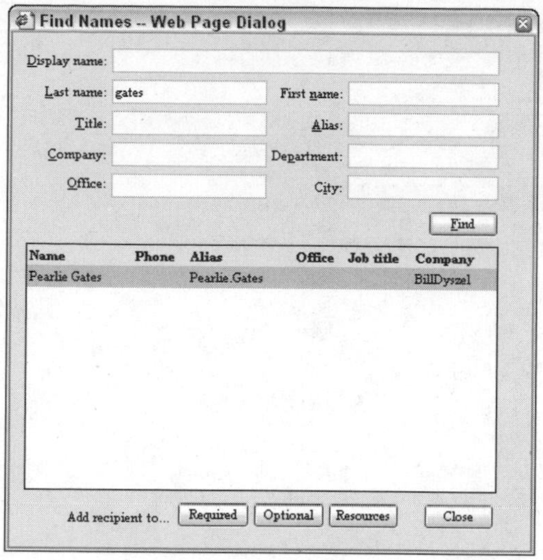

Figure 17-8:
Search
and you will
find — at
the bottom
of the Find
screen.

6. Click a name to select it; then click one of the three boxes at the bottom of the screen.

You can choose either Required or Optional, depending on how crucial that person's attendance is to the meeting. When you click Required, the name of the person you chose appears as a link in the Web dialog box.

The third choice, Resource, is where you request something you may need for the meeting, such as a conference room or a projector. Some organizations don't set up this option, but the resource box appears anyway.

7. Repeat Steps 5 and 6 until you've chosen everyone you want to add to the meeting.

The names you select appear as underlined text on the appointment form.

8. Click the Close button in the Find Names Web dialog box.

At this point, you can click the Send button to send off your invitation, but you might want to check everyone's availability first. No use inviting people to a meeting they can't attend.

9. Click the Availability tab.

The Availability page appears, showing a diagram of everyone's schedule (as shown in Figure 17-9). If you've picked a time that doesn't fit all attendees' schedules, use the Start Time and End Time boxes at the bottom of the screen to pick workable times.

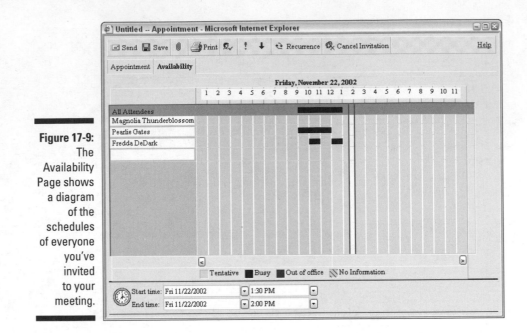

Figure 17-9:
The
Availability
Page shows
a diagram
of the
schedules
of everyone
you've
invited
to your
meeting.

10. **Click Send.**

    Your meeting request goes to the people you've invited.

Although the regular version of Outlook offers slicker planning tools than you'll find in Outlook Web Access, the Web version is a big help when you need a quick-and-dirty way to plan a meeting while you're away from the office.

Respond to a meeting request

If you travel a lot, you may need to check in frequently to see whether other people in your organization have summoned you to attend meetings when you return. Outlook Web Access enables other people to send you a special e-mail that invites you to a meeting. You can then accept that request to be automatically included in the meeting. To respond to a meeting request, follow these steps:

1. **Click the Inbox icon in the Outlook Bar.**

    Your list of messages appears.

2. **Click the message that includes a meeting request.**

    The message you click opens, displaying a special toolbar with buttons labeled Accept, Tentative and Decline. Meeting requests appear in your Inbox (as with any other e-mail message), but the icon in front of a meeting request looks different from the icon in front of other messages. (Normal e-mail messages have an icon that looks like a tiny envelope; the meeting request icon is an envelope with two faces in front of it.)

3. **Click one of the buttons in the Toolbar; then click Send.**

Your response is sent to the meeting organizer.

When you accept a meeting request, the meeting is automatically added to your calendar and the meeting organizer's calendar reflects the fact that you've agreed to attend the meeting. (To find out more about sending and responding to meeting requests, see Chapter 14.)

Using Public Folders

Many organizations set up a system called Public Folders — a forum for sharing information and for conducting ongoing group discussions. You can use Outlook Web Access to see your group's Public Folders and participate in the group discussion even when you're out of the office.

Viewing Public Folders

Before you jump into a conversation, you probably ought to find out what's being discussed. If the conversation is being held in a Public Folder, you can do that by following these steps:

1. **Click the Folders divider in the Outlook Bar.**

Your list of Folders appears (as shown in Figure 17-10).

2. **Click the name of the Public Folder you want to view.**

A list of messages appears.

3. **Click the message you want to view.**

The text of the message you click appears.

You can really zip through the contents of a Public Folder by taking advantage of the Preview Pane. The Preview Pane is a box that appears at the bottom of the screen in Outlook Web Access that displays the contents of whatever message you've selected at the top of the screen. Clicking the Preview Pane icon in the toolbar (the little square icon in the toolbar between the black X and the word View) toggles the Preview Pane on or off. With the Preview pane on, you can zoom through the messages in the folder you've selected by pressing the up and down arrow keys on your keyboard.

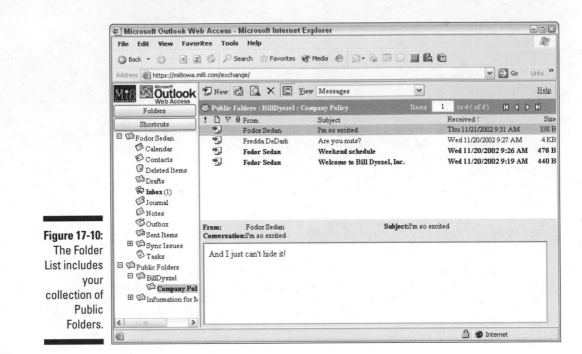

Figure 17-10:
The Folder
List includes
your
collection of
Public
Folders.

Adding items to a Public Folder

When you read a discussion in a Public Folder and you just can't resist putting your two cents in, don't (resist, that is). You can post your words of wisdom for all to see by following these steps:

1. **Click the Folders divider in the Outlook Bar.**

   Your list of Folders appears.

2. **Click the name of the Public Folder to which you want to post a new message.**

   A list of messages appears.

3. **Click the New button in the toolbar.**

   The new message form appears (as in Figure 17-11).

4. **Enter the subject and text of your message, then click the Post button.**

   Your message is posted to the Public Folder you chose.

Bear in mind, Public Folders can be set up so most people can only read messages but not write messages to that folder. Don't be offended if your masterpiece doesn't get posted to a certain Public Folder; just ask your system administrator to tell you who owns the folder and ask them to give you rights to post to that folder. (For more about Public Folders, see Chapter 14.)

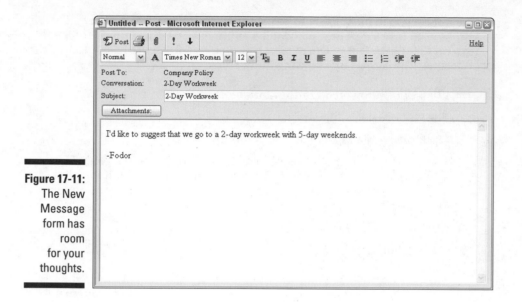

Figure 17-11:
The New
Message
form has
room
for your
thoughts.

Options

You can adjust a limited number of options through Outlook Web Access. To see what options are available, click the Options icon in the Outlook Bar. You may want to adjust the e-mail notification options or the way dates are displayed. For the most part, however, you won't miss much if you leave the options alone.

Out of Office

If you have to call in sick, remember these two important rules:

- ✔ Don't come back from your "Sick Day" with a glorious new suntan.
- ✔ Turn on your Outlook Out of Office message so people don't think you're avoiding them (even if you are).

Of course, it's pretty silly to come into the office just to turn on your Outlook Out of Office message. With Web view, you can just log on from home (or Tahiti, or wherever you are) and set up an Out of Office message — which automatically sends a response to all incoming e-mail messages saying that you're not immediately available.

The option you're most likely to use is the Out of Office notice. After all, if you have to take a sick day, you don't want to have to drag into the office to turn on that pesky Out of Office message. Spare yourself the hassle (and your colleagues the germs) by following these steps:

1. **Click the Options icon in the Outlook Bar.**

   The Options page appears.

2. **Click the words I'm Currently Out of the Office.**

   The circle next to the words you clicked darkens, to show you've selected them. You can also add a detailed message, describing all the gory details of why you're absent. (Figure 17-12 shows a typical piteous example.)

3. **Click Save and Close.**

   The Options page closes.

Now you can stop feeling guilty about not coming in. (Well, okay, maybe you'll still feel a teeny bit guilty, but you've done your part.) Try to remember to turn your Out of Office message off when you get back to the office, otherwise your co-workers will think you're still at home, lounging around and not at the office lounging around.

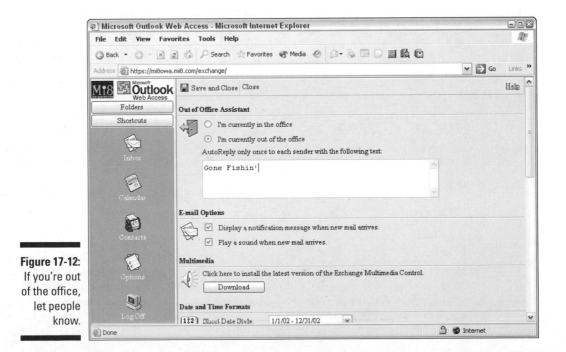

Figure 17-12:
If you're out of the office, let people know.

Part VI
The Part of Tens

The 5th Wave   By Rich Tennant

It's an e-mail from my mother. She says that the honeymoon suite is fantastic and she'll have the covers turned down when we arrive.

In this part . . .

Top-ten lists are everybody's favorite. They're short. They're easy to read. And they're the perfect spot for writers like me to toss in useful stuff that doesn't easily fit into the main chapters of the book. Flip through my top-ten lists for tips you'll want to use, including a timesaving look at things you *can't* do with Outlook (so you don't have to waste your time trying).

Chapter 18

Top Ten Accessories for Outlook

*O*utlook can do plenty for you without any outside help, but a few well-considered accessories can make your life even easier. Some of my favorite accessories make up for capabilities that Outlook ought to have (in my humble opinion) but doesn't. Some of my other favorite accessories help me to use my Outlook data anywhere, anytime.

Palm Organizer

The Palm handheld computer is far and away my favorite "accessory" for Outlook. Although I can enter and manage data in a snap with Outlook, I can carry my most important Outlook info in my pocket on my Palm device. I can even read my e-mail on the subway using the Palm organizer (something I wouldn't try with a laptop).

Several types of handheld computers are on the market today, but I prefer the ones that use the Palm operating system. Those products include the Palm-brand devices, Handspring Treo, Sony Clie, and certain phones by Kyocera and Samsung. Some new handheld computers use the Pocket PC system that Microsoft makes. You might think that the Microsoft Pocket PC system is more compatible with Outlook, but it's not. Palm still offers better value for the money in my view. To find out more about Palm computers, take a look at one of my other books, *Palm For Dummies* or *Treo and Visor For Dummies,* both published by Wiley Publishing, Inc.

Microsoft Office

When Outlook was first released, it was a part of the Microsoft Office 97 suite. Now that you can buy Outlook as a standalone product (or in a package with Internet Explorer), you may not have the benefits of using Microsoft Office and Outlook in concert. Office enables you to do all sorts of tricks with outgoing e-mail and graphics, while Outlook makes it a snap to exchange the work you've created in Office via e-mail. I recommend using both, if possible.

A Business-Card Scanner

You can use several brands of business-card scanners to copy contact information into Outlook from the business cards you collect at conferences and trade shows. Of course, you *can* enter all the info manually, but if you collect more than a few dozen cards per week, a business-card scanner can save you lots of work. (Personally, I use a business-card scanner from Corex because I find it connects to Outlook seamlessly.)

A Large, Removable Disk Drive

The second most common question I hear is, "How do I back up my Outlook data for safekeeping?" Again, because the Outlook data file is much too big to save on a floppy disk, you may want a large-capacity device for storing your data. The Iomega Zip drive costs about a hundred bucks, hooks up to your USB or printer port, and gives you lots of space.

You might also consider a CD burner for backing up your Outlook data. Many new computers come with a CD burner already installed, so if you have one, take advantage of it.

CopyTalk

Entering information into Outlook is pretty easy, as long as you're near a computer. If not, an even easier method is to make a phone call. A service called CopyTalk enables you to add appointments, tasks, and contact information — even send e-mail messages — by making a phone call and telling their system what you want to do. With CopyTalk, any time your cell phone works, you can too. You can find out more at www.copytalk.com, but please remember to turn off your phone at the movies, okay?

Nelson E-mail Organizer

Lots of people are deluged with e-mail; it's not uncommon to meet someone who gets over a thousand e-mail messages a week. If you live and die by e-mail, the Nelson E-mail Organizer, or NEO, is designed to help you sort, organize, and manage e-mail collections with blazing speed. NEO uses a technique called *indexing*, which enables it to display any message you search for almost instantly. For more information about NEO, go to www.caelo.com.

Address Grabber

The quickest way I know of to fill up your Address Book is to capture addresses from the Internet by using a product called Address Grabber, which costs $49 from eGrabber.com. If you've installed Address Grabber on your computer, just highlight any address that appears on-screen — from a Web page, a document, or an e-mail message — and the address is automatically sorted out and transferred to your Outlook Contacts list. It's a wonderful timesaver.

Quicken

Quicken, the world's most popular personal finance program has an address book that you can now synchronize with the names in your Outlook contact list. When you add Quicken to Outlook, you get a single source of information about the people with whom you do business, making it easier to send messages, money, or mail.

MindManager

The tasks you save in Outlook appear in nice tidy rows and columns. In real life, your tasks probably come at you from all angles, up, down, and sideways. That's why I was happy to discover that of my favorite planning and brainstorming programs, MindManager now connects with Outlook. When you view your Outlook tasks in MindManager, you get an elaborate, weblike arrangement that helps you visualize the relationships among the many things you do. You can find out more about MindManager from the developers' Web site at www.mindjet.com.

Dymo LabelWriter

The people who designed Outlook got so excited about e-mail that they completely forgot about that old-fashioned stamp-and-paper system that some people still prefer (how quaint!). Outlook alone can store zillions of mailing addresses, but it doesn't do a very good job of putting an address on an envelope. I use a Dymo LabelWriter to bridge that gap. The LabelWriter prints any address from Outlook to a convenient gummed label that you can stick on a package or envelope faster than you can say "United States Postal Service."

Chapter 19

Ten (Or So) Things You Can't Do with Outlook

Maybe I sound crabby listing the things that Outlook can't do, considering all the things it *can* do. But it takes only a few minutes to find out something that a program can do, and you can spend all day trying to figure out something that a program *can't* do. I could easily list *more* than ten things that Outlook can't do (walk the dog, deflect incoming asteroids — the usual); this chapter lists just the first big ones that I've run into.

The Top Ten List

Bear in mind that Outlook can't do these ten things when you first get it. Because Outlook can be reprogrammed with the Visual Basic programming language, however, a clever programmer could make Outlook do many of these things.

Insert a phone number into your Calendar

When you're entering an appointment, it would be nice if Outlook could look up the phone number of the person you're meeting and insert the number into the appointment record. If you have a Palm organizer, you may be used to doing just that with the Address Lookup feature, but you can't get Outlook to follow suit. Maybe some other time.

"Reverse-search" phone numbers

You probably have Caller ID on at least one of your phones, so it sure would be handy if you could punch in the number of an incoming call to get the skinny on the person you're about to speak with from your Contacts list. You'll have to hold the phone a little longer for that feature.

Choose different Outlook signatures in Microsoft Word

The Signature feature gives you a very handy way to choose a "billboard" to add to the end of your message, but when you're creating a document in Microsoft Word (or when you use Microsoft Word to create your e-mail), you can't choose Insert⇨Signature and pick a Signature. You can use a standard signature on all your outgoing messages, but where's the fun in that?

Perform two-sided printing

Some people like to print their schedule and keep it in a binder to look just like one of those old-fashioned planner books. I guess they're just sentimental for the good ol' paper-and-pencil days. The only problem with that is that Outlook doesn't know how to reorganize printed pages according to whether the page is on the left side or the right side of the book when you look at it. This is a very small quibble, but if it's important to you, sorry, you'll have to live with one-sided printing.

Search and replace area codes

It seems like the people at the phone company change area codes more often than they change their socks these days. If you need to change all your 312s to 708s, Outlook can't do that automatically; you'll have to change them one by one.

Turn off AutoPreview globally

Sometimes the AutoPreview feature is pretty handy, but other times you want to see a simple list of items without seeing the preview in order to save screen space. Your view of each folder is controlled separately, so if you want to turn off AutoPreview in all your folders, you need to go to each folder and turn off the feature one folder at a time.

Embed pictures in notes

You can copy and paste a picture, file, or other item into the text box at the bottom of any item when you open the item's form. You can paste a photo of a person in the text box of the person's Contact record, for example. But those little, yellow stick-on notes don't let you do that; they accept only text.

Automatically record all contact stuff in the Journal

You can open the Tools⇨Options dialog box and check off all the names of contacts you want to record, but you can't click a single button that checks 'em all. When you click the Activities tab for a contact, Outlook searches for all items related to that contact so that you can see where you stand with your important clients.

Calculate expenses with Journal Phone Call entries

You can keep track of how much time you spend talking to any person, but you can't calculate the total call time or total call cost for billing purposes.

Cross-reference items to jump to different modules

You can include a Contact record in a Journal Entry, for example, but when you double-click the icon for the record in the Journal, Outlook only opens that person's record; it doesn't jump to the Contacts module. If someone from XYX Company calls, and you want to look at the names of your other contacts from that company, you have to switch from the Journal module to the Contacts module and search for the names you want.

Ten More Things Outlook Can't Do for You

Alas, Outlook is also deficient in some other ways, though you may prefer to do these things for yourself, anyway.

Outlook can't

- Do the Locomotion.
- Play *Misty* for you.
- Pierce any body parts.
- Catch the Energizer Bunny.
- Stop tooth decay.
- Take the *Jeopardy!* Challenge.
- Refresh your breath while you scream.
- Fight City Hall.
- Predict the lottery.
- Find Mr. Right (unless you send e-mail to me!).

Oh, well. Aside from all that, it's a pretty neat program. You can save scads of time and work more smoothly by mastering all the things Outlook *can* do for you.

Chapter 20

Ten Things You Can Do After You're Comfy

*I*f Outlook is an iceberg's-worth of capabilities, I can only show you the tip in this book. You can already do some formidable tasks with Outlook. Time will tell (and pretty quickly at that) how much more you'll be able to do with future versions of Outlook, Internet Explorer, and all the other powerful technology that will be associated with those applications.

You can't do much to really mess up Outlook, so feel free to experiment. Add new fields, new views, new icons — go wild. This chapter describes a few Outlook adventures to try out.

Opening a Web Page from Outlook

If you like to surf the Net, your best bet is to use a Web browser, such as Internet Explorer, which was made for the job. If you want to browse a page now and then from Outlook, that's possible, too.

To open a Web page from Outlook, follow these steps:

1. **Choose View⇨Toolbars⇨Web.**

   The Web toolbar appears, along with any other toolbars you have open.

2. **Click the Address box on the Web toolbar.**

   The Address box contains strange-looking text, something like `outlook: \\personal%20Folders\Inbox`. When you click that text, it turns blue to show that you've selected it.

3. **Type the address of the Web page you want to view.**

   You've seen Web addresses everywhere: those odd strings of letters that begin with *www*, such as `www.outlookfordummies.com`.

4. **Press Enter.**

   The address of the page you've entered appears in the main screen of Outlook.

The Web toolbar also contains some of the same browser buttons you find on Internet Explorer to help you navigate around the Internet.

Office E-Mail

If you're using Microsoft Office, you can create an e-mail message for Outlook to send without even opening Outlook. All Microsoft Office programs have an e-mail button on the toolbar that you can click to turn any document you're creating into an e-mail message. When you click the e-mail button on the Microsoft Word toolbar, for example, boxes labeled *To, CC,* and *Subject* appear at the top of your document. Just enter an e-mail address exactly the way you would if you were creating a message from the Outlook Inbox. (For more about creating e-mail messages, see Chapter 5.)

The person getting your message may not be equipped with an e-mail program that can read messages with all the fancy formatting that you can use in Word. If the person to whom you're sending your message is in your office and uses the same programs as you do, you'll have no problem. If you're sending a message to someone outside your office and you want to make a good impression, your best bet is to keep your message simple.

AutoText

You can create AutoText entries to avoid typing the same word or phrase over and over. For example, if you often need to type **Subject to change without notice**, you can type that phrase once, select it, choose Insert⇨AutoText⇨New, and type an abbreviation for that phrase (such as **subj**). Then every time you want to insert that phrase, just type the abbreviation you chose and press the F3 key. Voilà — the whole phrase appears like magic.

Themes

If you want to make a Microsoft Word document a bit more colorful and zippy, apply a *Theme*. Themes are predesigned backgrounds and color schemes that you can apply to a document to create a mood or image. Just choose Format⇨Theme and double-click the name of the theme you want to use. Well, okay, the fancy formatting and backgrounds that you can apply so easily as a Theme can be lost just as easily on the way to your recipient when you send e-mail to people outside your office. But themes are fun and easy to use, so why not give 'em a try?

Creating a Form Letter from the Contacts List

Today I received a personalized invitation to enter a $250,000 sweepstakes that had my name plastered all over the front of the envelope. How thoughtful and personal! (At least it sort of looks that way.) Whenever you get a sweepstakes letter with your name already entered, you're getting a form letter. A *form letter* is a letter with standard text that's printed over and over but with a different name and address printed on each copy. You can send form letters, too, even if you're not holding a sweepstakes. An annual newsletter to family and friends is one form letter you may want to create.

To create a form letter from Outlook, follow these steps:

1. **Click the Contacts icon in the Navigation Pane.**

   Your list of contacts appears.

2. **Choose Tools⇨Mail Merge.**

   The Mail Merge Contacts dialog box appears.

3. Choose Form Letters from the Document Type list.

The document type list is at the lower-left corner of the Mail Merge Contacts dialog box. The words *Form Letters* appear after you make your choice.

4. Choose New Document from the Merge To list.

The Merge To list appears just to the right of the Document Type list at the bottom of the dialog box. Normally the words *New Document* appear automatically (so you don't have to do anything), but you may want to check to be sure.

5. Click OK.

Microsoft Word starts, displaying a blank document.

6. Type your form letter, inserting merge fields as you go.

You insert a *merge field* by clicking the Insert Merge Field button (sixth from the left end of the toolbar) wherever you want data from your Outlook Address Book to appear in your form letter (as in Figure 20-1).

Now you don't have to settle for sending impersonal, annoying form letters to dozens of people; you can send a *personal,* annoying form letter to hundreds of people. (If you're planning to send an annoying form letter to me, my address is 1600 Pennsylvania Avenue, Washington, D.C.)

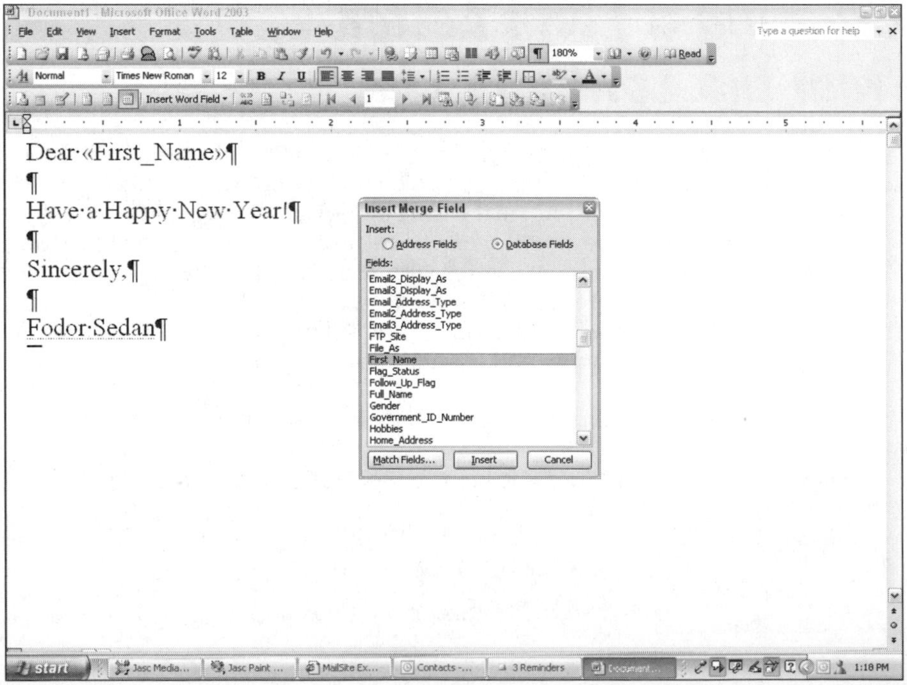

Figure 20-1:
Adding merge fields to your letter.

Merging to E-Mail

Another appealing feature of the Mail Merge tool is the capability to create merged e-mail. Usually, you don't need to use mail merge for e-mail because you can send a single e-mail message to as many people as you want. But if you want to send an e-mail message to a bunch of people *and customize each message,* you can do that with a mail merge to e-mail. That way, you won't send your "Dear John" message to George, Paul, or Ringo.

To merge to e-mail, follow the same steps you use to create a form letter (see the preceding section), but choose E-Mail instead of New Document from the Merge to List in the Mail Merge Contacts dialog box.

If you're using Outlook on a Microsoft Exchange network, Outlook is probably set up to send your document directly to your recipient as soon as you click the Merge button. If you've made a mistake, there's no chance to fix it. I recommend turning off the automatic send feature while creating a merged e-mail message so you can check your work. Choose Tools➪Options➪Mail Setup and see if there's a check mark next to the words "Send Immediately when connected." If so, click the check mark to make it disappear, then click OK. When you're sure you've said what you want to say, press Ctrl+Shift+O to switch to your Outbox (as shown in Figure 20-2) and see the collection of messages before pressing F9 to send your messages.

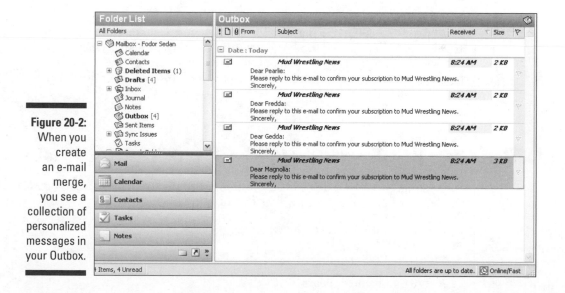

Figure 20-2:
When you create an e-mail merge, you see a collection of personalized messages in your Outbox.

Merging Selected Records

You probably don't want to send a letter to every person on your Contacts list. It's easy to end up with thousands of names on your list — the postage alone could cost a fortune. To limit your list of letters or mailing labels to just a handful of contacts, hold down the Ctrl key and click the names of the people you want to include. After you've selected everyone you want, choose Tools➪Mail Merge. The Mail Merge tool then creates letters or labels for only those people whose names you've selected.

Selecting Dates as a Group

When you're viewing a range of dates, you don't have to limit yourself to fixed days, weeks, or months. Suppose you want to look at a range of dates from September 25 to October 5. Click September 25, and then (while holding down the Shift key) click October 5. All the dates in between are selected, appearing in the Information Viewer.

Turning on Additional Toolbars

Outlook has several toolbars to choose from if the mood strikes you. The Standard toolbar is the one that shows up when you first start Outlook. You can only see the Advanced toolbar if you turn it on by choosing View➪Toolbars➪Advanced. You don't have to be advanced to use the Advanced toolbar, so give it a try. You can also flip on the Web toolbar by choosing View➪Toolbars➪Web.

Creating Your Own Type of Outlook Field

You can create your own fields in any Outlook module, form, or view. You can even define what type the field will be and how it will look.

To create your own type of Outlook field, follow these steps:

1. **Right-click the heading of any column.**

   A shortcut menu appears

2. **Choose Field Chooser.**

   The Field Chooser appears.

3. **Click New.**

   The New Field dialog box appears.

4. **Type the name of your new field in the Name box.**

5. **In the Type box, choose the type of field from which you want to make your new field.**

   The Type box enables you to choose what kind of information will go in the field — text, time, or percentage. Feel free to experiment; it's easy to change the type later by using the Format➪Fields command.

6. **In the Format list, choose the format of the information that you want to put in the field.**

   Some types of information have several possible formats. Dates, for example, could have the format 7/4/98, July 4, 1998, or Sat 7/4/98. Some types of information, such as plain text, have only one format.

7. **Click OK.**

   Your new field appears in the Field Chooser.

8. **Drag your new field to the position where you want it to appear.**

You have a plethora of different ways to customize and use Outlook; I've only begun to scratch the surface. Feel free to experiment; you really can't break anything, and most features of Outlook are easiest to understand when you see them in action.

Chapter 21

Ten Shortcuts Worth Taking

*E*ven though computers are supposed to save you time, some days this just doesn't seem to be the case. Juggling menus, keys, and buttons can seem to take all day. Here are some shortcuts that can really save you time and tension as you work.

Using the New Item Tool

To create a new item in whatever module you're in, just click the New Item tool at the far-left end of the toolbar. The icon changes when you change modules, so it becomes a New Task icon in the Tasks module, a New Contact icon in the Contacts module, and so on. You can also click the arrow next to the New Item tool to pull down the New Item menu.

 When you choose an item from the New Item menu (see Figure 21-1), you can create a new item in an Outlook module other than the one you're in without changing modules. If you're answering e-mail, for example, and you want to create a note, pull down the New Item menu, choose Note, create your note, and then go on working with your e-mail.

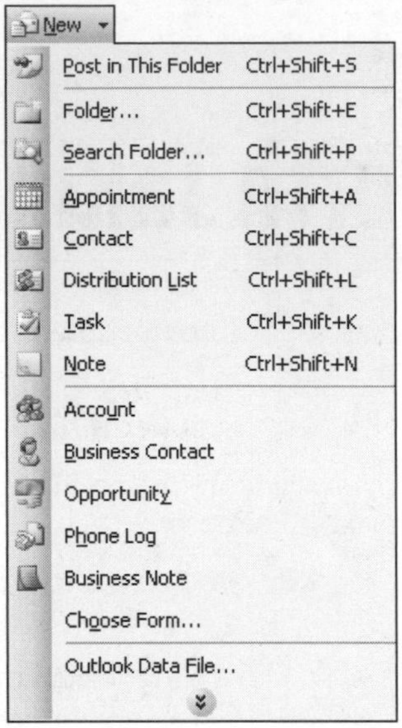

Figure 21-1:
The New
Item tool
with the
New Item
menu pulled
down.

Sending a File to an E-Mail Recipient

You can send a file via Outlook e-mail with only a few mouse clicks, even if Outlook isn't running. When you're viewing files in Windows Explorer, you can mark any file to be sent to any e-mail recipient. Here's how:

1. **Right-click the file that you want to send after finding the file with Windows Explorer.**

   A menu appears.

2. **Choose Send To.**

   Another menu appears.

3. **Choose Mail Recipient.**

   A New Message form appears. An icon representing the attached file is in the text box.

4. **Type the subject of the file and the name of the person to whom you're sending the file.**

   If you want to add comments to your message, type them in the text box where the icon for the file is.

5. **Click Send.**

   Your message goes to the Outbox. Press F5 to send it on its way. (If you send your files by modem, you also have to press F5 to dial your e-mail service.)

Sending a File from a Microsoft Office Application

You can e-mail any Office document from the Office application itself, without using the Outlook e-mail module. Here's how:

1. **In the application that created it, open an Office document that you want to send.**

2. **Choose File⇨Send To⇨Mail Recipient (As Attachment).**

   A New Message form appears, displaying an icon for the file in the text box to indicate that the file is attached to the message.

3. **Type the subject of the file and the name of the person to whom you're sending the file.**

   If you want to add comments to your message, type them in the text box where the icon for the file is.

4. **Click Send.**

   Your message goes to the Outbox. (If you send your files by modem, you also have to switch to Outlook and press F5 to dial your e-mail service.)

Microsoft Word actually gives you two ways to send someone a file via e-mail. The method I describe in the preceding step list sends the Word file as an attachment to a message. If you choose File⇨Send To⇨Mail Recipient, not as an attachment, Word sends the document as the body of your e-mail message. That's a better method when you're sending the message to someone in your office who uses all the same hardware and software as you do — but not when you send a message to a person over the Internet (sometimes the other person's computer makes a mess of the message if you send it from Word). As a general rule, send Word documents as attachments to people outside the office.

Taking a Note

How often do you need to take a quick note in the course of a busy day? (A lot, I bet.) If Outlook is running, you can take a quick note by choosing File⇨New⇨Note (or pressing Ctrl+Shift+N), typing your note and pressing the Escape key. In just a second, your note is stored away for future reference in your Outlook Notes module.

Finding Something

It doesn't take long to amass quite a large collection of items in Outlook — which can then take a long time to browse through when you want to find one specific item. Outlook can search for items at your command if you press the Find button on the toolbar (or press Alt+I). The Find button toggles the Find window on and off, so you can get to it in a flash.

Undoing Your Mistakes

If you didn't know about the Undo command, it's time you heard the good news: When you make a mistake, you can undo it by pressing Ctrl+Z or by choosing Edit➪Undo. So feel free to experiment; the worst you'll have to do is undo! (Of course, you must undo what you've done right away, before you do too many things to undo at one time.)

Using the Go To Date Command

You can use the Go To Date command (as shown in Figure 21-2) in all Calendar and Timeline views . If you're looking at the Calendar, for example, and you want to skip ahead 60 days, press Ctrl+G and type **60 days from now**. The Calendar advances 60 days from the current date.

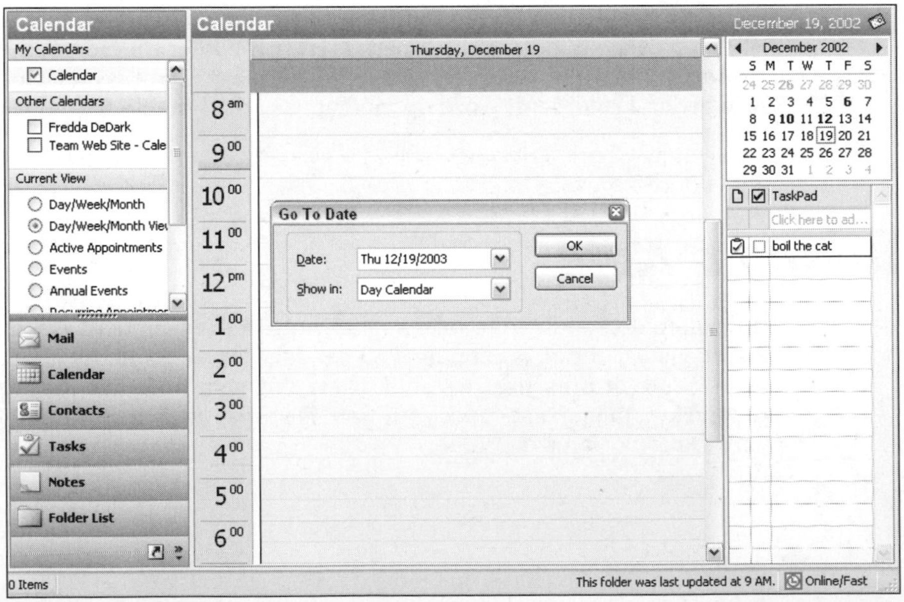

Figure 21-2:
The Go To Date dialog box.

Adding Items to List Views

Many Outlook lists have a blank line at the top where you can type an entry and create a new item for that list. When you see the words `Click here to add a new task`, that's exactly what you do. Just click the line and type your new item.

Sending Repeat Messages

I have one or two messages that I send out over and over, so I've stored the text of those messages as either an Outlook signature or as a Word AutoText to save time. For example, when I'm writing a book about Handspring Visor, I send a message to every company I encounter that makes things for the Visor that says something like this:

> I'm currently writing the next edition of *Treo and Visor For Dummies,* and I'd like to evaluate your product, XX, for discussion in the book. Could you send me a Press Kit?

Because I've saved that message as a signature, all I have to do when I find a new Treo accessory vendor on the Web is to double-click the company's e-mail address in my browser, choose that signature, change the XX to the name of its product, and click Send. I can have a request out in less than 30 seconds and get on to my next task. (If you're using Word as your e-mail editor, you have to save your message text as AutoText instead.)

Navigating with Browser Buttons

You can use Outlook to browse the World Wide Web if the mood strikes you. Just choose View⇨Toolbars⇨Web to open the Web toolbar. The Web toolbar appears at the top of your screen, right next to the Standard toolbar, and contains an Address box and browser buttons for navigating the Internet.

If you're accustomed to using Web browsers such as Netscape or Microsoft Internet Explorer, you'll find that the browser buttons on the Outlook Web toolbar work exactly the same way as the navigation buttons in your Web browser. (Honestly, I think you're better off browsing the Web with a normal browser program such as Internet Explorer, but if you want to make Outlook do the job, go right ahead.)

Index

creating folders in, 80–81, 226–227
defined, 28–29
deleting default forms, 235–236
dragging border under, 26
in Outlook Express, 208, 209
showing, 29
viewing two accounts in, 252–253
folders, e-mail. *See also* Junk E-mail
folder
arranging mail by, 99
creating, 80–81, 226–227
moving messages to, 81–82
overview of, 79
Search Folders, 82–83
folders, public. *See also* collaboration
using Outlook and Exchange
defined, 256, 261
flaming and, 259
moving Outlook items to, 259, 260–261
in Outlook Web Access, 307–309
posting messages, 258
posting replies, 259, 260
viewing, 257
Format Columns dialog box, 281–282
formatting text
contacts information, 109–110
dates, 281–282
in e-mails with Word, 49–50
in Table view columns, 281–282
Formatting toolbar, 109
forms, 225. *See also* Outlook forms
Forms Manager dialog box, 235–236
forwarding e-mail
with attached notes, 191–192
overview of, 59–61
setting style options, 73, 74
warning, 60

• G •

Global Address List, 255
Go button, 24, 25
Go To Date command, 131–132, 332
Group By dialog box, 287–288
grouped views. *See specific Outlook
views;* Outlook Table views, grouping
by columns

• H •

hackers, 265
Help system
via F1 key, 31, 32–33
Office Assistant, 32–33
online help, 31
toolbar button, 32
holidays, adding to calendar, 149
home use. *See* Outlook at home

• I •

icons used in book, 7–8
Icons view in Notes, 180, 181, 276
Identities feature in Outlook Express,
212–213
importance options, e-mail, 51–52, 100
Inbox, 24
indexing, 315
Information Viewer, 23–24, 26–28. *See
also specific Outlook views;* Outlook
main screen
Insert File dialog box, 74–75
Internet. *See also* Outlook at home; Web
page addresses
cable modem access, 217
DSL access, 217
ISP access, 215–216, 217–218

Notes

Notes

Notes

Notes

Notes

Notes

Notes

Notes

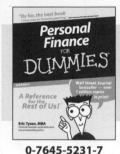

FOR DUMMIES®

The easy way to get more done and have more fun

PERSONAL FINANCE

0-7645-5231-7   0-7645-2431-3   0-7645-5331-3

Also available:

Estate Planning For Dummies
(0-7645-5501-4)
401(k)s For Dummies
(0-7645-5468-9)
Frugal Living For Dummies
(0-7645-5403-4)
Microsoft Money "X" For Dummies
(0-7645-1689-2)
Mutual Funds For Dummies
(0-7645-5329-1)

Personal Bankruptcy For Dummies
(0-7645-5498-0)
Quicken "X" For Dummies
(0-7645-1666-3)
Stock Investing For Dummies
(0-7645-5411-5)
Taxes For Dummies 2003
(0-7645-5475-1)

BUSINESS & CAREERS

0-7645-5314-3   0-7645-5307-0   0-7645-5471-9

Also available:

Business Plans Kit For Dummies
(0-7645-5365-8)
Consulting For Dummies
(0-7645-5034-9)
Cool Careers For Dummies
(0-7645-5345-3)
Human Resources Kit For Dummies
(0-7645-5131-0)
Managing For Dummies
(1-5688-4858-7)

QuickBooks All-in-One Desk Reference For Dummies
(0-7645-1963-8)
Selling For Dummies
(0-7645-5363-1)
Small Business Kit For Dummies
(0-7645-5093-4)
Starting an eBay Business For Dummies
(0-7645-1547-0)

HEALTH, SPORTS & FITNESS

0-7645-5167-1   0-7645-5146-9   0-7645-5154-X

Also available:

Controlling Cholesterol For Dummies
(0-7645-5440-9)
Dieting For Dummies
(0-7645-5126-4)
High Blood Pressure For Dummies
(0-7645-5424-7)
Martial Arts For Dummies
(0-7645-5358-5)
Menopause For Dummies
(0-7645-5458-1)

Nutrition For Dummies
(0-7645-5180-9)
Power Yoga For Dummies
(0-7645-5342-9)
Thyroid For Dummies
(0-7645-5385-2)
Weight Training For Dummies
(0-7645-5168-X)
Yoga For Dummies
(0-7645-5117-5)

Available wherever books are sold.
Go to www.dummies.com or call 1-877-762-2974 to order direct.

FOR DUMMIES®

A world of resources to help you grow

HOME, GARDEN & HOBBIES

Feng Shui FOR DUMMIES
0-7645-5295-3

Gardening FOR DUMMIES
0-7645-5130-2

Guitar FOR DUMMIES
0-7645-5106-X

Also available:

Auto Repair For Dummies
(0-7645-5089-6)

Chess For Dummies
(0-7645-5003-9)

Home Maintenance For
Dummies
(0-7645-5215-5)

Organizing For Dummies
(0-7645-5300-3)

Piano For Dummies
(0-7645-5105-1)

Poker For Dummies
(0-7645-5232-5)

Quilting For Dummies
(0-7645-5118-3)

Rock Guitar For Dummies
(0-7645-5356-9)

Roses For Dummies
(0-7645-5202-3)

Sewing For Dummies
(0-7645-5137-X)

FOOD & WINE

Cooking FOR DUMMIES
0-7645-5250-3

Cookies FOR DUMMIES
0-7645-5390-9

Wine FOR DUMMIES
0-7645-5114-0

Also available:

Bartending For Dummies
(0-7645-5051-9)

Chinese Cooking For
Dummies
(0-7645-5247-3)

Christmas Cooking For
Dummies
(0-7645-5407-7)

Diabetes Cookbook For
Dummies
(0-7645-5230-9)

Grilling For Dummies
(0-7645-5076-4)

Low-Fat Cooking For
Dummies
(0-7645-5035-7)

Slow Cookers For Dummies
(0-7645-5240-6)

TRAVEL

Italy FOR DUMMIES
0-7645-5453-0

Hawaii FOR DUMMIES
0-7645-5438-7

Las Vegas FOR DUMMIES
0-7645-5448-4

Also available:

America's National Parks For
Dummies
(0-7645-6204-5)

Caribbean For Dummies
(0-7645-5445-X)

Cruise Vacations For
Dummies 2003
(0-7645-5459-X)

Europe For Dummies
(0-7645-5456-5)

Ireland For Dummies
(0-7645-6199-5)

France For Dummies
(0-7645-6292-4)

London For Dummies
(0-7645-5416-6)

Mexico's Beach Resorts For
Dummies
(0-7645-6262-2)

Paris For Dummies
(0-7645-5494-8)

RV Vacations For Dummies
(0-7645-5443-3)

Walt Disney World & Orlando
For Dummies
(0-7645-5444-1)

FOR DUMMIES®

FOR DUMMIES

Helping you expand your horizons and realize your potential

INTERNET

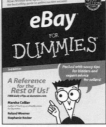

0-7645-0894-6

0-7645-1659-0

0-7645-1642-6

DIGITAL MEDIA

0-7645-1664-7

0-7645-1675-2

0-7645-0806-7

GRAPHICS

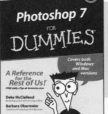

0-7645-0817-2

0-7645-1651-5

0-7645-0895-4

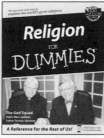

FOR DUMMIES®

The advice and explanations you need to succeed